CHALLENGE FOR A THRONE

CHALLENGE FOR A THRONE

THE WARS OF THE ROSES

by

Robert Silverberg

Writing as Franklin Hamilton

THE BORGO PRESS

MMX

www.wildsidebooks.com

FIRST WILDSIDE EDITION

INTRODUCTION TO THE BORGO EDITION

From Franklin Hamilton to Robert Silverberg

Since 1955 I have primarily been a writer of science fiction, but in the early 1960s, when I was about six years along in what had been a very successful career, science fiction fell into hard times, with diminishing sales of books and magazines and a corresponding aversion to artistic risk by most of the editors who remained at work in the greatly shrunken field. (Things were so bad that many leading writers, editors, and readers took part in a famous symposium, *Who Killed Science Fiction*, that won an award at the next World Science Fiction Convention.)

Since it now had become impossible for me to continue earning a living as a full-time freelancing specialist in science fiction, I turned my writing activities elsewhere, and soon, drawing on my own interests in history and science, had established myself as a writer of non-fiction books for high school and college readers. The major publishers of such books—Holt, Putnam, Doubleday, Macmillan, and several more—welcomed them, and quickly I began winning awards for them and the attention of librarians, who readily bought each new one as it appeared. The first of the books was *Lost Cities and Vanished Civilizations* (1962), swiftly followed by several others on archaeological subjects—*Empires in the Dust, Man Before Adam, Sunken History, To the Rock of Darius*, etc. I wrote a book about Socrates. I wrote one about great medical men. I wrote one on Copernicus and Galileo. I wrote one about nuclear physics. I wrote one on the Indians of the Pueblos. It was a busy decade.

I wrote so many books on so many themes between 1961 and 1970, in fact, that it started to seem implausible that one writer could master such a wide range of subjects, although I have always been a good researcher and a very prolific writer. My publishers and I feared that book buyers would begin to question the quality of the work. So it became commercially desirable to conceal my prolificacy behind pseudonyms. When I did a couple of books about famous explorers, I used the byline "Walker Chapman." A biography of Winston Churchill was credited to "Edgar Black." And when, in 1964, I wrote a book about the Norman conquest of England, it was published (by the Dial Press, an important publisher of the day) under the name of "Franklin Hamilton."

There were three Franklin Hamilton books in all: *1066*, the Norman Conquest book, followed in 1965 by *The Crusades*, and in 1967 by *Challenge for a Throne*, which dealt with the Wars of the Roses. (A projected fourth book about the Byzantine Empire got caught in a publishing change and was abandoned.) They were good, solid books, beautifully illustrated by my friend Judith Ann Lawrence (the wife of science-fiction writer James

Blish), they were well received by reviewers, and they sold very well for many years.

Now, after several decades in publishing limbo, here they are back in print again—and, since I am no longer so prolific that my books jostle against each other for the attention of readers, I see no reason to continue to hide them behind a pseudonym, so I have placed my own name on them at last.

—Robert Silverberg
Oakland, California
August, 2010

maps and illustrations

GeneaLogical tables

Of comfort no man speak:
Let's talk of graves, of worms, and epitaphs;
Make dust our paper, and with rainy eyes
Write sorrow on the bosom of the earth;
Let's choose executors and talk of wills:
And yet not so—for what can we bequeath
Save our deposed bodies to the ground?
Our land, our lives, and all are Bolingbroke's,
And nothing can we call our own but death,
And that small model of the barren earth
Which serves as paste and cover to our bones.
For God's sake, let us sit upon the ground
And tell sad stories of the death of kings:
How some have been depos'd, some slain in war,
Some haunted by the ghosts they have depos'd,
Some poison'd by their wives, some sleeping kill'd;
All murder'd: for within the hollow crown
That rounds the mortal temples of a king
Keeps Death his court. . . .

Shakespeare: *Richard II*, ACT III, SCENE II

# of kings and kingdoms

T WAS a war of brother against brother, of cousin against cousin, a cycle of blood and death that lasted nearly a century. Three crowned kings died by violence; earls and dukes and lords perished like cattle in a slaughterhouse. It was a murderous time, a dangerous time to be alive and an Englishman. For England it was a time of testing. An uncertain nation, divided against itself, entered that crucible of blood; and when the last battle was fought, the last act of villainy performed, a different kind of nation emerged. Out of the terrible English civil wars of the fifteenth century came the splendid, mighty England of the sixteenth.

We call those wars the Wars of the Roses. No one who fought in them would have recognized them by that name. It was coined by Sir Walter Scott in a novel published in 1829, *Anne of Geierstein*. The roses were real enough, symbols of the two great families of Lancaster and York that fought for England's throne. The red rose was the rose of

1

Lancaster; the white, the rose of York. But Lancaster and York had many badges other than their roses, and the warrior of 1471, say, did not think of himself as fighting a "war of roses." He was fighting a war of men, a war of rival kings. The roses of Lancaster and York had sharp thorns, and pricked deeply into the flesh, bringing forth rivers of blood. Sir Walter Scott has given us a pretty name for a brutal, ugly, dreadful century of conflict.

If it takes fighting to make a war, then the Wars of the Roses began in 1455 and ended in 1471. But a war sends echoes rumbling through time in two directions; what erupted in 1455 had been smoldering since 1399, and what was extinguished in 1471 remained aglow until 1485. For those who lived at that time, the shape of events was unclear and tangled, a muddled twisting and turning of the course of power. Now one family ruled, now another, and no man could predict fate's next grim prank. But the passing of centuries gives a pattern to long-ago happenings. It draws together the great moments and erases the dull years between them, so that we see only the climaxes, the highlights. Thus we receive impressions that are too simple, though not false. It seems to us that the powerful forces of fate must have been at work, balancing injustice with injustice, crime with crime, usurpation with usurpation, so that the rhythm of history would come out cleanly and symmetrically.

To us the pattern of the Wars of the Roses is particularly well balanced. At the beginning, a king was pushed from his throne and a usurper took his place. After many years of troubled rule, the usurper's family was thrust aside by a second line of usurpers, who claimed with some justice to be the rightful kings. Then this second line turned on itself in a ghastly torrent of blood; and out of the western mists came a man of royal blood to overthrow the last of the false kings and give England a new dynasty of greatness.

Such is the broad outline of that century of the sword. Richard II's downfall gave the throne of England to the Lancastrian kings, Henry IV, Henry V, and Henry VI. Then Lancaster was put aside by York: Edward IV ruled, and after him came his dark-souled brother, Richard III, taking the rightful place of the boy who should have been King Edward V. Finally, Henry VII, an exile returning to his native land, restored order, united by marriage the warring houses, and laid the foundations for England's greatness; his descendants have worn the royal crown to this day.

As we will see, the real story is something more than a shuttling succession of Richards, Henrys, and Edwards. Each change of dynasty was nothing less than a revolution; and nations are shaped by their revolutions. The issues were complex, the questions raised were difficult to answer, and nothing in the story is quite what it seems to be at first glance. There are few heroes and few villains. The neat pattern we impose on events proves, upon close examination, not to be so neat.

To understand any of it, we must begin somewhat earlier than the beginning. . . .

England has always been a land set apart from the rest of Europe, not merely by design of geography, but by something more subtle. England stands at the rim of the continent, cut off by miles of water from the feuds and migrations of Europe. Over thousands of years, shifting groups of men and women crossed those miles of water, putting their own distinct stamp on the life of the island.

The names of the earliest comers are lost in time; all that remains are the mounds in which they buried their dead, and the ruins of the great prehistoric temples, like Stonehenge. By Julius Caesar's day, two thousand years ago, the island was held by a people called the Britons. Then the conquering Romans came and turned the island of the Britons into the province of Britannia, or Britain. The Romans ruled Britannia for four centuries. After they departed, about A.D. 450, tribesmen out of Germany invaded the land. These barbarians—the Angles, the Saxons, and the Jutes—drove the Britons beyond the mountains, into the regions we call Wales and Scotland. What had been called "Britain" now came to be known as "Angle-land," or simply "England."

Under the Angles, the Saxons, and the Jutes, England became a rich and pleasant land. At first each little district in Anglo-Saxon England had its own tribal chieftain, who called himself a king; but in time one king established himself as supreme over all the others. Hardly had this royal dynasty grown secure on the throne, though, than fierce new invaders came—Viking pirates out of Denmark. The Danes raided England from 835 on, taking possession of large sections of it. In the year 1013 the Danish king made himself King of England.

But the Danes were overthrown and briefly men of Anglo-Saxon blood ruled England again—until that memorable year of 1066, when William, Duke of Normandy, came to conquer and reign. The blood of the Vikings flowed in the veins of William and his Normans, but they were French in language and French in culture. They shattered the power of the old Anglo-Saxon nobility and carved up England to please themselves. William—now King Wil-

liam I of England—kept the best land for himself and his
family, but rewarded his loyal followers with fine estates.

Thus a new ruling class was grafted onto the English
stock. The peasants and commoners of the towns were
Anglo-Saxons, often with a mixture of Danish blood; but
the nobles were the sons of the conquerors. They were the
masters, these French-speaking ex-Normans. Gradually, as
the centuries passed, they blended into the population they
had conquered. But there was always a wide gulf separating the proud nobles—who spent their time feasting, hunting, or making war—from the men who tilled the soil and
kept the shops.

William the Conqueror gave England a form of government quite different from that of most other lands. France,
for instance, was ruled by a king; but France had many
dukes who controlled whole provinces that were virtually
kingdoms within the kingdom. Sometimes these local dukes
had more power than the king himself. William, in fact,
had been just such a mighty duke in France, and he wanted
no local rulers of this sort to plague him now that he had
won a country of his own. He took good care to scatter
the estates of his earls and barons, giving them strips of
territory here and there but not letting any of them gain
power over a single great domain.

In William's England the king was supreme. He made
the laws and the important decisions; he could create earls,
and he could strip them of their lands; he led troops personally in battle; he was the greatest landowner in the kingdom. Surrounding the king were chosen advisers, but he
could listen to them or not, as he wished. Most important,
the throne belonged to the king's family; it was a piece of
property that could be handed down from father to son.

William intended that his direct descendants should rule England forever.

And so it has happened. The present royal family of England can trace its ancestry back to King William I. But there have been many zigs and zags in that ancestral line over the nine centuries since William conquered England.

When King William died, his son William Rufus became William II. William II met a mysterious death after ruling for thirteen years, and since he had no children, he was succeeded by his younger brother, Henry.

King Henry's son, Prince William, died before Henry did. That created a problem. The only other direct heir to the throne was King Henry's daughter Matilda. However, according to the custom of the day, a daughter could inherit her father's property but not his title. Matilda could not become Queen of England. Who would rule?

William the Conqueror had not anticipated such a problem. He had assumed that there would always be plenty of sons in his family, so that the crown could descend from generation to generation. But neither he nor anyone else had worked out fixed laws for the succession. Everything had been left to chance, in the hope that there would always be a male heir.

When King Henry died in 1135, Matilda tried to take the throne. But the barons hesitated to give the throne to a woman. Nor could the throne go to Matilda's husband, Count Geoffrey Plantagenet of Anjou. Geoffrey was not descended from William the Conqueror, and so, as a mere 'in-law" of the royal family, was disqualified. Matilda and Geoffrey had a two-year-old son, Henry Plantagenet; but it was unthinkable in such dangerous times to allow an

infant to become king. The king must be a man and a
warrior.

During this period of confusion, Matilda's cousin Stephen
came forward and seized the throne. Stephen was a grandson of William the Conqueror, so at least he had the right
to say he was of royal blood. But he was the son of William's
only daughter, Adela. His descent from the Conqueror,
therefore, was in the so-called female line. That introduced
another complication. Did a member of the female line
have a right to take the throne? Or could the kingdom
descend only through *male* descendants of William I? No
one had any satisfactory answer on this point, either, so
vague were the laws of succession, and in any event no heir
in the male line existed.

What was not vague at all was Stephen's determination
to be King of England. Once he was on the throne, he
stayed there for nineteen years, even though some of the
nobles backed the claim of Princess Matilda and her baby
son. Civil war broke out; Matilda was forced to flee to
France.

Did it really matter—except to the few people directly
involved—who was king? That question naturally arises as
we look back to the year 1135 and the quarrel between
Stephen and Matilda. It is a question that will arise again
and again as we make our way through the story of the Wars
of the Roses.

The answer is that it did matter, very much. Today the
monarch of England is merely a symbolic figure; but in the
Middle Ages the king was the government. The safety of
the realm depended on his valor, his wisdom, and his skill
in ruling. A successful king had to be trained from childhood to perform the tasks that one day would be his. If the

king were weak or lazy or cruel, the welfare of the nation was threatened.

So it was an important concern, this business of who was to be king; and it was important, too, that the king be chosen in a legal way. Men had to respect the king. They could not respect a man who had stolen the throne. King William I had won the throne in a way that all could honor —through his bravery and strength. Therefore, so it was agreed, his descendants had the right to be kings of England. But each of those descendants had to come to power in a proper manner.

In the United States we are guided by a written Constitution that sets forth the way in which our leaders are chosen. We follow the regulations that were set down when our country was born, subject to the modifications that proved to be necessary in the original plan. Hence, every four years we hold an election and decide who is to be our President.

But England has never had such a written document. Instead of a formal constitution, she simply has a body of tradition, developed over the centuries. The English do things the way they have always been done in England— and when it turns out that the traditional way has ceased to work, they abandon it and try a new way.

But in 1135 the traditions were very new. There had been only three kings since the Norman Conquest: William I and his sons, William II and Henry I. When Henry I died without leaving a prince as his heir, no guidance could be found in past events. That left room for Stephen to take power. All during Stephen's reign the faction of Matilda's son, Henry Plantagenet, insisted that he was the rightful king. In the end, since King Stephen had no sons, he named young Henry as his heir. And in 1154 Stephen died and Henry Plantagenet became King Henry II.

England's unwritten tradition of royal inheritance now had grown a little. Both Stephen and Henry II had come to the throne through the female line. And so, although it was still agreed that the daughter of a king could not become queen and reign herself, it was now accepted that her children might inherit the throne.

As it happened, there was no need to invoke that tradition for hundreds of years. The Plantagenet family produced an ample quantity of sons in generation after generation. Henry II was followed as king by his son Richard the Lion-Hearted; and when Richard died without a son, the crown passed to his brother John. King John's son was the next king—Henry III. Some new difficulties arose at that point, for Henry III was only nine when his father died. But the leading barons of the realm placed him on the throne and ruled in his name until he was of age. England thus received her first boy-king; and his reign was a troubled one. It was an omen for a later time when other boys would mount the throne.

Henry III ruled for more than half a century. At his death, his oldest son became King Edward I, who was in turn succeeded by *his* son, Edward II, in 1307. In Edward II's time another problem arose. This Edward was a foolish and idle man, the first member of his family who was unfit to be king. England was threatened by war and inner turmoil. What was to be done? The king was deemed God's anointed ruler, a mighty and nearly sacred figure. It was a serious matter to rip the crown from a legitimate king. But if Edward II remained on the throne much longer, disaster and chaos would result.

It was a desperate time, and desperate measures were taken. Roger Mortimer, the first Earl of March, led a rebellion against the king. Supported by King Edward's own queen, Mortimer seized the king and put him to death in 1327. But the rebellious nobleman did not dare to make himself king in Edward's place, although the thought probably occurred to him. Mortimer was not of royal blood, and the country would accept as its king only a man descended from William the Conqueror. So Mortimer allowed the fourteen-year-old son of the murdered monarch to become King Edward III. Another article had been added to England's growing unwritten constitution: If a king is unworthy of the throne, his people may cast him aside.

Edward III proved to be one of the strongest kings in England's history. While still in his teens he brought order out of the chaos that his deposed father had left. Roger Mortimer attempted to act as the real ruler, using Edward III as a puppet, but the young king would have none of that; in 1330, when he was eighteen years old, he arrested Mortimer, accused him of the slaying of Edward II, and had him hanged.

With England under control, the vigorous king turned to foreign war. The relations between England and France had been tense for decades. In the time of Henry II more than half of France had actually been controlled by England, through inheritance from William as Duke of Normandy, through the dowry of Henry's French-born queen, and through later conquest. But these possessions had nearly all been lost under Edward II. All that remained to England was a narrow strip of land along the western coast.

Edward III resolved to win back the French territories England had lost. He opened war in 1337—scarcely imagining that he was commencing what history would call the Hundred Years War. English troops commanded by the valiant king invaded France and in 1346 won a great victory at Crécy. Then the frightful plague known as the Black Death, which killed a third of the population of Europe, interrupted the war for several years. In 1356 came another great English triumph at Poitiers; the King of France himself was taken prisoner and carried off for ransom.

Through the victories of Crécy and Poitiers, Edward III had regained England's old possessions in France and gained a rich harvest of treasure as the ransom for the French king. England hailed her warrior king with ringing cheers—and also praised his stalwart sons, who had fought as brilliant generals in the French campaigns.

No other King of England has ever had so many sons as Edward III. When he was fifteen, four months after the murder of his father, he married his second cousin, Philippa of Hainault, and between 1330 and 1355 she presented him with seven sons and five daughters. Two of the sons and three of the daughters died young. The others lived and had many descendants, so that England was filled with the family of Edward III in a way that created powerful rivalries and ultimately led to civil war.

The eldest son was Edward, known as the Black Prince —a magnificent soldier who spent most of his life fighting in France. The Black Prince was the hero of Poitiers, and as the first son of the king was the heir to the throne; for the tradition had long since been established that the crown descended in order of age, from the king to his first son, and then to the first son of that son. If the oldest son of the king had no male heir, the throne went to the second oldest son of the king, and so on down the line of seniority.

King Edward III invented a special honor for the Black Prince in 1337: he gave him the title of Duke of Cornwall. There had never been dukes in England before, although the title was common in France. The highest-ranking nobles, next to the king himself, had been the earls; but now the Black Prince, as Duke of Cornwall, outranked all the earls of the land.

King Edward III's second-born son died in childhood. The second to reach manhood was Lionel of Antwerp, who was made Duke of Clarence in 1362. A quarter of a century had passed between the creation of the first and the second royal duke of England, as though perhaps King Edward did not think it was wise to give such an exalted rank to all of his sons. On the same day that Lionel received his dukedom, King Edward's next oldest son, John of Gaunt, was honored. John became Duke of Lancaster, though he was generally still known simply as John of Gaunt, after his birthplace, the Belgian city of Ghent, which the English called "Gaunt." King Edward did not offer dukedoms to his two youngest sons, Edmund of Langley and Thomas of Woodstock.

The last years of Edward III's reign were sad ones. He had ruled England all his adult life, and the strain of power had worn him out. France, which had seemed beaten in 1356, had found new strength and had regained some of the territory Edward had taken from her; Edward, as he aged, could not summon the strength to launch a new war, and so there were many years of uneasy truce in the middle of the century-long struggle with France. The death of Edward's son Lionel, the Duke of Clarence, in 1368, came as a heavy blow to the monarch. But far more severe was the news that came to him eight years later: Edward the Black Prince, exhausted by battle, had gone to his grave. The heir to the throne had died. King Edward, his life sinking fast, withdrew in despair to a hunting lodge in a quiet part of his land, and death came to him on a June day in 1377, in the sixty-fifth year of his life and the fiftieth year of his reign.

He was survived by three sons—John of Gaunt, Edmund of Langley, and Thomas of Woodstock. But none of them could take the throne. By recognized tradition the right to the crown had passed through their generation entirely to their ten-year-old nephew, Richard, the son of the dead Black Prince.

No one openly questioned Richard's right to be king. So for the second time a boy would wear the crown of England. The coronation of Richard II ushered in the beginning of the time of troubles for the country. By all the laws of inheritance the young monarch had a clear title to the throne. But he was the last King of England who could say that he came to his position by certain line of descent from William the Conqueror. After the tragic reign of Richard II, various side branches of the family would occupy the throne, and the crown would bound like a football from king to king.

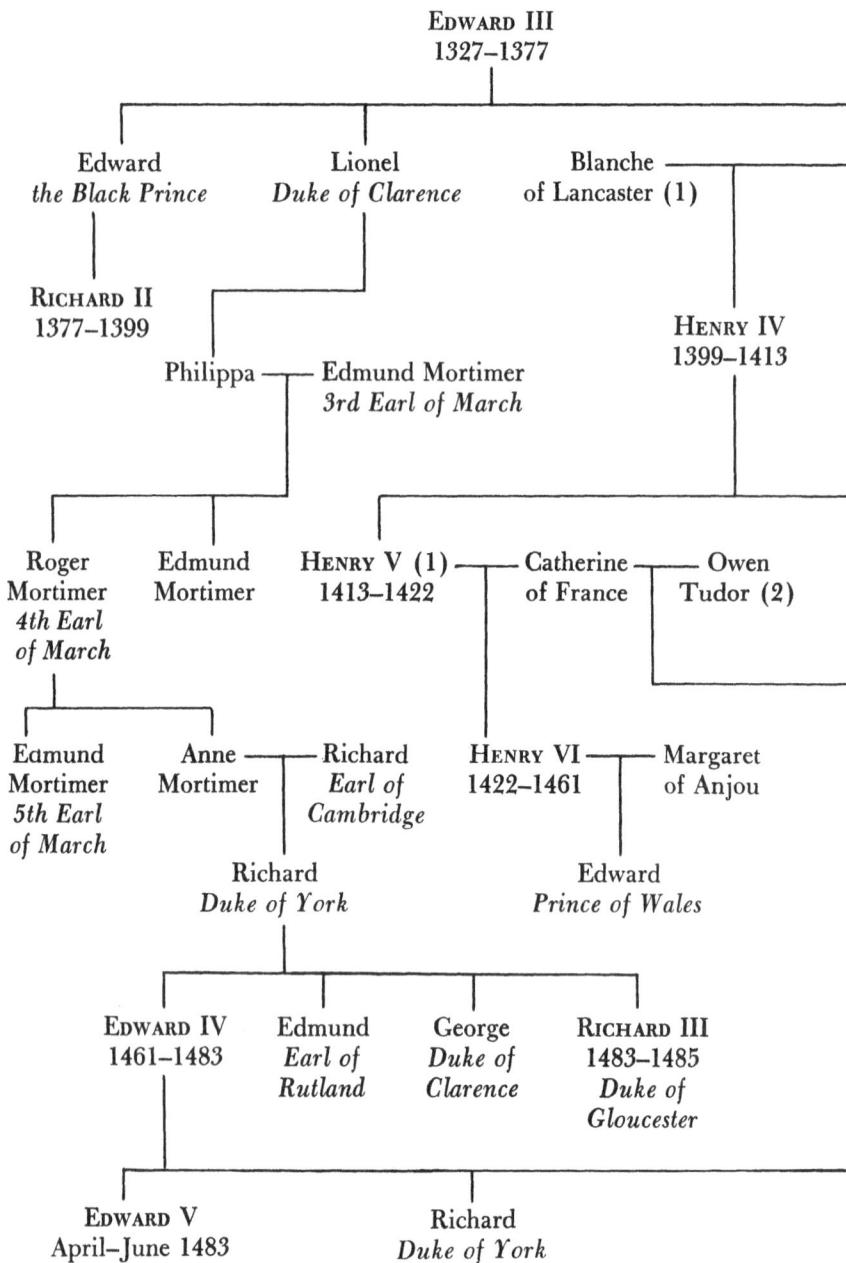

EDWARD III
1327–1377

Edward
the Black Prince

Lionel
Duke of Clarence

Blanche
of Lancaster (1)

RICHARD II
1377–1399

HENRY IV
1399–1413

Philippa —— Edmund Mortimer
3rd Earl of March

Roger
Mortimer
*4th Earl
of March*

Edmund
Mortimer

HENRY V (1) —— Catherine —— Owen
1413–1422   of France   Tudor (2)

Edmund
Mortimer
*5th Earl
of March*

Anne —— Richard
Mortimer   *Earl of
            Cambridge*

HENRY VI —— Margaret
1422–1461   of Anjou

Richard
Duke of York

Edward
Prince of Wales

EDWARD IV
1461–1483

Edmund
*Earl of
Rutland*

George
*Duke of
Clarence*

RICHARD III
1483–1485
*Duke of
Gloucester*

EDWARD V
April–June 1483

Richard
Duke of York

John of Gaunt ———— Catherine   Edmund   Thomas
Duke of Lancaster   Swynford (3)   *Duke of York* *Duke of*
                                                     Gloucester

John   Henry   Thomas   Edward   Richard
Beaufort Beaufort Beaufort *Duke of York* *Earl of*
Earl of   *Cambridge*
Somerset   married Anne Mortimer

Thomas   John   Humphrey   Henry   John   Edmund
Duke of *Duke of* *Duke of*   Beaufort Beaufort II Beaufort
Clarence *Bedford* *Gloucester*   *Duke of*
                                        Somerset

Edmund ———————— Margaret
Tudor   Beaufort
Earl of
Richmond

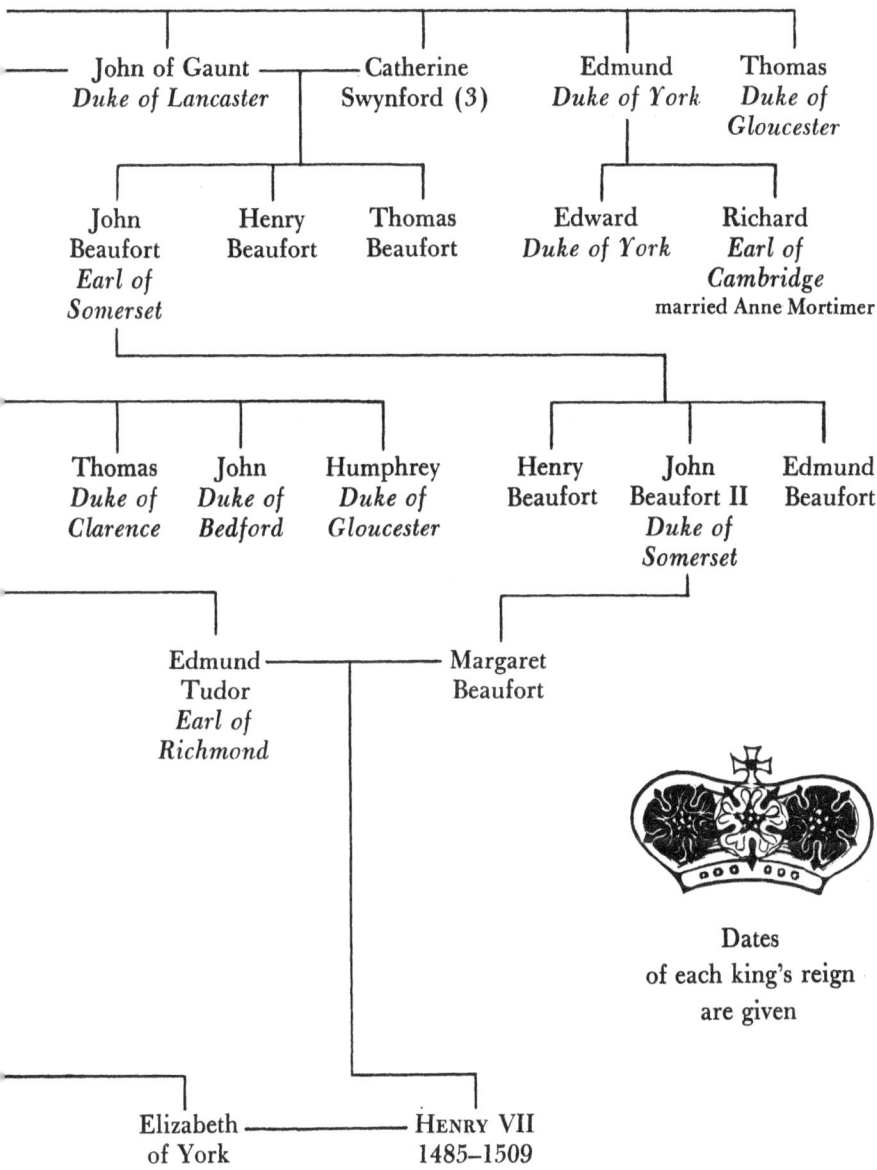

Dates
of each king's reign
are given

Elizabeth ———————— HENRY VII
of York   1485–1509

the royal cousins

HE CORONATION ceremony in honor of Richard II was a grand event, carried out with
medieval pomp and pageantry on July 16, 1377. At the
head of the splendid procession rode the new king's oldest
uncle, John of Gaunt; the slender ten-year-old king followed, surrounded by the richest nobles of the land. The
parade passed through the city of London to the royal
palace at Westminster. Then the chief participants went on
foot from the palace to Westminster Abbey, where the
crown would be placed on Richard's head. This time John
of Gaunt walked beside the fair young king. Behind them
were Richard's two younger uncles, Edmund of Langley
and Thomas of Woodstock. Then came the third Earl of
March, Edmund Mortimer. His great-grandfather, Roger
Mortimer, had been executed by King Edward III for the
murder of Edward II; but the Mortimer family had come
back into royal favor since then.

To the rear of the Earl of March walked the Archbishop

of Canterbury, England's highest-ranking churchman, who would anoint Richard with the holy oils marking his kingship. With the Archbishop marched the Bishop of London and the Bishop of Winchester. Among the other figures in the coronation procession was a small boy, seven months younger than the new king himself, who proudly carried a ceremonial sword. He was King Richard's cousin, Henry, the son of John of Gaunt. That day all eyes were on the youthful king; cousin Henry was simply a royal relative, one of many. But Henry—called Henry of Bolingbroke after the place of his birth—was marked to play an important role in the drama of English history. One day he too would stand in Westminster Abbey to be crowned King of England. But no one could foresee that then.

Even as Richard II took his coronation oath, donned his crown, and accepted the homage of his subjects, men were giving thought to his eventual successor. The boy was frail, and life was always risky. What if Richard died before he was old enough to father a son and heir?

In that case, the one who stood next in line was a three-year-old child named Roger Mortimer, the son of the third Earl of March. It was a strangely ironical twist that had made the great-great-grandson of the outlawed rebel of 1330 the heir to the throne in 1377. It had come about because Edmund, the third Earl of March, had married Philippa, the daughter of the dead Lionel, Duke of Clarence. Lionel had been the third-born son of Edward III, the second to live to manhood. Richard II traced his own line of descent from his grandfather Edward III by way of the Black Prince, Edward III's eldest son. It was a complicated bit of genealogy, but England would hear much more of it in years to come.

Richard's closest friend and playmate in his youth—if a king can be said to have friends and playmates—was his cousin Henry of Bolingbroke. Henry was third in line for the throne, since his father, John of Gaunt, was the fourth-born son of Edward III. But both Richard II and little Roger Mortimer would have to die without heirs before Henry could become king, and no one seriously expected that to happen. In any event, the royal cousins did not spend their days drawing up diagrams of family trees. They learned to ride horses, to wield swords and bows, to hunt and to fight. And they watched as the older members of their family governed the kingdom.

Beyond a doubt the most powerful man in England was Henry's father, John of Gaunt, the Duke of Lancaster. He was the oldest living son of King Edward III; he was a shrewd and complex man, and he had distinguished himself in battle overseas. Above all else, John of Gaunt was rich. He was the wealthiest man in the country, thanks to the cleverness and ambition of many of his ancestors over the past century, and especially to his luck in marrying the heiress Blanche of Lancaster.

The fortunes of the house of Lancaster went back to the time of Edmund Crouchback, the younger son of King Henry III. Edmund's older brother Edward had become King Edward I; but Edmund, who did not have to bear the burden of ruling England, spent his time collecting estates. In 1267 Henry III gave Edmund the title of Earl of Lancaster and loaded him with valuable land. At that time a title of nobility still carried with it the lordship of a particular district; the Earl of Lancaster thus was the landlord of the whole county of Lancaster, entitled to collect rents from all those who lived on and farmed his land. (Later such titles often became strictly honorary, marks of rank rather than tokens of power over a specific place.)

Edmund Crouchback's land holdings included no less than 632 properties, stretching from Wales to the borders of Scotland, and from Lancashire in the west to the coast of Yorkshire in the east. Through marriage he added still more property to this domain. His son Thomas, the second Earl of Lancaster, brought new estates into the family holding by wedding Alice Lucy, the heiress of the property of the Earls of Salisbury and Lincoln. Among the castles she brought to him was Bolingbroke, in Lincolnshire, where a future king would be born.

Thomas of Lancaster rebelled against Edward II and was beheaded for treason in 1322. All the estates of Lancaster were declared forfeited to the king. But after the fall of Edward II, Thomas' brother Henry was made Earl of Lancaster and received back the lands taken from his brother. Henry's son, also Henry, continued the family policy of acquiring land. This second Henry had no sons, but his daughter Blanche became the wife of John of Gaunt. The vast Lancaster possessions descended to her and through her became the property of John of Gaunt. In his own right, as a king's son, John had already accumulated much land in addition.

As Duke of Lancaster after 1362, John enjoyed some special powers. On his own land he had the right to appoint judges, to execute the law, and to do virtually everything else that was normally the power of the king. The king reserved the right to levy taxes in the duchy of Lancaster, but otherwise John of Gaunt, by permission of King Edward III, was the master of a kingdom within the kingdom. Though only a duke, John of Gaunt in 1377 held more power than many kings had enjoyed.

Now he ruled all of England on behalf of his nephew Richard II. Though he could have seized the throne himself, he never wavered in his loyalty to Richard. So long as John had the power of a king, there was no reason for him to commit the outrage of usurping the throne. He worked vigorously to bring the kingdom out of the difficulties that had assailed it in the years of Edward III's old age.

But it was an uneasy time. Many injustices had been practiced. Taxes had been raised again and again to pay the cost of the French war and the occupation of the conquered territory; the common people were grumbling against their masters. In the summer of 1381 a terrifying revolt swept through the country. Peasants led by a man named Wat Tyler rose in arms; there were riots in many cities, and the rebels swarmed across London Bridge into London itself, murdering and looting. Several noblemen were beheaded. The palace of John of Gaunt was burned. The rebels demanded to speak with King Richard and present a list of their grievances.

Richard had been taken for his own safety to the Tower of London, that grim old fortress begun by William the Conqueror. From the walls of the Tower Richard and his cousin Henry of Bolingbroke looked out and saw London in flames. John of Gaunt could do nothing to halt the violence. Richard took a bold step; he appeared in a turret of the Tower and asked the angry peasants to go peacefully to their homes. When they refused, he offered to leave the Tower and meet with their leaders at a place called Mile End the next morning.

The king was not yet fifteen years old. He had volunteered to quit his sanctuary and go among murderous rioters. In the morning, after a night of disorder and destruction, Richard kept his word. Accompanied by the Mayor of London and a handful of lords and knights, he proceeded to Mile End and listened to the petitions of the rebels. He agreed to grant some of their demands if they would return to their villages.

The next day the king met with another band of rebels, this time including Wat Tyler himself. Once more Richard assured the peasants that their wishes would be granted; but Tyler was suspicious, and tempers flared. Suddenly the Mayor of London pulled Tyler from his horse and another man of the royal party stabbed him to death. The peasants set up a great cry of rage and rushed forward. Coolly, Richard cried out, "Sirs, will you shoot your king? You shall have from me all you seek. Only follow me to the fields outside!" He rode away, leading the peasants out of the city, and order was restored.

Though disturbances continued in parts of England for most of the summer, Tyler's death had deprived the rebellion of its leader, and in a few months it petered out. Young King Richard had demonstrated his courage magnificently by daring to meet the rebels in person. For the moment it seemed that England had a king of whom to be proud, a worthy son of the Black Prince. But that early promise was not to be fulfilled.

John of Gaunt had extensive property on the European mainland, and from 1384 on he spent much of his time overseas. That left a group of lesser nobles to guide the king. Richard resented their guidance. Having shown his courage during the revolt of 1381, he felt that the time had come to be king in his own right and to escape from the domination of older men. In 1385 he was eighteen years old; his grandfather Edward III had been unquestioned ruler of England at that age, but Richard was still hampered by a council of older advisers.

A group of court officials backed Richard in his attempt to gain full authority. He was opposed by his uncle, Thomas of Woodstock, who was hungry for power himself. Thomas, the youngest son of Edward III, had received the title of Duke of Gloucester from Richard. At the same time, Richard made his third uncle, Edmund of Langley, the Duke of York. Becoming a royal duke seemed to spur Thomas of Gloucester's ambitions, and soon he was plotting against the king.

In 1386 Thomas and several other powerful nobles launched an attack on Richard and his friends. Thomas ordered the king to dismiss his court favorites and obey Thomas' policies. When Richard refused, his uncle went to Parliament to ask for a grant of special powers over the king.

Parliament was something William the Conqueror had never had to contend with. He had ruled as an absolute king. The first substantial weakening of the king's powers had come in 1215, when a group of strong earls and barons had forced King John to sign a document called Magna Carta, limiting his right to tax them. This gathering of mighty noblemen was hardly a Parliament in the true sense of that word, though, for it represented neither the smaller landowners nor the commoners.

During the reign of another weak king, Henry III, a rebellious baron named Simon de Montfort summoned a true national assembly. Not only lords, but minor knights and townsmen, took part in Simon de Montfort's Parliament of 1265. By the time of Edward I, a generation later, Parliament was meeting every few years and was gradually winning power from the king. The idea became established that the king could not tax his subjects without the consent of Parliament, and that Parliament could act to curb a king's unwise actions. When Roger Mortimer overthrew the worthless Edward II in 1327, he went to the trouble of getting Parliament's permission for the deed.

While Edward III was on the throne, Parliament assumed its modern form, dividing into a House of Lords and a House of Commons that met separately to vote. The Lords consisted of forty or so earls and barons, nearly all of them related to the king by blood or by marriage, together with the leading archbishops and abbots of the realm. Commons was made up of representatives of the towns and cities, elected each time a Parliament was summoned by the king. It was a long way from being a truly democratic system; only rich men were allowed to vote for members of Commons, and only knights and landowners could run for office. Yet the power of Parliament—and particularly of the Commons—steadily grew all during the fourteenth century. By the time of Richard II, Commons was demanding the right to inquire into public abuses, to impeach royal ministers, and to pass judgment on the actions of the king himself.

Why did the kings allow such power to slip into the hands of Parliament? The kings had no choice. They needed money—money to run the royal household, money to pay the royal soldiers, money to meet all the expenses of the kingdom. To raise this money the kings were forced to turn to their subjects; and by a slow, steady process the subjects were able to extract concessions from their rulers in return for their cash. When a spendthrift king was on the throne, Parliament generally managed to improve its position, and then it fought hard to keep that position during the next reign.

Thomas of Gloucester, King Richard's uncle, went before Parliament in 1386 and was given a virtual grant of the royal powers. The king fled from London and began to gather forces for a civil war. The Duke of Gloucester also assembled an army. Richard marched back to London at the head of his troops; but when the moment of collision arrived, Richard's support collapsed. His friends took to their heels and the humiliated young king had to submit to his uncle the duke.

In December of 1387 one of Richard's exiled supporters raised a new army and marched toward London. Once more the ruling barons sent troops to drive off the king's men. A battle took place at Radcot Bridge, in Oxfordshire, and Richard's army was routed. Of the men who fought on Gloucester's side, one of the bravest that day was twenty-year-old Henry of Bolingbroke—the king's cousin!

This was a bitter blow to King Richard II—that his relative and boyhood friend should have turned against him. But Henry had good reason for joining Gloucester's party. The king had handed out honors, titles, and grants of land to many of the young courtiers about him, but had almost entirely overlooked his cousin of Bolingbroke. Although Henry, as the son of the fabulously wealthy John of Gaunt, was in no need of property, he resented being overlooked. So it was easy for the sinister Thomas of Gloucester—Henry's uncle as well as the king's—to tempt him into rebellion.

King Richard now was at the mercy of the nobles. Early in 1388 they met to determine his fate. In a long, heated argument, they quarreled over the future of the throne. Thomas of Gloucester wished to kill the king and don the crown himself, but the others would not permit that. Young Henry of Bolingbroke argued for a more moderate course: let Richard live, he said, but force him to yield all power.

Bolingbroke's suggestions were adopted. Richard, brooding in defeat, remained king, but only as a puppet. Thomas of Gloucester summoned a Parliament picked in advance to be cooperative. This "Merciless Parliament" of 1388 gave the ghost of a legal status to the new arrangement. Richard's friends were hunted down and brutally executed; even the king's elderly tutor was hanged. Richard retired to his palace, suffering the shame of a deposed king.

For a year the faction of Thomas of Gloucester ruled England. But Richard, working with quiet cleverness, unveiled a surprise in the spring of 1389. He appeared before Gloucester, Bolingbroke, and the three other great lords who had usurped his powers and asked mildly to be told how old he was. Three-and-twenty, they replied. Then he declared that he had certainly come of age, and was minded to rule his kingdom without their help. The five lords were taken off guard; before they could act, Richard had sent word to the nation that he was in command. He moved with such swiftness that his scheme succeeded. By September of 1389 Richard at last was master of his own realm.

A more determined king would have beheaded the five

usurping lords at once—for, in the rough politics of the day, death was the usual penalty for choosing a losing side. But Richard II was a curious mixture of weak and bold, of tender and ruthless. Though he harbored cold hatred in his breast for Gloucester, Bolingbroke, and the other three, he allowed them not only to live but to retain high office. Perhaps he feared the consequences of destroying them even when they were in his power. Or perhaps it was the calming influence of old John of Gaunt, who had returned from Spain late in 1389 when Richard had so suddenly asserted himself.

For the next eight years Richard II governed England. More than any previous king he paid heed to the troubles of the common man, easing the lot of the peasants in many ways. With great tact he concealed the bitterness he felt toward the five usurpers. Indeed, Henry of Bolingbroke became one of Richard's closest companions again. During the occasional quarrels between the king and his nobles during those eight years, Bolingbroke always spoke up on the king's side. The nobles were restless, for they disliked Richard and feared his sympathies for the commoners; but Richard remained in charge.

The king was now a man. But the king had no son. In 1382 Richard had married a foreign princess, Anne of Bohemia; she died, childless, twelve years later. In 1396 Richard married again, wedding Isabel, the daughter of King Charles VI of France. Cousin Henry had carried on the negotiations for the wedding, which was intended to symbolize the end of the long hostility between England and France. As a move in the chess game of international politics, Richard's second marriage was wise. But Queen

Isabel was only seven years old. It would be many years before King Richard could have an heir for his throne.

Richard feared that the restless, ambitious men who had overthrown him in 1388 might seek to push him from his throne again and replace him with someone more pliable. The nearest in line—the "heir presumptive," as he was called—still was Roger Mortimer, the fourth Earl of March by now. This great-grandson of Edward III, seven years younger than King Richard, had grown to manhood as a strong, well-liked soldier. Richard, who was on friendly terms with him, had sent Roger to Ireland in 1394 to put down a revolt of the fierce Irish chieftains. If anything should happen to Richard, Roger would be king.

At the beginning of 1397 Richard chose to strike against his old enemies before they could move against him. Showing that he had forgotten no grudges in the past eight years, he ordered the arrest of his uncle, Thomas of Gloucester, and two of the other lords of the 1388 overthrow: the Earl of Arundel and the Earl of Warwick. He did not arrest Bolingbroke, nor the fifth of the usurpers, Thomas Mowbray, Earl of Nottingham. These two had become loyal to Richard since that troubled time.

The king now showed what fierce resentments had burned in his breast. Arundel was declared a traitor and was beheaded. Warwick was exiled. Thomas of Gloucester, men were told, had mysteriously "died" in his prison cell— and it was not difficult to see that he had been murdered by the king's henchmen to avoid the ugly need of placing a royal duke on trial.

For the two loyal lords, Richard had rewards. He gave Henry of Bolingbroke the title of Duke of Hereford, and made Mowbray the Duke of Norfolk. At the same time he persuaded Parliament to declare that neither man shared the guilt of the king's overthrow in 1388. Parliament was willing to approve any decree Richard might make; for the king had abruptly emerged as a dynamic, almost terrifying figure bent on vengeance, and no man dared thwart him.

In fact, Richard was out of control and on the verge of becoming a tyrant. Sensitive, even poetic by nature, highly intelligent, ambitious, Richard had been forced to endure a great deal in his youth, compelled to stand by while first John of Gaunt and then Thomas of Gloucester enjoyed the royal powers. Essentially a weak man with a strong man's ideas, Richard had destroyed his enemies by patient craft and cunning, and now, in a sudden surge of pleasure, he showed himself willing to rule without paying heed to barons, friends, or Parliament. He had forced the powerless Parliament of 1398 to suspend many of the fundamental rights and liberties of the realm, placing total control in his own hands.

But an absolute monarch, holding the power of life and death at a whim, could no longer be tolerated in England. Despotism of the kind Richard now was practicing had been common in the ancient world, perhaps, in the blood-thirsty empire of Assyria and in Rome under the Caesars. But this was a different era. The theory had long been established that the king ruled by grace of God and by the consent of the governed; his subjects had elevated him to his high place so that he might protect their lives, laws, and property. The king could not stand above the law, striking off heads as it pleased him, nor could he casually abolish any laws that menaced his strength. That was tyranny, and the English, over many generations of slow progress, had moved past the stage of permitting a tyrant to rule. The modern theory of government had been stated clearly enough about 1375 by Nicholas of Oresme, a French bishop: "Whenever kingship approaches tyranny it is near its end, for by this it becomes ripe for division, change of dynasty, or total destruction, especially in a temperate climate . . . where men are habitually, morally and naturally free."

Among those who watched in alarm as the Richard II of 1398 ran amok was Henry of Bolingbroke. Henry watched as Richard's extravagance mounted, as he demanded heavy "loans" from the nobles to pay his debts, as he stripped away the cloak of law to slay all who opposed him. To Henry, Richard's abrupt explosion seemed a mark of the king's madness; it appeared that Richard was embarked on the same disastrous course of misrule that had brought the downfall of their great-grandfather, Edward II.

Bolingbroke began to consider ways of removing Richard from the throne.

There was more on Henry's mind than simply preserving the kingdom from a mad king. He was looking out for his own ambitions. His father, John of Gaunt, was old and near death. Soon Henry would inherit the vast holdings of the Duke of Lancaster. But what if Richard turned on him in a burst of greed and confiscated that fantastic inheritance? True, Henry was in favor just now; but he saw a possible rival in the person of the other new duke, Thomas Mowbray. Richard had made Mowbray the Duke of Norfolk even though Mowbray was an upstart with no royal blood in his veins. Did Richard have some bigger plans yet for Mowbray, Henry wondered uneasily?

And in August of 1398 Roger Mortimer was killed while fighting in Ireland. He left several daughters and a son, Edmund Mortimer, who became the fifth Earl of March and also, as great-great-grandson to Edward III by descent from Edward's second oldest son, the heir presumptive to the throne of England. But the new Earl of March was only seven years old. As Henry saw it, no one stood between him and the throne but a madman and a child. Could he persuade the country to make him its king?

A tense triangle of uncertainty linked Richard, Henry, and Mowbray. None of them knew the extent of the other's ambitions; each feared both the others. Mowbray, like Henry, was troubled by Richard's new display of headstrong self-determination. As they were riding together one day, Mowbray voiced to Henry his fears about the king. Could Richard be trusted, Mowbray asked? Perhaps at this very moment he was scheming to dispose of the two men he had just honored with dukedoms!

Henry used Mowbray's indiscreet words as a weapon against this man whom he regarded as a rival. Hastily he rushed to Richard and accused Mowbray of uttering treason. It was a rash and not overly scrupulous thing to do—and, for perhaps the only time in his life, Henry of Bolingbroke had made a serious miscalculation. In his hurry to ruin Mowbray, he failed to realize that Richard might see the situation as a chance to rid himself of both ambitious dukes with one stroke.

Henry went before Parliament to denounce Mowbray. Mowbray replied that Henry was lying and that he had never spoken words disloyal to Richard. The quarrel grew heated, and it was decided to settle it in a fine old medieval way: trial by combat. On September 16, 1398, Mowbray and Bolingbroke would appear in full armor at the city of Coventry and prove by force of arms which man was guilty of the act of treason.

England had not known such excitement in many years. A huge crowd journeyed to Coventry to watch these young, strong lords do battle. The accuser and the accused stood forth in the arena, hands to their weapons. The trumpets sounded. The marshal of the combat turned to each man, asking him to state his name and cause. Shakespeare puts resounding words into the mouths of the two men:

> *My name is Thomas Mowbray, Duke of Norfolk*
> *Who hither come engaged by my oath,—*
> *Which God defend a knight should violate!—*
> *Both to defend my loyalty and truth*
> *To God, my king, and his succeeding issue,*
> *Against the Duke of Hereford that appeals me;*
> *And, by the grace of God and this mine arm,*
> *To prove him, in defending of myself,*
> *A traitor to my God, my king, and me:*
> *And as I truly fight, defend me heaven!*

To which Shakespeare's Bolingbroke replies:

> *Harry of Hereford, Lancaster, and Derby*
> *Am I; who ready here do stand in arms,*
> *To prove by God's grace and my body's valour,*
> *In lists, on Thomas Mowbray, Duke of Norfolk,*
> *That he's a traitor foul and dangerous,*
> *To God of heaven, King Richard, and to me:*
> *And as I truly fight, defend me heaven!*

But King Richard, always the master of the unexpected stroke of drama, threw down his baton just as the combatants were ready to charge, ending the duel before it had

begun. The disappointed spectators learned that they were
to be deprived of the thrilling, barbaric show. There would
be no duel. For the sake of the kingdom's peace, Richard
said, he was banishing Henry of Bolingbroke from England
for a term of ten years. Then, turning to Mowbray, Richard
pronounced a sentence of exile for life.

Both men were stunned. Once again the wily Richard
had taken stronger men than himself off guard, and willy-

nilly they obeyed. Mowbray departed for Germany, but his exile was a brief one; within twelve months he was dead. Henry, astounded by Richard's trick, left for France.

Richard was now supreme. By execution or banishment he had rid himself of all five of the powerful men who had crushed him in 1388. The kingdom was his, to use as a plaything. As a boy, he had shown promise of greatness, but in young manhood his desire for revenge led him only into folly.

Folly upon folly was his path in 1399. On February 3 of the new year John of Gaunt died, undoubtedly weakened by the shock of his son Henry's disgrace and banishment. The lands of Lancaster were bequeathed to Henry, no longer Henry of Bolingbroke or the Duke of Hereford, but now the Duke of Lancaster, wealthier even than the king. But Henry was in exile; and Richard, wallowing in extravagance, needed money. With the connivance of Parliament, Richard disinherited his cousin and ordered the estates of Lancaster forfeited to the crown.

He could have done nothing more likely to turn the other nobles of the realm against him. Richard's act struck at the security of every landowner in the kingdom. If he could disinherit the Duke of Lancaster so easily, the king might in his avarice take any man's land. To quiet the nobles, Richard distributed portions of the Lancastrian lands to his noble supporters, though keeping the best properties for himself. Still there was murmuring. This time the king had gone too far. The exiled Henry of Lancaster in France began to gather a band of sympathetic friends who urged him to return to England and avenge the outrage that had been committed.

Now Richard made a second error. In May of 1399, immediately after his reckless seizure of the Lancastrian lands, the king chose to go to Ireland and make war against the chieftains that had slain Roger Mortimer. He named as "guardian" of the realm the only living son of Edward III: Edmund of Langley, the Duke of York. This duke, Richard's last surviving royal uncle, was a meek and retiring man wholly incapable of governing the kingdom. Yet Richard went off to Ireland, leaving a "man of straw" in his place and the entire land disordered and chaotic.

In pleased amazement Henry of Lancaster learned that his cousin had been so foolish as to depart from the country. The coast was clear for Henry's return. On a day early in July, 1399, Henry and a small band of loyal men crossed the English Channel from France and landed at a place called Ravenspur, on the Yorkshire coast.

He had come back to England, he announced, only to claim what was rightfully his: the properties of Lancaster. He wanted no more than that, he declared. He did not speak just then of his true ambition—which was to push Richard II from his throne and place the crown of England on the brow of John of Gaunt's son Henry.

the downfall
of a king

THE PRECEDENT for deposing an English king had been set in 1327, when Parliament, spurred by the first Earl of March, had approved the removal from authority of Edward II. So Henry of Lancaster did not need to fear that he was going against established law and order in plotting to overthrow his royal cousin Richard. And through his recent despotism the once-popular Richard had made himself hated throughout the land.

Yet the situation was not the same as in 1327. When Edward II had been deposed, the throne had gone to his son and legitimate heir, Edward III. Now the legitimate heir was a child of eight, Edmund Mortimer, the fifth Earl of March. Henry was not about to make a child into a king. Yet if he seized the throne himself, ahead of the rightful heir, he would be no more than a usurper. Though he was qualified by training and personality to be a king, he lacked that all-essential blessing: the proper ancestry.

So he hesitated to let anyone think that he had royal ambitions. During the summer of 1399 he maintained, with apparent sincerity, that he merely wished to claim what was

his by inheritance from his father, the revered John of
Gaunt. Taking up a strong position in Yorkshire during
Richard's absence overseas, Henry soon found himself surrounded by willing allies. Most of the great nobles of the
realm, afraid that Richard might some day treat them as
he had treated Henry, came to the duke's support. The most
powerful of Henry's friends were two lords whose territory
lay in the north, near the borders of Scotland: Ralph
Neville, the Earl of Westmorland, and Henry Percy, the
Earl of Northumberland. More than twenty years earlier
these men—and ten-year-old Henry—had marched in the
coronation procession of Richard II. Now they planned his
destruction.

Gathering a huge army as he went, Henry of Lancaster
marched across England, from York to Bristol, from Bristol
to Chester. Meanwhile word had come to Richard II in
Ireland of what was happening, and he hurried back. By
the time he arrived, few men in England dared to support
his cause; his strength simply ebbed away, and even Edmund
of York, the "guardian" of the realm, had pledged himself
to Henry. Landing in Wales, Richard surveyed the situation
and realized that all was over for him. The power that he
had cunningly built in a decade of scheming had evaporated
like the morning dew. In a single month Henry of Lancaster
had conquered England without striking a blow.

Richard surrendered and threw himself on his cousin's
mercy. He hoped, perhaps, that Henry would be content
with taking power, and would leave him his crown. That
was what had been done in 1388, and Richard had re-
bounded to triumph ultimately over his persecutors. But it
was not to happen again. Now Henry demanded the king's
abdication in his favor. The claim of Edmund Mortimer

would be conveniently overlooked; against all law, Henry of Bolingbroke, the Duke of Lancaster, would make himself king.

It was a grave step, and it was solemnly debated among Henry and his supporters. Everyone agreed that Richard II must be stripped of authority; but many held back from the idea of usurpation. Let Richard remain king, some lords said, while Henry rules in his name. Shakespeare, writing two centuries later, gives eloquent words to one of these backers of Richard, the Bishop of Carlisle:

> And shall the figure of God's majesty,
> His captain, steward, deputy elect,
> Anointed, crowned, planted many years,
> Be judg'd by subject and inferior breath,
> And he himself not present?

Knowing what events were to follow, Shakespeare had his bishop utter a terrible prediction of the consequences of crowning Henry:

> The blood of English shall manure the ground
> And future ages groan for this foul act. . . .
> And in this seat of peace tumultuous wars
> Shall kin with kin and kind with kind confound;
> Disorder, horror, fear and mutiny
> Shall here inhabit.

Henry of Lancaster now was too close to high power to turn from his course. With Richard a prisoner, he rode to London. The unfortunate king was jailed in the Tower of London, and on September 29, 1399, it was announced that Richard II had "voluntarily" abdicated from the throne, making a "pure and free resignation." The next day Henry came before Parliament to claim the crown.

He did not have the legal right to be king, and everyone

knew it. Assuming that it had been proper to depose Richard II, the throne belonged to the heir of Lionel of Clarence,
Edward III's next oldest son. That heir was the boy Edmund Mortimer. Henry of Lancaster, as the son of Edward
III's fourth son, had only a junior claim to the crown he
was about to grasp.

In the feverish days preceding the forced abdication of
Richard II, Henry and his closest followers had worked
hard to concoct a plausible argument that would allow him
to put himself forth as the legitimate heir. Henry's first suggestion was an utterly fantastic one. He was, he pointed out,
descended from King Henry III of the thirteenth century
both through his father and his mother. His father was the
great-grandson of Henry III's elder son, King Edward I.
His mother, Blanche of Lancaster, was the great-great-
granddaughter of Henry III's younger son, Edmund Crouchback.

Somehow a fable had begun to circulate that Edmund
Crouchback had actually been the *older* son of Henry III
and had been wrongfully set aside in favor of his brother
Edward because he was a humpback and so not thought fit
to rule. If that had really happened, Edward I had been a
usurper, and Edward II, Edward III, and Richard II had
all come wrongfully to the throne. Therefore Henry of
Lancaster, by virtue of his descent from Edmund Crouchback through his mother, was merely restoring the rightful
line to power by taking the crown.

The trouble with this theory was that it was wholly false.
The records showed that Edward I had been born six years
before Edmund Crouchback; and Edmund, despite his nickname, had not even been deformed. Henry's friends told

him that if he put forth such a preposterous claim, he would do himself more harm than good.

Very well, then, Henry said; he would claim the throne by right of conquest, as William the Conqueror had done in 1066.

This was even more disturbing to the friends of Henry. A conqueror Henry certainly was; but a conqueror was free to wipe out the existing laws and reshape the kingdom to his own liking, as William had done. To allow such sweeping grounds for Henry's rise to power would be to destroy all the traditions of law that had been collected in the past three and a half centuries.

But there was no other legal way for Henry to take the throne. True, he was the grandson of King Edward III, but that in itself did not give him the right to be king, not so long as little Edmund Mortimer was alive. In the end, Henry simply sidestepped legality altogether. Standing before a hand-picked committee of Parliament on September 30, 1399, he made a vague reference to his descent from Henry III, and claimed the crown "through the right that God of his grace hath sent me, with the help of my kin and of my friends to recover it."

It was usurpation, undisguised. But Richard was deemed unfit to rule, and Edmund Mortimer was too young. Henry of Lancaster, although not lawfully entitled to be king, was the man best qualified in this time of crisis. By common consent the lords of England winked at the irregularity, and Henry became King Henry IV. The hapless Richard II was packed off to the Lancastrian castle of Pontefract, to be imprisoned there for the rest of his life, however long that might be.

On Monday, October 13, 1399, Henry IV celebrated his coronation day. The medieval chronicler, Sir John Froissart, tells us that two days earlier "the new king went from Westminster to the Tower of London, attended by great numbers, and those squires who were to be knighted watched their arms that night; they amounted to forty-six; each squire had his chamber and bath. The next day after mass the duke created them knights, and presented them with long green coats with straight sleeves lined with minever, after the manner of the prelates. . . .

"This Sunday after dinner the duke left the Tower on his return to Westminster; he was bare-headed, and had round his neck the order of the King of France. The Prince of Wales, six dukes, six earls, and eighteen barons accompanied him; and of the nobility there were from 800 to 900 horse in the procession. The duke, after the German fashion, was dressed in a jacket of cloth of gold, and mounted on a white courser, with a blue garter on his left leg. He passed through the streets of London, which were at the time all handsomely decorated with tapestries and other rich hangings; there were nine fountains in Cheapside and other streets through which he passed, and these perpetually ran with white and red wine. . . . That same night the duke bathed, and on the morrow confessed himself, and according to his custom heard three masses.

"The prelates and clergy who had been assembled then came in procession from Westminster Abbey, to conduct the king to the Tower, and back again in the same manner. The dukes, earls, and barons wore long scarlet robes, with mantles trimmed with ermine, and large hoods of the same. The dukes and earls had three bars of ermine on the left arm a quarter of a yard long, or thereabout; the barons had but two. . . . In the procession to the church the duke had borne over his head a rich canopy of blue silk, supported on silver staves, with four golden bells at the corners. . . . The procession entered the church about nine o'clock. In the middle of the church was erected a scaffold covered with crimson cloth, in the center of which was the royal throne of cloth of gold. When the duke entered the church, he seated himself on the throne, and was thus in regal state, except having the crown on his head. The Archbishop of Canterbury proclaimed from the four corners of the scaffold how God had given them a man for their lord and sovereign, and then asked the people if they were consenting parties to his being consecrated and crowned king. Upon which the people unanimously shouted 'ay,' and held up their hands, promising fealty and homage."

A new dynasty—the House of Lancaster—had been established. And, looking about him on his coronation day, Henry IV had no reason to fear for heirs. Four strong sons stood beside him. The eldest, Henry, called Prince Hal, was twelve years old and now the heir to the throne. Hal's brothers, Thomas, John, and Humphrey, were further assurance to King Henry that in one way or another his line would take root and flourish in England. But usurpation breeds usurpation, and the House of Lancaster was destined to reign a mere sixty years.

The continued presence of Richard II in the world proved to be awkward. Soon after he had taken power, Henry IV quarreled with several of the men who had backed him. They claimed he had not paid them well enough for their aid, and stirred up a revolt designed to restore Richard to the throne. Henry fell ill—there was talk of poison—but recovered quickly and quelled the uprising. Several lordly heads were lopped off. And in Pontefract Castle, the former King Richard came to the end of his days perhaps somewhat too soon. His death was announced in February of 1400. Some whispered that he had been starved to death by order of King Henry; others, defending Henry, insisted that the deposed king had pined away from grief. No one will ever know the truth; Richard, like Edward II before him and two English kings after him, met death in the darkness of a stone-walled chamber, and the details of what happened remain the eternal secrets of those walls.

The reign of Henry IV, having begun with usurpation and possible murder, was tinged with shadow from its start. The shadows deepened as the king grew older. As Henry of Bolingbroke he had been a high-spirited cavalier, fond of sports and music, a reader of books, even a student of

THE LANCASTRIAN LINE

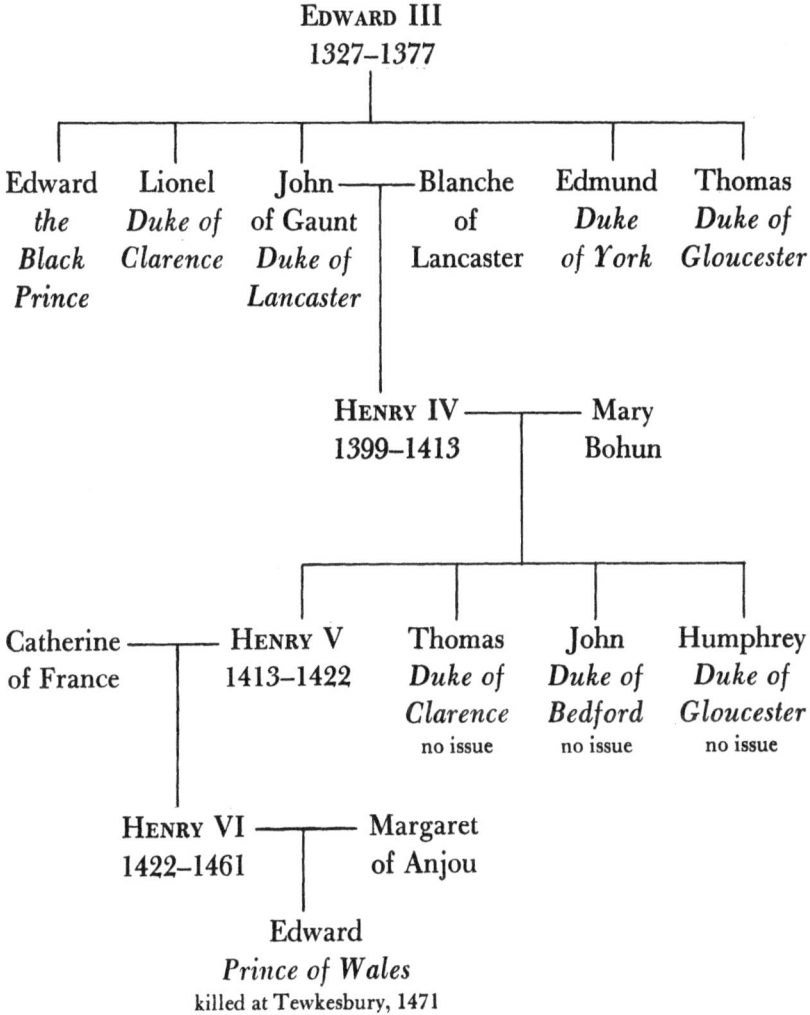

EDWARD III
1327–1377

Edward | Lionel | John ——— Blanche | Edmund | Thomas
the | *Duke of* | of Gaunt | of | *Duke* | *Duke of*
Black | *Clarence* | *Duke of* | Lancaster | *of York* | *Gloucester*
Prince | | *Lancaster* | | |

HENRY IV ——— Mary
1399–1413 | Bohun

Catherine ——— **HENRY V** | Thomas | John | Humphrey
of France | **1413–1422** | *Duke of* | *Duke of* | *Duke of*
| | *Clarence* | *Bedford* | *Gloucester*
| | no issue | no issue | no issue

HENRY VI ——— Margaret
1422–1461 | of Anjou

Edward
Prince of Wales
killed at Tewkesbury, 1471

philosophy. As Henry of Hereford he had been an uneasy noble swirled about by a headstrong king. As Henry of Lancaster he had been first an embittered exile, then a shameless usurper. And as King Henry IV he was a man of doubt and guilt, tormented by inner uncertainties and weakened in health by his responsibilities. Shakespeare's Henry IV speaks the truth when he tells Prince Hal:

> *Heaven knows, my son,*
> *By what by-paths and indirect crook'd ways*
> *I met this crown; and I myself know well,*
> *How troublesome it sat upon my head.*

There were few sunny moments in the thirteen years of Henry IV's reign. For all his strength and forcefulness, he could never succeed in gaining full control over the country whose crown he had seized. Much of a king's authority among his subjects stemmed from his nearly divine state of majesty: he was thought to be chosen by God to rule. But everyone in England knew that there was nothing divine about the former Henry of Bolingbroke. He was merely a man, a man who had muscled his way to the highest power of the land. And they never let him forget it.

Parliament in particular gave Henry trouble. If he had any valid claim to the throne at all, it was a Parliamentary one; since Parliament had voted to make him king, he was monarch more by election than by natural right of inheritance. If Parliament could make a king, it could also try to rule him. And so Henry found himself saddled with a Parliament that criticized his actions and demanded changes in the operations of his government. When Henry tried to ignore Parliament's wishes, Parliament retaliated by refusing to vote the taxes he had requested. No English king before Henry had ever had to put up with such a haughty, domineering Parliament. But no English king before Henry had ever had such a shaky claim to the throne, either. He was in a weak position, and Parliament took advantage of it. A king with a guilty conscience was at the mercy of the legislators.

There were constant rebellions against the usurper, too. In the first year of his reign came an attempt to restore Richard II to the throne, which, as we have seen, ended in the defeat of the rebels and the death of Richard. But new conspiracies were born.

Henry's problem was one of money; the king was expected to pay the expenses of the government out of his own pocket, and not even all the wealth of Lancaster could meet the debts. Hampered by a stingy Parliament, Henry could not levy taxes and was constantly short of cash—so short that he was unable properly to reward the nobles who had helped him take the throne. Henry Percy, the Earl of Northumberland, was the most disappointed man of all. He had spent a fortune to raise troops for Henry IV; but when Northumberland presented a bill for his services, the king was able to pay only part of it.

Northumberland angrily took back his oath of allegiance to the king. He and his fiery son, Harry Percy, known as "Hotspur," denounced Henry IV as a man who had no right to the throne. Coolly the Percies insisted that they had never intended to make Henry a king but merely to aid him in gaining his rightful rank as Duke of Lancaster. As Hotspur says in Shakespeare's *Henry IV:*

> *A poor unminded outlaw sneaking home,*
> *My father gave him welcome to the shore;*
> *And, when he heard him swear, and vow to God,*
> *He came but to be Duke of Lancaster,*

To sue his livery, and beg his peace
With tears of innocency and terms of zeal,
My father, in kind heart and pity mov'd,
Swore him assistance, and perform'd it too.

The Percies launched an armed uprising against the king. At the same time, a Welsh chieftain named Owen Glendower had declared himself independent of Henry IV and was raising an army in the unruly western land of Wales. Glendower found an ally in Edmund Mortimer, the brother of Roger Mortimer, the late fourth Earl of March. He was the uncle of the boy named Edmund Mortimer who was the fifth Earl of March and the rightful King of England now that Richard II was dead. The elder Edmund Mortimer had married a daughter of Owen Glendower. At about the same time Mortimer's sister had become the wife of Hotspur. Mortimer formed a league with his brother-in-law Hotspur and his father-in-law Glendower to overthrow Henry IV and place the little Earl of March on the throne.

In the summer of 1403 Hotspur led a small army across England to join forces with Glendower's Welsh troops. But Henry IV moved too swiftly for him. Henry hurried north and intercepted Hotspur's men at the town of Shrewsbury on July 21. In the fierce battle that followed, Hotspur was killed, and Henry IV's son, the fifteen-year-old Prince Hal, showed for the first time on the field his exceptional gifts for warfare.

That ended the rebellion for a while; but Glendower, Mortimer, and the old Earl of Northumberland, Hotspur's father, still seethed with hatred for the king. Early in 1405 a much greater plot was put into action. The three conspirators were joined by several other nobles, including young Thomas Mowbray, the son of Henry of Lancaster's old rival.

In March the rebels attacked Windsor Castle, where King Henry had placed the Earl of March and his younger brother Roger for safekeeping. The two boys were carried off, and an attempt was made to proclaim the earl, now fourteen, as king.

Several influential men backed the rebels, among them Richard Scrope, the Archbishop of York, who had taken part in Henry IV's coronation ceremony. But when the time of battle came, the king again was triumphant. Northumberland was beaten and forced to take refuge in Scotland. Mowbray and Archbishop Scrope were captured and beheaded. Glendower was driven back into the mountains of Wales, and the two Mortimer boys were recaptured.

In another few years Henry completed his rout of those who would depose him. The Earl of Northumberland was defeated and put to death in February, 1408, and a year later the troublesome Glendower's power was broken in Wales. The elder Edmund Mortimer ceased to plot against the king, and his nephew of the same name, the Earl of March, never showed any desire to claim the crown that should have been his.

But Henry emerged from these civil wars shattered in health. Prematurely aged, made tense and wary by guilt and struggle, he kept many doctors occupied with diseases that evidently were mainly in his mind. In 1405, after the execution of Archbishop Scrope, the king was smitten with a skin rash, and men murmured that he had been afflicted with leprosy as a punishment from God. A year later he complained of pains in his legs; in 1407 it was plague that he thought endangered his life, and a chronicler tells us that his "failing health" brought on a nervous dread of infection, "and constant change of place was deemed the only safeguard when the air was charged with pestilence." He suffered from fainting fits, palpitation of the heart, and what was probably a light stroke. By December of 1408 he felt that he was at the point of death; but he recovered some of his strength and continued to rule.

During these years of the king's illnesses and torments Prince Hal had come to share more and more of the burdens of government. The handsome, dashing prince had been given his first military responsibilities in 1400, when he was only thirteen; by 1406 he was regularly attending meetings of the high governmental councils, and repeatedly proved himself ready to assume the kingship whenever the scepter should slip from his father's weary hands. At this time, also, three other men had emerged as leading figures of the kingdom: King Henry's half-brothers, John, Henry, and Thomas Beaufort.

The brothers Beaufort were illegitimate children of John of Gaunt. During the lifetime of his first wife, Blanche of Lancaster, John had fallen in love with one of Blanche's ladies-in-waiting, a girl of common birth, Katherine Swynford. Sometime after the birth of Henry of Bolingbroke in 1367, Katherine became the mother of a son named John, called John Beaufort after a castle owned by John of Gaunt.

Blanche of Lancaster died in 1369, and two years later John of Gaunt married the heiress to the throne of the Spanish kingdom of Castile. But at the same time he continued his affair with Katherine Swynford. Two more Beaufort sons followed: Henry and Thomas. It was not at all unusual for a powerful lord like John of Gaunt to have a few children by a woman who was not his wife, and John made no attempt to conceal the fact that he was the father of the Beaufort boys. They were raised with all the advantages of wealth, and in childhood spent much time with their half-brother Henry of Bolingbroke and their cousin King Richard II. John of Gaunt intended that his three illegitimate sons should reach high rank and influence in the kingdom despite the irregularity of their birth.

In 1394 John of Gaunt's second wife died. Two years later he committed an astonishing act: he married Katherine Swynford, his mistress for more than twenty-five years, making this humble woman the Duchess of Lancaster. By this time there was a fourth Beaufort child, a girl named Joan.

John of Gaunt then approached his nephew King Richard with an urgent request. He wished the Beauforts to be made legitimate by royal decree. This was an uncommon but not illegal arrangement, and Richard was glad to grant his uncle's wish. After gaining the approval of Pope Boniface IX, Richard pronounced the Beauforts legitimate on September 1, 1396. The following year Parliament confirmed the decision.

The stain on their birth thus was wiped away by retroactive legislation. Now there was nothing to bar the Beauforts' rise to power, for in the eyes of the law they were as properly descended from John of Gaunt as was Henry of Bolingbroke himself. John Beaufort, the eldest, was granted the title of Earl of Somerset. Henry Beaufort, who had entered the church, became Bishop of Lincoln in 1398, and six years later received the more important post of Bishop of Winchester. Thomas Beaufort eventually was awarded the title of Earl of Dorset, and still later became Duke of Exeter. As for their sister Joan, she was to marry Ralph Neville, the first Earl of Westmorland, and in time to become the mother of nine children and the grandmother of two kings of England.

At the time of the overthrow of Richard II, the Beauforts naturally supported their half-brother, Henry of Lancaster, and he rewarded them well when he came to power. Step by step, he brought them into the highest councils of the realm. Henry Beaufort in particular, the Bishop of Winchester, came to serve as adviser and guardian to the royal heir, Prince Hal. Because of the manner of the Beauforts' birth, King Henry IV found it necessary to reaffirm their legitimacy through a new act of Parliament. It was passed in February of 1407, and declared the Beauforts legitimate in all respects but one. Although they were grandchildren of King Edward III, Parliament decreed that no member of the Beaufort family might ever inherit the throne. Since Henry IV had four healthy sons, that clause seemed like a mere technicality at the time. But it would come to have great importance years later.

Henry IV sank into an early old age. By 1411 his health was broken; trembling and feeble, the king had all but abandoned the pretense of ruling. Prince Hal, guided by Henry and Thomas Beaufort, made most of the decisions of government. (John Beaufort had died in 1410.) Since Hal was king in all but name, Henry Beaufort pressed him to urge his father to abdicate in his favor.

But there was fire in Bolingbroke yet. Henry IV reacted with fury to the suggestion that he should step down. There was an angry confrontation between father and son, and Prince Hal gave way. Temporarily in disgrace, the prince was rarely seen at court in 1412, and the dying sovereign clung tightly to his scepter. Though he could scarcely walk, Henry IV talked of invading France, even spoke of making a pilgrimage to Jerusalem and leading a new Crusade to

win the Holy Land away from the infidel Turks. But his time had come. "Uneasy lies the head that wears a crown," Shakespeare's Henry IV declares; and for Henry, the terrible weight of that stolen crown had come to bear crushingly on him. His life ebbed away. Worn with care and sorrow, King Henry IV died on March 20, 1413.

There was no question about his successor. The new dynasty of Lancaster was firmly entrenched. "The king is dead!" went out the cry. "Long live the king! Long live King Harry!" And handsome Prince Hal mounted the throne to reign as King Henry V.

Lancaster—
Glory and Decline

HE NEW king, at twenty-six, seemed to be fortune's favorite. For the first time in more than a century, a reign was beginning in joy and hope. Henry IV had come to power as a usurper; Richard II had been crowned as a child overshadowed by mighty and ambitious uncles; Edward III's reign had commenced with his father's murder. But here was a vigorous, attractive, intelligent king in the full flower of his young manhood, who promised to lead the country into an era of renewed greatness.

He could count on the loyalty of everyone—or nearly everyone. Those who had rebelled against his father were dead or powerless. The great nobles of the realm, those who could make or break a king, were fewer in number now than they had been in the time of Edward III's many sons, and they were generally favorably disposed to the new monarch. If Henry V's title to the throne was tinged with illegality, he could at least say that he was the son of a king, however that king might have gained his crown, and so he was in a better legal position than his father.

Only a few lingering bitternesses remained in the land. Henry V did his best to wash them away with love. He declared a general pardon against those who had opposed his father, and had the body of Richard II buried solemnly and splendidly at Westminster Abbey. Young Henry Percy, dead Hotspur's son, had been taken prisoner in Scotland; King Henry V negotiated with the Scots for his release and restored him to the Percy family's title of Earl of Northumberland. In every way Henry V attempted to bind the wounds his father had opened. As Shakespeare makes him say:

> *Think not upon the fault*
> *My father made in compassing the crown!*
> *I Richard's body have interred new;*
> *And on it have bestow'd more contrite tears,*
> *Than from it issued forced drops of blood.*

Urged by Bishop Beaufort, Henry V shortly was seeking to unify the country in the way most likely to succeed: by waging a foreign war. A brave young king carrying England's banner overseas would be a symbol no Englishman could fail to support. There had been a long intermission in the Hundred Years War with France; Henry V felt that the time had come to renew the struggle, to equal the triumphs of his great-grandfather Edward III. Thus he embarked on the war that would occupy him for the rest of his life, the war that would cover him with glory and at the same time strain England's financial resources to their limits. The military campaigns of Henry V were among the most magnificent in English history, but they left behind a heritage of debt and weakness that ultimately destroyed the dynasty of Lancaster.

All during 1414 King Henry gathered his forces. He built a great fleet, with six large vessels and hundreds of smaller ones. He collected a corps of 6,000 archers, of whom half were mounted warriors, and 2,500 noble and knightly soldiers in armor, each with two or three squires and aides. In the spring of 1415 Henry's army assembled at the port of Southampton. It was a mighty force for its day. Spearsmen, pikemen, surgeons, armorers, clerks, drummers, pipers, fiddlers, gunners, carpenters, servants of all kinds, knights in heavy armor equipped with lances, swords, and daggers, pages, minstrels, cooks, attendants—an entire universe of war waited at the port for the king's arrival. All these men would have to be paid out of the king's own funds. Henry had several ways of raising the enormous sum needed for his army's wages. First, from the rents and revenues derived from the land he owned both as King of England and as Duke of Lancaster. Second, from the customs duties and other fees that were granted to the king for his expenses. Third, from the taxes he could persuade Parliament to levy. Fourth, from the money he could borrow from such rich men as his half-uncles, the Beauforts. And finally, the king could hope to repay his debts and replenish his exchequer from the loot and ransom he might obtain in the conquest of France.

The omens were good for a successful campaign of war.

And then, on the very eve of his departure for France, came an unexpected development: a plot against the king's life, a conspiracy to replace him on the throne with the Earl of March.

The plot sprang from the intricate rivalries among the descendants of King Edward III—rivalries that had grown vastly more complicated through the marriage of close relatives. Edmund of Langley, the next-to-youngest son of Edward III, had been made Duke of York in 1385 by Richard II. He had earlier been given the title of Earl of Cambridge. After he died in 1402, these titles passed to his two sons. Edward, the elder, became the second Duke of York. Richard, the younger, was made Earl of Cambridge, though not at once; he received his title from Henry V in 1413.

Richard of Cambridge took as his wife Anne Mortimer, the sister of Edmund Mortimer, the fifth Earl of March. That made him the brother-in-law of the man whose genuine claim to the English throne had been set aside by the usurping Henry IV in 1399. Although the Earl of March was not inclined to seek the throne, Richard of Cambridge and a few confederates hatched the notion of assassinating King Henry and his three brothers and placing the earl at the head of the kingdom.

While King Henry was at Southampton in July of 1415 the plans of the conspirators moved rapidly toward fulfillment. But at length the Earl of March learned of the murderous deed that was to be done in his name. Hurriedly he gave the whole story away, on August 1, the very day on which the assassinations were to take place. Richard of Cambridge and two co-conspirators were arrested and placed on trial the next day. They were found guilty at once and executed. A few days later King Henry sailed to France at the head of his superb army. He had met and dealt with the only threat to the House of Lancaster that would arise during his reign. But Richard of Cambridge left a three-year-old son, also named Richard; and that Richard would be heard from in years to come.

The English landed without opposition at the mouth of the Seine and soon were laying siege to the strategically placed French fortress of Harfleur. Henry was confident of victory in France. King Charles VI of France had gone insane, and his country was without strong leaders; while the mad king still lived, the French armies were headed by his son and heir, the Dauphin (or prince) Charles. But the Dauphin was a weak, uncertain general. Worse, the ruling family of France had quarreled with the strongest noble of the realm, the Duke of Burgundy. Burgundy was virtually a kingdom within the kingdom, and its duke was wealthier and stronger than his supposed royal master. He let it be known that he would welcome the defeat of the King of France by the King of England, though officially Burgundy still remained neutral.

Harfleur fell to the English in the middle of September. King Henry left a garrison there, sent his sick and wounded home, and set out to cross a hundred miles of hostile territory to the port city of Calais, which had belonged to England since 1347. On the way, Henry's men—about a thousand knights and four thousand archers—were attacked by twenty thousand French soldiers at a place called Agincourt. The French drew up in three lines of battle and prepared to annihilate the English king and his army. It was a dark moment. Henry offered to withdraw from Harfleur and surrender all his prisoners if he would be allowed to go unharmed to Calais. The French, knowing they had the invader trapped, refused. Henry realized then that he must do battle against these overwhelming odds.

The English have always been at their finest when things look most black. With ringing words King Henry rallied his men. A chronicler of the day tells us that he asked them, "Do you not think that the Lord with these few can overthrow the pride of the French?" And Shakespeare's Henry V cries out:

> *We . . . shall be remembered,*
> *We few, we happy few, we band of brothers;*
> *For he today that sheds his blood with me*
> *Shall be my brother; be he ne'er so vile*
> *This day shall gentle his condition.*

The alarms and trumpets of war sounded shortly after eleven o'clock on the morning of October 25. A storm of arrows rained down on the French, who were packed so tightly that they were unable to use effectively their powerful crossbows and their booming cannon. The English longbows slew with deadly accuracy. As the French churned in dismay, the English archers put by their bows and seized their swords to rush foward for hand-to-hand combat. King Henry was in their midst. A French prince struck down Henry's brother Humphrey, the Duke of Gloucester; Henry rushed to his wounded brother's rescue and was wounded himself. But the French gave way. The massacre was ferocious, and within a few hours the flower of French nobility lay dead on the field. More than fifteen hundred French knights and nearly five thousand common soldiers had perished. On the English side the dead numbered less than three hundred. Among them was Edward, Duke of York, the loyal brother of the treacherous Richard of Cambridge.

The great victory at Agincourt shattered the French might and made Henry V a place among history's most famous generals. To the English, Henry became and long

remained a hero among heroes; and in the bleak days of 1940, when Great Britain fought on alone against the German military machine that had engulfed all the rest of Europe, the harried defenders often looked for inspiration to the memory of King Henry V at Agincourt. It was a finer triumph even than those of Crécy and Poitiers, those glittering achievements of Edward III and his son the Black Prince.

But the expense of fighting a foreign war drained Henry's treasury, and he could not immediately follow up his first success. A slow, dreary time of sieges and small battles ensued. Throughout 1417 and 1418 the English hacked their way through the province of Normandy, conquering piecemeal the land from which William had come in 1066. Then, in 1419, agents of the Dauphin rashly murdered the Duke of Burgundy. The new duke instantly allied himself with England, and now there could be no hope for France in the war. By May, 1420, the French admitted defeat.

The peace treaty was signed at the town of Troyes. Representatives of the insane King Charles VI agreed to disinherit the Dauphin and make Henry the heir to the throne of France. Henry was to marry Katherine, the beautiful daughter of the French king. When Charles VI went to his grave—which surely could not be long in happening—Henry would become King of France as well as King of England. Two of Europe's greatest nations would be bound together under the rule of the House of Lancaster.

It was a brilliant stroke of diplomacy, but it had one hidden flaw: Henry had agreed to marry the daughter of a madman. The insanity of Charles VI had made Henry's conquest of France all the easier, but now Henry proposed to import that insanity to England. What if the weakness that clouded the mind of Charles VI should pass through his daughter Katherine to the heir of Henry V? What then for the House of Lancaster? In the excitement of triumph no one cared to ask that question; and so tragedy was brought upon Henry's house and upon his kingdom.

The wedding of Henry V and Katherine took place at Troyes on June 2, 1420. The honeymoon was brief, because certain fortresses loyal to the Dauphin had refused to accept the terms of the treaty, and Henry left his bride within two days to lead the siege against them. By November the fortresses surrendered. On the first of December Henry V and Charles VI entered Paris side by side, accompanied by the Duke of Burgundy, Philip the Good. Final approval of the Treaty of Troyes was obtained there.

Next Henry toured the conquered territories in Normandy. January of 1421 saw him in Rouen, where his great ancestor William the Conqueror lay buried. Then, accompanied by his queen, his brother John, whom he had named Duke of Bedford, and the Earl of March, loyal Edmund Mortimer, King Henry proceeded to the port of Calais and set sail for England. He landed at Dover on February 1. On his way to London he stopped at Canterbury to make a solemn offering of thanks. On February 23 Queen Katherine was crowned at Westminster Abbey, and a splendid banquet followed. King Henry was home, after an absence of three and a half years.

He returned glowing with triumph, but the state of the kingdom was not good. Gold had run in a swift river from the treasury to pay for Henry's war. The king's ministers had raised taxes as high as they dared, and the common people were grumbling. The king was heavily in debt, hav-

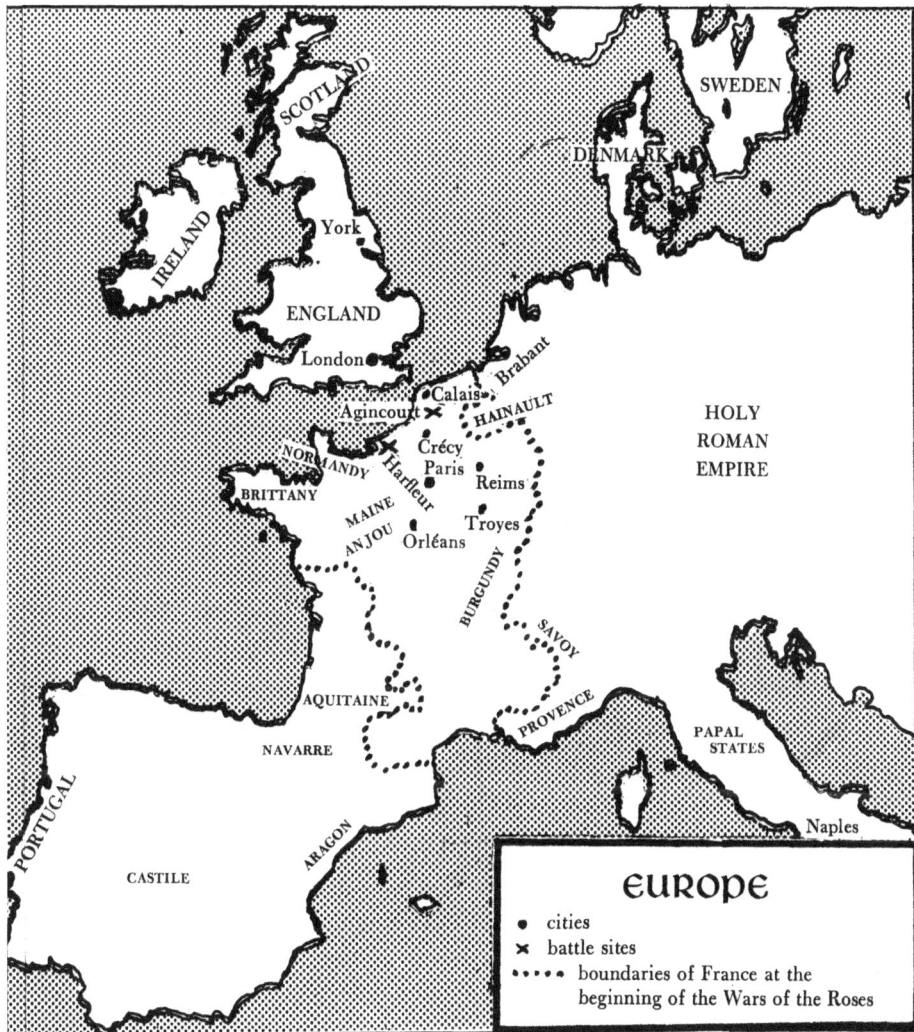

SWEDEN

DENMARK

SCOTLAND

IRELAND

York

ENGLAND

London

Calais
Brabant
Agincourt
HAINAULT
Crécy
Harfleur
Paris
NORMANDY
Reims
MAINE
Troyes
ANJOU
Orléans
BRITTANY

BURGUNDY

SAVOY

AQUITAINE

PROVENCE

NAVARRE

PORTUGAL

CASTILE

ARAGON

HOLY
ROMAN
EMPIRE

PAPAL
STATES

Naples

EUROPE

- cities
- ✗ battle sites
- •••• boundaries of France at the
  beginning of the Wars of the Roses

ing mortgaged everything to pay his expenses. In 1421 he had borrowed £17,666 from his half-uncle Bishop Beaufort alone—a monstrous sum at a time when the royal revenues were only £55,000 a year, and a skilled workman's annual wages amounted to some five pounds sterling. Touring his land in the spring of 1421, Henry sensed the discontent over the cost of the war. But he could not halt now; the Dauphin was still at large in France, refusing to accept the terms of the Treaty of Troyes, and King Henry knew that he must soon return to complete the conquest. That meant more taxes, more loans.

In May he appeared before Parliament and submitted the terms by which he had become heir to the throne of France. Parliament was pleased to ratify the treaty, though that was a mere formality. By August Henry was on his way back to France. There was talk that the Dauphin meant to besiege the city of Chartres; but Henry led his troops against the French prince and drove him into retreat. Then, late that fall, Henry concentrated on besieging the city of Meaux, at a well-fortified site in northern France. Meaux resisted stubbornly, and Henry was still involved in the siege when happy news came to him in December. Queen Katherine had given birth to a son on December 6, 1421. The child was named Henry. Until the spring of that year the heir to the throne had been the king's oldest brother, Thomas, Duke of Clarence. But Thomas had been killed in battle in April, putting King Henry's next oldest brother, John, Duke of Bedford, in line to inherit the throne. Now, however, Henry V had the comforting knowledge that his crown would go some day to a child of his own seed.

Destiny reserves its most somber jests for those who rise too swiftly to the heights. In the moment of his victory over

France, almost in the very moment that his son and heir had been born, Henry V fell ill. An epidemic of dysentery swept through the English who besieged Meaux. Many men died, and the ailing Henry left the siege to recover his strength at a country estate. During the new year the king's illness gnawed at his life. In the spring the Duke of Burgundy asked him to relieve a Burgundian garrison that was under attack by the Dauphin's forces, and Henry agreed to go. But he was too weak to ride his horse and had to turn command over to his brother John of Bedford. When death took him on the last day of August, 1422, King Henry V was thirty-five years old and had ruled England little more than nine years. Shakespeare, depicting the king's funeral at Westminster Abbey, gives these lines to John of Bedford:

> *Hung be the heavens with black, yield day to night!*
> *Comets, importing change of times and states,*
> *Brandish your crystal tresses in the sky,*
> *And with them scourge the bad revolting stars,*
> *That have consented unto Henry's death!*
> *King Henry the Fifth, too famous to live long!*
> *England ne'er lost a king of so much worth.*

And the dead king's other surviving brother, Humphrey of Gloucester, adds:

> *England ne'er had a king until his time.*
> *Virtue he had, deserving to command:*
> *His brandish'd sword did blind men with his beams;*
> *His arms spread wider than a dragon's wings;*
> *His sparkling eyes, replete with wrathful fire,*
> *More dazzled and drove back his enemies*
> *Than mid-day sun fierce bent against their faces.*
> *What should I say? his deeds exceed all speech.*
> *He ne'er lift up his hand but conquered.*

It was a time to lament, a time to gasp in wonder at the cruelty of fate. Men found it hard to believe that a king so young and strong and fair could be cut down in all his gleaming greatness. That in itself was cause for grief; but those who looked to the future had another reason to feel sorrow. England had a new monarch, King Henry VI. But the king was an infant nine months old. Twice before, England had crowned a child as king: nine-year-old Henry III in 1216, ten-year-old Richard II in 1377. Both their reigns had been times of turmoil and civil war. To place a baby on the throne, though, was far more ominous. It meant fifteen or twenty years without a king at all, while powerful ministers governed the realm. What disasters would that bring?

Bewildered, troubled, the many relatives of the royal infant gathered to plan the course of government.

The senior members of the family were the Beaufort brothers: Henry, the Bishop of Winchester, and Thomas, the Duke of Exeter. Certainly they would have a powerful influence over future events. There was also a new generation of Beauforts, the sons of John, the late Earl of Somerset: John Beaufort II, the second Earl of Somerset, and Edmund Beaufort, the Earl of Dorset. But they were both less than twenty years old and just beginning to establish their positions in the kingdom.

Closer in blood to the new king were his uncles, John of Bedford and Humphrey of Gloucester. These two royal dukes were but a year apart in age; John was thirty-three, his brother Humphrey thirty-two. Until Henry VI had fathered a son—many years in the future, obviously—John and Humphrey, in that order, would be the next heirs to the throne. For the moment, though, the question was not who would inherit but who would hold the highest office.

A title was revived that had first been used in the time of the boy-king Henry III, two centuries earlier: Protector and Defender of the Realm. The protector would exercise many of the powers of the king, but only subject to the authority of a council of nobles and, of course, to that of Parliament.

Which royal uncle would be the protector? The man preferred by most was John of Bedford, a brave soldier and a wise, even-tempered man. But John himself felt that his place was in France, continuing his late brother's campaign of conquest. Henry VI's other uncle, Humphrey of Gloucester, put himself forth eagerly for the protectorship. Humphrey, though, was a strange, hot-blooded man, stormy by nature, brilliant of mind, much given to reading difficult books and becoming embroiled in passionate disputes. To many, Duke Humphrey seemed too unstable, too turbulent, to be entrusted with such a high office. His half-uncle Bishop Beaufort in particular was his bitter enemy and fought against his appointment.

In the end a compromise was reached. Humphrey of Gloucester would hold the office of protector, and John of Bedford would serve as military commander-in-chief in France. But whenever John was in England, he would automatically replace Humphrey as protector so long as he remained. The Beauforts worked quietly behind the scenes to see to it that Humphrey, as protector, would have as little real power as possible.

On that uneasy footing did the new reign begin.

The chief nobles of the land met on November 5, 1422, to give their assent to the arrangement of the protectorship. Several weeks earlier a significant event had taken place:

King Charles VI of France had died. Under the terms of the Treaty of Troyes, little Henry VI was now King of France—the only person in history to hold both the thrones of England and of France.

The child laughing in his cradle knew nothing of that, of course. While his relatives bickered, he lay in innocent happiness, a cheerful, mild-mannered baby surrounded by worshiping nurses. The radiant glory of the dead hero of Agincourt glowed like a halo about the infant. Those who could never forget his father's fame piously wished that one day this sixth Henry would equal those bold exploits—a wish that was never remotely fulfilled.

Soon the king took his first steps; soon he uttered his first words. He seemed unusually tender and sweet, almost a saintly child. Over his head his elders continued to quarrel. In October of 1425 Duke Humphrey and Bishop Beaufort nearly came to blows over the question of which should have custody of the king. The child was at London, in Humphrey's care, when word came that a band of armed men in the pay of the bishop was about to invade the city. The duke called for the officials of London and bade them to "keep well the city that night and make good watch." At their orders, chains were placed across the southern end of London Bridge.

The next morning Beaufort's men began to tear away the chains. A great many Londoners flocked to the bridge to defend their king against these kidnappers, and it seemed that there would be a pitched battle. Wiser heads prevailed; after some mediation, the attackers withdrew. Humphrey for the moment retained custody of the king. But the bishop hastily summoned John of Bedford from France, and when John arrived, just before Christmas, Duke Humphrey ceased to be protector. Bedford called the high nobles of the realm together for a reconciliation. Humphrey uttered bitter charges against Beaufort, and the bishop hurled back charges of his own. In the end the dispute was smoothed over, and on the surface all appeared well, Humphrey resuming the protectorship when his brother John returned to France. But the feud between duke and bishop continued to simmer.

Another event of note during 1425 was the death at the age of thirty-four of Edmund Mortimer, the fifth Earl of March. Since he had no children, and his brother had died some years earlier, the title of Earl of March left the Mortimer family forever. It passed to Edmund Mortimer's nephew—a boy who already held the much greater title of Duke of York.

He was Richard Plantagenet, the son of that Richard, Earl of Cambridge, who had been executed for treason by Henry V in 1415. Young Richard was three years old when his father was put to death. Later that same year, the boy's uncle, Edward, Duke of York, was slain at Agincourt and the dukedom passed to Richard. Since Richard of Cambridge had married Anne Mortimer, sister of the Earl of March, the earl too was his uncle, and in that zigzag way Richard Plantagenet, thirteen years old in 1425, inherited a second title from a childless uncle.

He inherited much more than that from Edmund Mortimer. He inherited a claim to the English throne.

Richard Plantagenet—Richard of York—was linked by a double line of descent to King Edward III. His father, Richard of Cambridge, had been the son of Edmund of Langley, Edward III's next-to-youngest son. Through that line Richard of York was of royal blood, as the great-grandson of a king; but descent from a junior member of Edward III's family did not provide a strong claim on the throne.

On the other hand, Richard of York's mother could trace her lineage back to Edward III's second oldest son. She was the daughter of Roger Mortimer, the fourth Earl of March, who was the son of Philippa Mortimer; and Philippa was the daughter of Lionel of Clarence, second son of Edward III to reach manhood. By this maze of genealogy, Richard of York could say that his branch of the family was senior to that of King Henry VI; for the king, grandson of the usurper Henry IV, was of the line of John of Gaunt. And John of Gaunt was merely the third oldest of the five sons of Edward III who lived to adulthood. Through his mother, Richard of York had a more legitimate right to be king than Henry VI, at least by strict tracing of the family tree. In 1425, however, no one—certainly not the young Duke of York himself—paid heed to that. The greatness of Henry V had wiped away all thought of dynastic strife. It would be an insult to that brilliant monarch's memory to suggest that there could be a rival claimant for the throne. That throne, everyone declared, belonged to Henry VI—if not by strict legitimacy, then certainly by virtue of his father's heroism.

So it was that the child who was King Henry VI grew into boyhood. And so it was that England moved steadily toward a time of disaster.

the saintly king

OUNG HENRY VI grew tall, though not strong;
he took little interest in sports and hunting, but
became a devout child, often spending long hours
kneeling in prayer or poring over some religious book. In
person he was gentle of manner, tender of expression. Some
of his teachers and relatives thought that he was unusually
brilliant, with a wide-ranging intelligence and sensitivity.
Yet others who watched the king closely insisted that in
truth he was something of a simpleton who could barely tell
right from wrong. Was his placid smile a smile that hid
inner complexity, or one that indicated an inner hollowness?
It was hard to tell. In boyhood as in manhood, Henry VI
remained a person apart, revealing nothing of what went on
within his mind.

He was king of two realms, thanks to his father's valor.
But one of those realms, the one beyond the English Channel, was swiftly slipping away.

The Dauphin Charles, disinherited by the Treaty of Troyes in 1420, had continued to fight for his lost throne. Though himself an uncertain and hesitating man, the Dauphin had been aided by two unexpected developments— first, the removal from the scene of England's greatest general, Henry V, and then the emergence in France's time of peril of a peasant girl, Joan of Arc, who seemed herself a greater general than any man.

The miraculous Joan served at the inn of the forest town of Domrémy, and tended sheep in the fields. While she was with her flock one day, heavenly voices spoke to her: St. Michael, bidding her command the armies of the liberation of France, and St. Margaret and St. Catherine as well, repeating the divine orders. Joan was frightened at first, but gathered strength, purchased shining armor, and made her way to Chinon, where the Dauphin and his courtiers were staying. Though she had never set eyes on the Dauphin before, she picked him out from a crowd of nobles and knelt before him. "Most noble Lord Dauphin," she cried, "I am Joan the Maid, sent on the part of God to aid you and the kingdom, and by His order I announce that you will be crowned in the city of Rheims."

It was an impudent, improbable, fantastic thing for a peasant girl to do. Yet Joan seemed to glow with an inner conviction that her heavenly voices were true voices and that she alone could lead France out of defeat. Throughout history certain individuals have had a mystic gift of leadership, a radiant assurance that inspires devotion. Jesus had that gift, as did Mohammed and Moses and Napoleon. So, too, did the Mongol warrior Genghis Khan, and Mohandas Gandhi of India, and that titan of evil, Adolf Hitler. And this strange glow of command belonged also to Joan of Arc.

Somehow she persuaded the Dauphin and his advisers that she was divinely inspired. In the spring of 1429 she rode at the head of the French troops toward the city of Orléans, which lay under siege by the English. Brushing aside the besiegers, Joan led the French into the city and brought relief to its exhausted defenders. Word spread among the awed English that God had sent a supernatural being to aid France.

The tides of war had surged in England's favor for fourteen years, since Henry V had led his men into Harfleur. Now those tides shifted, and ran against the invaders. Fearful, frozen in sudden terror, the English faltered and Joan spurred the Dauphin's troops to victory after victory. English forts fell; English garrisons were slain. The siege of Orléans was broken. Onward moved the triumphant Joan, insisting that the Dauphin march to Rheims to be crowned on the throne of his ancestors. Charles hesitated, for Rheims was far within the boundaries of English-occupied France. Incredibly, Joan's spell worked its magic, and the Dauphin met with little opposition as he journeyed to Rheims to be anointed as Charles VII of France.

Joan's mission now was complete. She said that her voices had ceased to speak to her, and she asked to be allowed to return to her sheep and her duties at the inn. But the French generals could not allow this symbol of liberation to slip back into obscurity. Against Joan's protests they insisted that she lead them in an attack on Paris. The attack was disastrous; Joan was wounded and the French were forced to retreat.

Though the cause of France now gleamed with new vigor, Joan herself was no longer aglow with her old confidence. In May of 1430 she was again involved in an unsuccessful assault. This time she was captured by Burgundian soldiers, and the Burgundians immediately sold her to their allies, the English.

John of Bedford, the English commander, was delighted to have the troublesome Joan in his power. To him she was a witch, and her voices not those of saints but of demons. For a year bishops and judges questioned her, trying to get her to admit that she had had dealings with the forces of black magic. Under pressure Joan wavered once, but quickly regained her faith and renewed her insistence that her voices came from heaven. She was convicted of heresy and witchcraft, and condemned to die at the stake. On May 30, 1431, she was tied to a pyramid of faggots in the marketplace at Rouen. As the flames engulfed her, an English soldier was heard to say, "We are lost. We have burnt a saint."

Joan was dead, though, and for the moment the English rejoiced, hoping they could swing the tide of war once again in their favor. John of Bedford chose this moment for what in modern terms would be called a counteroffensive of propaganda: to inspire his troops as Joan had inspired the French, John had his nephew Henry VI brought to Paris to be crowned King of France.

In December of 1431 the nine-year-old king stepped solemnly down the majestic aisle of the Cathedral of Notre Dame to come before his late father's half-uncle, Bishop Beaufort. The bishop pronounced the sacred words and placed the crown of France on the boy's brow, giving him formal possession of the double title that he had inherited before his first birthday.

But the gesture was a hollow one. Kings of France were crowned at Rheims, not at Paris; and there had already been a king lately crowned at Rheims. Young Henry might have the right to call himself King of France, but the true king was the former Dauphin, now Charles VII. When Henry was paraded through the streets of Paris after the ceremony, the faces of his "subjects" were as chilly as the gray December skies.

England had lost the Hundred Years War, though the fact was not yet apparent. In her single year of glory, Joan of Arc had fetched France from the brink of despair, and in her death she had given her country an eternal symbol of courage. In Joan's name the French armies fought with strength reborn. The Maid's execution had horrified all of Europe; the English now were tainted with guilt and self-reproach, while even the Burgundians, who had given Joan over to her slayers, were dismayed by her burning. The alliance between England and Burgundy began to fall apart. Duke Philip of Burgundy had entered into secret negotiations with King Charles VII three months before Henry VI's coronation at Paris. John of Bedford fought on, but now it was in the numbing awareness that he was losing his dead brother's war.

The ceremony at Paris had an unexpected effect on the meek boy-king. For the first time he began to behave like a monarch, holding himself with regal pride and taking a precocious interest in the affairs of the realm. A nobleman who was serving as his tutor in governmental matters reported that the ten-year-old king was "grown in years, in stature of his person, and also in conceit and knowledge of his royal estate, the which causes him to grudge any chastising." He showed signs of being impatient for the day when he could push his guardians aside and come into his kingly powers.

In 1435 the alliance between England and Burgundy, feeble for four years, collapsed altogether. Burgundy and France had patched up their long-standing feud, and henceforth England could not count on Burgundian aid. Ten days after the breach with the Burgundians John of Bedford died, still a young man but sick with fatigue. England had no general to equal him, and now the loss of Henry V's conquests became inevitable. At home, the removal of Bedford left no one to act as an intermediary in the always fierce struggle for power between Bishop Beaufort and Duke Humphrey of Gloucester. The powerful, wealthy Beaufort had won a new title; the Pope had awarded him the red hat of a prince of the Holy Roman Church, and now he was Cardinal Beaufort, with great influence at Rome. But Duke Humphrey, as Protector of the Realm, clung savagely to his own authority despite the cardinal's schemes.

Younger men were coming to prominence now. In 1434 Richard of York took part for the first time in a meeting of the Great Council at Westminster. The following year, the twenty-four-year-old York was appointed Lieutenant and Governor of France and Normandy. When John of Bedford died a few months later, York, who had had little experience of actual warfare, became the commander of the English troops in France. He was well liked, this distant cousin of King Henry VI, and wise men predicted a brilliant future for him.

Among the other important new men were the younger Beauforts, nephews of the cardinal: John, Earl of Somerset, and Edmund, Earl of Dorset. Also in great esteem was the Earl of Buckingham, Humphrey Stafford, a great-grandson of King Edward III by descent from his treacherous youngest son, Thomas of Gloucester. And King Henry VI himself, no longer a child, was beginning to exert some authority in the kingdom. In December of 1436, at the age of fifteen, Henry signed his first royal decree. He was regularly attending council meetings and occasionally was permitted to take part in the reaching of decisions. Often the king showed a remarkable grasp of current events; but just as often he revealed a terrifying lack of understanding. He seemed wholly simple and saintly and guileless to some, while there were those who still contended that his guilelessness was merely a mask for guile. Time would tell.

Two marriages were celebrated in the royal household in 1437, and each caused a ripple of surprised comment—though no one then could foresee the great future consequences of these unions. Jacquetta, the widow of John of Bedford, married Sir Richard Woodville, who had been a member of her husband's staff. For a duchess, as Jacquetta was, to marry a man of Richard Woodville's lowly rank was mildly scandalous. Thirteen Woodville children would follow in due course; most would figure importantly in national events, and one would become not only a queen but the mother of a queen.

The other marriage was that of Katherine, the widow of King Henry V, to a pleasant young Welshman named Owen Tudor. This wedding was even more of a mismatch than that of Jacquetta and Woodville, for Katherine was the daughter of one king, the widow of another, and the mother of a third, while Owen Tudor, for all his charm and good looks, was a commoner without social standing. And the marriage was somewhat overdue; Katherine had been living with Tudor through most of her fifteen years of widowhood, and had already borne him three sons and a daughter. By virtue of that fact, Owen Tudor was destined to become the ancestor of five centuries of English monarchs. But no one could possibly imagine such a thing in 1437.

Now Henry VI was nearing manhood. His early precocity, though, seemed to have strained his abilities past the breaking point. No longer did he come among the nobles of his council and attempt to assert his authority. That brief flash of regal mien had vanished, and the meek, saintly Henry had returned. Whether he was a saint or a simpleton, opinions differed; but one fact was becoming clear to all: Henry VI lacked the strength and majesty a king must have. The baby on whom such high hopes had been lavished had grown into a vague and innocent young man, fit only to be a puppet shuttled back and forth by the various factions of his court. The ordinary people might love such a king, but the leaders of the realm knew that he could not govern. Already the lack of a strong king had cost England most of her hard-won French empire. And Henry was still young; what fresh disasters lay in wait for the land as the long, vacant years of his reign unrolled themselves?

One contemporary description of this ill-starred king has come down to us. It was written by John Blacman, Henry's personal chaplain, after the king's death. No doubt it idealizes Henry's saintly characteristics and passes too quickly over his flaws, but it is revealing all the same, for through the eyes of the priest Blacman we can see that Henry had the temperament of a monk, not of a king:

He was, like a second Job, a man simple and upright, altogether fearing the Lord God, and departing from evil. He was a simple man, without any crook of craft or untruth, as is plain to

*all. With none did he deal craftily, nor ever would say an untrue
word to any, but framed his speech always to speak truth. . . .*

*He took pains to pay in full the tithes and offerings due to God
and the church: and this he accompanied with most sedulous devotion, so that even when decked with the kingly ornaments and
crowned with the royal diadem he made it a duty to bow before
the Lord as deep in prayer as any young monk might have done.
. . . A diligent and sincere worshipper of God was this king, more
given to God and to devout prayer than to handling worldly and
temporal things, or practicing vain sports and pursuits; these he
despised as trifling, and was continually occupied either in prayer
or the reading of the scriptures. . . .*

*Concerning his humility . . . from his youth up he had been
accustomed to wear broad-toed shoes and boots like a countryman.
Also he had usually a long gown with a rounded hood after the
manner of a burgess, and a tunic falling below the knees, shoes,
boots, hose, everything of a dark grey color—for he would have
nothing fanciful. Also at the principal feasts of the year, but especially when of custom he wore his crown, he would always have put
on his bare body a rough hair shirt, that by its roughness his body
might be restrained from excess, or more truly that all pride and
vain glory . . . might be repressed.*

While pious Henry prayed, his relative Richard of York
pursued the dreary war in France. The French had recaptured Paris and had hammered deep into Normandy, right
to the gates of Rouen. In despair, York had asked to be
relieved of his command. But the royal council insisted that
he stay on. In the summer of 1440, after York had returned
to England, the council renewed his appointment as commander in France. But he hesitated to return to that losing
struggle, and only when total defeat threatened, in June of
1441, did he reluctantly go back to the fray.

He carried with him a decree issued by "Henry by the
grace of God King of England and of France and Lord
of Ireland," ordering the royal treasurer to pay over "great

and notable sums of money" to cover the cost of "the setting over the sea of our cousin the Duke of York into our realm of France and duchy of Normandy for the conservation and keeping of them." But the treasury held little except the record of previous debts. York was forced to pay the expenses of the war out of his own pocket, hoping to get the money back from the government at a later date.

York was wealthy enough. He had inherited not only the titles of his uncles the Earl of March and the Duke of York, but their great estates and possessions as well; and in addition he had the lands of his father, the Earl of Cambridge. The income tax records of the year 1436 have come down to us, showing that there were only some seven thousand men in all of England with taxable incomes as high as £5 a year. (Today £5 is slightly less than $15 in American currency, but in the fifteenth century the purchasing power of the pound sterling was far greater than it is today.) Of all the subjects on the 1436 tax rolls, Richard of York was listed as having the highest income: £3,231 for the year. His actual income was probably twice as high, since much of a man's earnings was exempt from tax. The revenues and rents of York's lands amounted to as much as a thousand common men could earn in a year.

Even so, he was hardly in a position to fight the country's war with his own funds. For the time being he advanced the cash needed to pay the soldiers, but it caused him financial difficulties. And when he applied to the ministers of the king for repayment, they treated him shabbily. A document of 1446 exists to show that York received from the royal treasury far less than he had been forced to spend on the war. It angered him, and left him brooding and resentful.

The trouble, York knew, lay not with the blameless, mild King Henry, but with certain of his closest advisers. They did not want to continue fighting the war at all, and certainly did not care to spend public money for what seemed like a doomed enterprise. By choking off funds for the war, they hoped to bring it to a quick end—even if that meant victimizing York, who was bearing the financial burden.

The chief leaders of this "peace party" were Cardinal Beaufort and his nephew, Edmund Beaufort, the Earl of Dorset. Allied with them was a new figure who had suddenly come to great power in England: William de la Pole, the Earl of Suffolk.

Suffolk was one of the few important men of this period who was not descended in some way from King Edward III. His grandfather, Michael de la Pole, had been a close friend and counselor to Richard II, and had been banished in 1388 when the king's relatives had seized power under Thomas of Gloucester. But the Pole family had returned to favor by 1399. William de la Pole, who was born in 1396, became Earl of Suffolk when his older brother was killed fighting at Agincourt.

By 1440 Suffolk was one of the elder statesmen of the realm, and he allied himself with the Beauforts to work for peace with France at any cost. As usual, anything favored by the Beauforts was opposed by Duke Humphrey of Gloucester; Humphrey was the most outspoken member of the war faction at court, demanding a great military offensive that would gain for England all that had been lost since the death of Henry V. Richard of York shared Humphrey's belligerent feelings.

But the king himself, for what little his influence was worth, had cast his lot with the peace faction, simply because peace was more to his liking than war. Furthermore, there was no money in the treasury for continuing the war. By necessity, matters were allowed to drift along until, in the spring of 1444, England and France concluded a truce. That was a sharp defeat for Duke Humphrey. The former protector was now very much in eclipse and rarely was seen at court. The Duke of Gloucester had earlier suffered a severe personal loss through the scheming of his enemies the Beauforts. In 1441 the cardinal had accused Humphrey's wife of witchcraft. It was said that she had made a wax figure of King Henry and had held it over a candle so that the wax would gradually waste away; the king's life was supposed to waste similarly away if the magic were properly performed. The duchess denied the charge, but she was found guilty, and Duke Humphrey was powerless to save her. She was forced to walk barefoot through the streets of London for three days, and then was sent to a distant castle under sentence of life imprisonment. Humphrey, broken in spirit, retired to his manor, where he consoled himself with his magnificent library of rare books. Thus it was that he

was unable to prevent Suffolk and the Beauforts from making peace with France in 1444.

The king, now twenty-three years old, was still unmarried. He had little interest in women and often protested the immodesty of the clothing worn by some of the countesses and duchesses at his court. If left to his own desires, he would probably never have married. But a bachelor king was an impossibility. The House of Lancaster needed an heir.

The Beaufort-Suffolk party was particularly eager to marry Henry off rapidly. The current heir to the throne was still the hated Humphrey of Gloucester, as he had been since the death of his brother John of Bedford in 1435. Humphrey, who was past fifty, childless, and of a tempestuous, erratic character, was hardly suited to be king, but in any case the Beauforts and Suffolk had no desire to see their detested enemy mount the throne. It was urgent to find a bride for Henry at once and for that bride to bring forth a son, lest some prank of fate make Humphrey king.

In February of 1444 Suffolk went to France to negotiate the terms of the truce. But he went also to find a wife for King Henry, and in this he succeeded. Suffolk found a girl who by heritage and character was meant to wear a queen's crown: a girl so fiery, so determined, so savage in the defense of her lawful rights that she brought the dynasty of Lancaster to ruin and presided over the wreckage of a divided England.

the
RISE OF YORK

HE DEMONIC strength of sixteen-year-old Margaret of Anjou could not have been apparent to the Earl of Suffolk at his first meeting with her on May 4, 1444. She was handsome to behold and well schooled in courtly manners, but Suffolk hardly was aware of the terrible force leashed within her slender body.

Margaret was the daughter of a king. Her father, though, was not Charles VII of France, but Charles's cousin, René of Anjou, a very different sort of monarch. René could call himself a king because he had inherited the shadowy title of King of Jerusalem, which had belonged to the leaders of the Crusades in the twelfth and thirteenth centuries. In fact, René was a king twice over; he was King of Sicily as well. But the Crusaders had been evicted from Jerusalem by the Turks in 1244, and Sicily did not recognize René's claim to its throne. The only land he actually owned was in the French provinces of Maine and Anjou, and most of that had been conquered by the English and still was held by them.

So René did not have much in the way of a dowry to offer with his daughter. Suffolk, however, was fascinated by young Margaret, and privately was driven by his desire to get Henry VI married and provided with an heir before anything could happen to him. As part of the marriage agreement Suffolk secretly promised that the English would withdraw within a few years from the province of Maine, restoring it to France. This secret clause verged on treason. Suffolk was giving away land that had been won by English blood merely to please the penniless father of England's future queen. Yet he felt that such a gift was the best way of insuring permanent peace between England and France; he and the Beauforts had already concluded that England's wisest course lay in drawing back from the expensive task of clinging to the lands obtained by Henry V's ambitions.

In March of 1445 the marriage of Margaret of Anjou to Henry VI was carried out—by proxy, with Suffolk placing the ring on the bride's finger in France while Henry remained in England. Escorted by Suffolk and Richard of York across Normandy, Margaret came to Harfleur, where she took ship for England. She landed, seasick and ill, at Portsmouth in April, and several weeks later her marriage to Henry was celebrated once again, now on English soil. On May 26 Margaret entered London for the first time, resting for the night at the Tower of London, which was a royal residence as well as a prison. The next day she made a grand procession through London to St. Paul's Cathedral. A chronicler who witnessed the scene wrote that Margaret was drawn in a chariot by "two steeds trapped all in white damask powdered with gold; and so was the vesture that she had on; and . . . her hair combed down about her shoulders, with a coronal of gold, rich pearls and precious

stones, with all lords on horseback, and ladies in chariots."
All of London turned out to hail the new queen. On May
30 she was crowned at Westminster, and joyous feasting
followed in the royal palace.

Suffolk and his relatives were heaped with honors for
his part in arranging the French truce and procuring the
royal bride. No one outside the Beaufort circle knew then
of the secret deal giving Maine back to France. If that tale
had become public, Suffolk would have been the target of
curses and jeers.

What Margaret, who was all fire and ambition, thought
of her dreamy, monkish husband can easily be guessed.
According to a story reported by an Italian diplomat of the
day in a letter to the Duchess of Milan, the first meeting of
king and queen was a strange one. It was said that Henry
came to Margaret disguised in the humble clothes of a
squire, "and took her a letter which he said the King of
England had written. When the queen read the letter the
king took stock of her, saying that a woman may be seen
over well when she reads a letter, and the queen never
found out that it was the king because she was so engrossed
in reading the letter, and she never looked at the king in his
squire's dress, who remained on his knees all the time.
After the king had gone, the Duke of Suffolk * said: 'Most
serene queen, what did you think of the squire who brought
the letter?' The queen replied: 'I did not notice him, as I
was occupied in reading the letter he brought.' The duke
remarked: 'Most serene queen, the person dressed as a squire
was the most serene King of England,' and the queen was
vexed at not having known it, because she had kept him on
his knees."

* Actually Suffolk's rank was not raised from earl to duke until 1448.

Margaret could scarcely have found mild-mannered Henry a fitting mate for her own soaring spirit. But royal marriages were rarely made for love, and Margaret was willing to overlook Henry's shortcomings. What mattered to her was that she was Queen of England, with all the power and advantage that that role conveyed. She would guard Henry against those who would mislead him; she would protect him against those who would betray him; and when his right to hold the throne was challenged, she would fight for him with all the fury of an outraged lioness.

Margaret lost no time discovering who were her friends at court and who her enemies. She allied herself with the faction of the men who had raised her to her lofty throne: Suffolk and the Beauforts. With them she shared a desire to maintain peace with France, her homeland. With them she came to regard Humphrey of Gloucester as her mortal enemy.

The aging duke, sulking in his library and deprived of his duchess, had had little part in public affairs since 1441. But he was still the heir to the throne and still a fierce advocate of renewing the war with France. When Humphrey learned of the agreement to turn the province of Maine over to the French, he spoke out angrily against it. His harsh words brought on his own swift downfall.

In February of 1447 Humphrey was summoned to appear before a meeting of Parliament at the town of Bury St. Edmunds. The unsuspecting Duke of Gloucester made the winter journey on February 18 and no doubt was puzzled to find a large royal army camped at the north side of town. Two officials met him and conducted him to his lodgings. As he rode to the inn where he was to stay, Duke Humphrey's route took him through a narrow, squalid lane. Halting a beggar that dwelled there, the duke asked, "What call ye this lane?"

The poor man replied, "Forsooth, my lord, it is called the Dead Lane."

Humphrey nodded. "As our lord will, be it all."

When he had dined, a party of nobles came to him, including Cardinal Beaufort's nephew Edmund, the Earl of Dorset, and Humphrey Stafford, formerly the Earl of Buckingham and now the Duke of Buckingham. (A general inflation of noble titles had been taking place all during the 1440's, and many earls had become dukes.) Humphrey of Gloucester was informed that he was under arrest. Soon after, a number of the duke's friends and aides were likewise arrested.

Five days later Duke Humphrey was dead.

The manner of his dying is unknown. Late in February his body was publicly displayed at his funeral so that men could see it bore no wounds. But there were ways of killing a man without mutilating his body, and whispers of murder went the rounds. However, historians today, examining the medical records, believe that Humphrey died of an apoplectic stroke. He was a man of short temper, easily excited to fury, and it appears that he collapsed in rage upon learning of his ruin, sank into a coma that lasted three days, and died. He is remembered today chiefly by the gift of his library to Oxford University, which contains, according to the chronicler of his day who noted the gift, "precious, beautiful, and sumptuous books of every science and branch of learning." A room called Duke Humphrey's Library still is found at Oxford today, although the unhappy duke's political mishaps of five centuries ago are nearly forgotten.

In that same year of 1447 died Duke Humphrey's archenemy, Cardinal Beaufort. The wily churchman died of natural causes, well weighed down by years and earthly treasure. Since the cardinal's brothers John and Thomas had preceded him to the grave by many years, and since his nephew John, the Earl and then Duke of Somerset, had died in 1444, the power of the Beaufort family now was concentrated in a single man: Edmund Beaufort, the surviving nephew of the cardinal.

Edmund Beaufort had become Duke of Somerset upon the death of his brother John three years earlier. Now, at the age of forty-three, this grandson of John of Gaunt came into full power in the realm. Since Queen Margaret was still childless after two years of marriage, Beaufort—or Somerset, as he was usually called—had come to regard himself as the heir to the throne. In this he had the important backing of Queen Margaret herself, as well as of William de la Pole, the Earl of Suffolk. (Suffolk had allied himself to the Beauforts by marriage, taking to wife a cousin of Somerset.)

There was only one serious flaw in Somerset's assumption that he could consider himself Henry VI's heir. By his decree of legitimacy of 1407, Henry IV had specifically banned the whole Beaufort family from aspiring to the throne. If that decree were valid at all, Somerset had no place in the line of succession. And another man happened to be alive with a far better title to the throne: Richard Plantagenet, the Duke of York.

Richard of York, in fact, had a better title to the throne than King Henry VI himself—though no one dared to mention that. Through a double line of descent from Edward III, York could claim with justice that he belonged on the throne. York did not choose to press that claim; but he would certainly not stand idly by if Somerset, with his clouded ancestry, tried to take the crown upon the death of King Henry.

Somerset and Suffolk, having disposed of Duke Humphrey, regarded York as the only really dangerous rival to their power in the land. While King Henry took no part and Queen Margaret urged them on, they wasted little time stripping York of influence. York had hoped to be re-appointed to the post of commander in France; his commission there had expired in 1445 during the truce arranged by Suffolk. It now seemed that the war was about to break out again. But Suffolk saw to it that his ally Somerset was placed in command of England's armies in France. In September of 1447, having been removed from his French command, York was "consoled" with the post of Lieutenant of Ireland on a ten-year appointment. He had hoped instead to receive a place of power at court, in the royal council.

To soften the blow, King Henry bestowed a number of valuable grants of land on the duke. But there was no mistaking what had taken place: Suffolk and Somerset, by sending York into the wilds of Ireland for a decade, had in effect banished their enemy from the court.

York seethed with resentment. He had served King Henry faithfully and well, often at great financial cost to himself. Unlike most of the other nobles at the court, he had shown neither greed nor excessive ambition. And this was his reward: to be thrust aside by the scheming Suffolk, a man not even of royal blood, and by the grasping Somerset, the son of one of John of Gaunt's bastard sons. For two years York remained in England, attempting to persuade King Henry to shift the balance of power. But the king stood aloof from the strife at his court. Queen Margaret, that woman of steel, was the true king now; and Margaret gave heed only to Suffolk, the man who had made her a queen. At last, late in 1449, York sorrowfully departed to take up his Irish command. He took with him his lively wife Cicely, who was the youngest of the twenty-three children of Ralph Neville, the first Earl of Westmorland. To Ireland, too, went York's children: his sons Edward and Edmund, his daughters Margaret, Anne, and Elizabeth. Edward, who was seven, carried the honorable title of Earl of March. Six-year-old Edmund was Earl of Rutland. The girls had no titles yet; those would come by marriage. Anne was ten, Elizabeth five, Margaret three. Soon after the York family arrived in Ireland, Cicely produced a third son, George. History had important places reserved for most of these children.

While York languished in savage Ireland, Somerset and Suffolk were bungling things in France. In 1448 came the transfer of Maine to the French, as agreed upon secretly four years earlier. The shameful transaction infuriated many Englishmen, lords and commoners alike, who cried that England had paid a province for a princess without a dowry. Suffolk, in England, had to face a storm of criticism. With Queen Margaret backing him, he tried to brazen it out, and might have succeeded but for the criminal avarice of one of Somerset's captains in France. With the probable knowledge of Somerset, a party of raiders attacked the town of Fougères, in Brittany, one night in March, 1449. Callously breaking the truce for the sake of plunder, they looted the rich town and made off with great wealth. Instantly an angry Charles VII came to the defense of Fougères, and the war was on again.

The English in France had grown soft and fond of their ease, and Somerset was no general. Peasants and merchants took up arms to drive the English from towns they had held for decades in Brittany and Normandy. By the fall of 1449 Somerset was besieged in Rouen, and bought his freedom by surrendering the city. In less than sixteen months—from May of 1449 to August of 1450—the English were swept clear of their French possessions everywhere except for the port of Calais and the province of Guienne. Calais was virtually an English-populated city; it had belonged to England for a century. As for Guienne, it had come to England as part of the dowry of Eleanor of Aquitaine, Henry II's queen, three hundred years before. It regarded itself contentedly as a part of England that happened to lie in France. But wherever the English were thought of as conquerors, they were driven out.

The loss was incalculable. English knights and lords lost French estates that had belonged to their families for generations. This final convulsion of the Hundred Years War, brought on by the perfidy of Somerset, completed the work of martyred Joan of Arc and sent the English in bloody fashion from France. William of Worcester, a contemporary chronicler, wrote a bitter lament:

Alas! We dolorous persons suffering intolerable persecutions and misery, as well in honor lost as in our livelihood there unrecompensed, as in our movable goods bereaved, what shall we do or say? Shall we in this dolor, anguish, and heaviness continue long thus? Way, nay, God defend that such intrusions, great wrongs, and tyranny should be left unpunished, and so great a loss . . . not repaired!

In England there was fierce outcry against the architects of this terrible disaster. Peasants, townspeople, soldiers, sailors, landlords, knights, barons, men of every class and rank spoke out against Somerset and Suffolk. They had given away Maine, they had lost Normandy and Brittany; too much, too much! In January of 1450 Adam de Moleyns, the Bishop of Chichester and a close associate of Suffolk, went to the harbor of Portsmouth to calm unruly sailors about to sail as reinforcements to France. The sailors, grumbling about their low pay and unwilling to serve under the leadership of Somerset, fell upon Moleyns and killed him. A few days later men began calling for the blood of Suffolk as well.

Parliament convened on January 22, seventeen days after the murder of Moleyns. The country was tense; rioting had begun in many places, and roving bands of brigands were taking advantage of the confusion to commit crimes by the score. Parliament sent for Suffolk and ordered him to explain his actions.

He was in a dangerous position; it behooved him to confess his errors, to beg for forgiveness. But Suffolk was a man swollen with pride. He had forgotten that he was once William de la Pole, whose great-grandfather had been merely a merchant. He was now the Duke of Suffolk, haughty and vain, the peer of those with William the Conqueror's blood in their veins. Before Parliament he denied all charges, scorning the "odious and horrible language that runneth through your land" as slander against him. In lengthy phrases he recited the valor of his family, the brother who had died at Agincourt, the father killed at Harfleur, his own military service in France during the reign of Henry V. But Suffolk's audience was unsympathetic. Since he had come to power, he had filled his pockets liberally at the public expense. He and the Beauforts had pried much royal land loose from the king. Parliament, which had had to raise taxes to make good the losses suffered while Suffolk and his friends grew rich, hated him as much for his grasping ways as for his catastrophic management of the government.

Four days after Suffolk spoke, Parliament demanded his imprisonment for treason and corruption. The indictment accused him of having gravely exceeded his authority; and in fact Suffolk had been a law unto himself since 1447, when he had arranged the fall of Duke Humphrey and the weakening of York. It was said—probably without justification—that he was guilty of "imagining and purposing, falsely and traitorously, to destroy your royal person," that is, to slay Henry VI and replace him on the throne with Somerset. Parliament's rage was such that Suffolk's execution seemed a certainty.

At the last moment Queen Margaret stepped in to save her favorite from condemnation. Obeying her wishes like a helpless puppet, King Henry VI halted the inquiry and banished Suffolk from England for five years, thus getting him beyond the reach of those who would punish him. In May of 1450 Suffolk set out across the Channel, carrying his treasure and his retinue of servants aboard two small ships.

He never reached the safety of exile. Pirate ships were waiting for the hated duke off the coast of Kent. Warned by Suffolk's enemies of his route, the pirates bore down on Suffolk and took him aboard their ship with the cold words, "Welcome, traitor!"

Shakespeare, in his early play *Henry VI*, gives us a vivid picture of the pirate captain berating Suffolk for his misdeeds:

> *Now will I dam up this thy yawning mouth*
> *For swallowing the treasure of the realm:*
> *Thy lips, that kiss'd the queen, shall sweep the ground;*
> *And thou, that smil'dst at good Duke Humphrey's death,*
> *Against the senseless winds shall grin in vain,*
> *Who in contempt shall hiss at thee again:*
> *And wedded be thou to the hags of hell,*
> *For daring to affy [betroth] a mighty lord*
> *Unto the daughter of a worthless king,*
> *Having neither subject, wealth, nor diadem. . . .*
> *By thee Anjou and Maine were sold to France,*
> *The false revolting Normans through thee*
> *Disdain to call us lord. . . .*

Shakespeare's Suffolk replies with the arrogance that was the mark of the man in real life:

> *O! that I were a god, to shoot forth thunder*
> *Upon these paltry, servile, abject drudges. . . .*

It is impossible that I should die
By such a lowly vassal as thyself.
Thy words move rage, and not remorse in me.

Suffolk's rage availed him little. His proud head was forced
down on a wooden block, and an executioner with a rusty
sword needed half a dozen strokes to sever it from his body.
The corpse was stripped of its fine robes and thrown naked
on the beach at Dover. Some accounts said that Suffolk's
head was mounted on a pole, by way of a grim, mocking
pun on his family name, Pole.

Suffolk was dead; Somerset shrewdly remained in
France; Queen Margaret raged; and King Henry sadly
prayed for the soul of his murdered duke. And now the
country erupted into a chaotic reign of terror.

An earthquake of violence shook
England. All the forces of savage anarchy held down in civilized realms by
government, burst loose in this land
whose king for so long had been a
saintly fool. The center of the fury was
in southern England, in Kent, where
Suffolk's body, cast ashore, inspired a
bloody uprising that threatened to become a revolution. Its leader was an ad-
venturer named Jack Cade, who falsely
claimed to be of the Mortimer family.

Wat Tyler's rebellion of 1381 had
been a rising of oppressed peasants,
the humblest subjects in the realm. But
Jack Cade's rebellion cut across many
social classes. Those who listened as
the firebrand Cade shouted his cries for

blood included merchants, shopkeepers, fishermen, sailors, a few priests, small landowners, a knight who had fought at Agincourt, and several former members of Parliament. Cade cried out against the misrule of those who surrounded the king. And in truth there was much to cry out against. In 1450 King Henry VI's debts amounted to £400,000. The annual income from what was left of the royal estates came to only £5,000. Suffolk and Somerset had obtained "gifts" of royal land with revenues of many thousands of pounds sterling a year; the officers of the royal household squandered and embezzled £24,000 a year.

Soon an armed band was marching toward London, gathering strength day by day. In June of 1450 Cade published a list of grievances against those whose false advice had injured the king: "His merchandise is lost, his common people is destroyed, the sea is lost, France is lost, the king . . . oweth more than any King of England owed. . . ."

Parliament was meeting at Leicester. The king and his nobles were there, with many followers. Each nobleman kept his own force of armed retainers, amounting to a private army. When word came of Cade's rebellion, it was easy to assemble these retainers into an instant army of considerable power, numbering more than ten thousand men. Henry VI himself, forced into action by Cade's threat to the safety of the realm, called for loyalty in suppressing the revolt. It was one of the few times in his reign that the king showed a willingness to lead.

He learned that the rebels were camped at Blackheath, not far to the south of London, and sent an advance guard of royal troops to deal with them. But the king's men were ambushed by the rebels and were cut down. Next Cade's forces burst upon the king's own camp, crying, "Destroy we these traitors about the king!" They called in particular for the death of the dreaded Lord Say, the royal treasurer. Henry VI and his courtiers managed a rapid retreat. The king sent Lord Say to the Tower of London for his own protection. Then Henry, Margaret, and the court lords abandoned the capital to Jack Cade and prudently withdrew to northern England. The rest of the royal army simply melted away, making no attempt to halt the progress of the rebellion.

On the first of July Cade and his rabble flooded into Southwark, just across the River Thames from London. Cade strutted forth proudly clad in spurs, armor, and helmet that he had stripped from a dead knight. Within the capital city on the far side of the river the frightened citizens, forsaken by their rulers, waited in terror.

The next day the rebels fought their way across London Bridge and entered the capital in triumph. "Up Fish Street!" cried Cade. "Down St. Magnus' corner! Kill and knock down! Throw them into the Thames!" He tapped his sword against the ground and boomed, "Now is Mortimer lord of this city!" The rebels paraded through London, pillaging and burning. One of the victims was Philip Malpas, a wealthy alderman disliked by many; Cade's men burst into his mansion and, says a chronicler, "bare away much good of his, and in specially much money, both of silver and gold, the value of a notable sum, and in specially of mechandises, as of tin, woad, madder, and alum, with great quantity of woolen cloth and many rich jewels, with other notable stuff of feather-beds, bedding, and many a rich cloth. . . ."

Lord Say was taken from the Tower on the morning of Saturday, July 4, given a mock trial, and beheaded. Also executed was William Crowmer, Say's son-in-law and the

Sheriff of Kent. The heads of Say and Crowmer were placed on long poles and marched through the city. That night Cade retired to his lodgings in Southwark.

There was more looting on Sunday; but that evening the people of London at last resolved to put an end to this violence. A body of armed citizens, reinforced by the garrison of the Tower and led by a veteran soldier named Matthew Gough, crossed London Bridge into Southwark and attacked the rebels. One man who took part in the fighting wrote to a friend soon after, "Then at night the captain put me out into the battle at the bridge, and there I was wounded, and hurt near to death; and I was six hours in the battle, and might never come out thereof." From early evening until eight in the morning "there was fighting upon London Bridge, and many a man was slain or cast in Thames, harness, body and all." Among the dead was Matthew Gough. But the rebels, full of wine and giddiness, began to give way. By morning their defeat seemed certain. When a delegation of bishops arrived, offering governmental pardon for Cade and his men if they would lay down their arms and go peacefully home, Cade accepted. The rioters scattered, laden down with booty. A few days later the pardons were revoked; Cade was proclaimed a traitor, and fled into hiding. A Sussex squire named Alexander Iden came upon him and slew him.

While London was suffering through the grim weekend of Jack Cade's marauding, atrocities were reported from other parts of the land. At Edington the Bishop of Salisbury was murdered by his own parishioners after he had said the Mass. The bishop was King Henry's confessor, and was thought to be a sinister influence at court. A chronicle tells how he was "drawn from the altar and led up to an hill there . . . and they slew him horribly . . . and spoiled him unto the naked skin, and rent his bloody shirt into pieces and bare them away with them, and made boast of their wickedness." And toward the end of July, soldiers coming home from France joined the movement toward anarchy. They were bitter over their defeat, hungry from lack of pay. Clad in battlefield armor and wielding axes and swords, the troops just back from Normandy stormed restlessly through towns and cities, venting their displeasure on anyone who crossed their path. One monk wrote in August: "The world was so strange at that time, no man might well ride or go in no parts of this land without a strength of fellowship but that he were robbed." Men sang jubilantly of the deaths of "Suffolk, Salisbury, and Say— slain were they that England betrayed."

England was in collapse and the king, helpless, allowed the violence to go on unchecked. The wealthiest and most secure state in the world was crumbling into barbarism and confusion. Government had all but vanished. At this critical time there seemed to be only one man who might bring order out of this turmoil. He was Richard, Duke of York. But York was in Ireland, where the schemings of Somerset and Suffolk had sent him.

A clause in York's commission allowed him to come to England in case of national emergency. Certainly this was such an emergency. He had governed well during his year in Ireland, bringing that unruly island under control through his strength and ability. The Irish, who hated their English masters with a fiery passion, had come to respect York as they did few other Englishmen; they saw in him a man of honor, virtuous and law-abiding. He did not wish to leave Ireland now. But there was need of him in England.

At the end of August, 1450, York crossed the Irish Sea and came home.

No one knew what he intended. After all, he had a strong right to the throne. Was he returning to cast weak King Henry aside and seize power? Or did he merely mean to offer his services to the troubled king in this moment of storm?

Queen Margaret felt that York was too dangerous to be trusted. As the duke made his way eastward across Wales, she sent agents to waylay and assassinate him. But York eluded these killers and safely reached his stronghold on the border between England and Wales. There he remained for several months, assessing the situation. Parliament was due to meet at Westminster in November. When it convened, Richard of York was present. Suddenly, after years of exclusion from power, the duke stood at the threshold of greatness. All eyes were on his short, stocky, muscular figure as he made his bid for power, and in so doing set in motion the conflicts that would bring England toward civil war.

challenge for a throne

ICHARD OF YORK's first act upon reaching Westminster in the fall of 1450 was to confront his kinsman King Henry, who had returned from his refuge in the north. The king, a pale, long-faced man with gentle eyes and a woman's pursed lips, must have felt little at ease as the sturdy York strode into his chambers. Yet York humbly knelt and proclaimed himself the king's true servant, loyal in all things. King Henry no doubt experienced a surge of relief; York meant to make no trouble. But virtually in the same breath, the duke demanded the place at the council table that had so long been denied him, and asked to know why agents of the queen had tried to murder him as he returned from Ireland. King Henry sidestepped that embarrassing point and tried to placate York. "We declare you our true subject and faithful cousin," the monarch said.

York now proceeded to Parliament. He met a warm reception there, both from the Lords and the Commons. The Lords looked to him as a relative and as a man who could end the agony brought on by the greed of the Beaufort family and the late Duke of Suffolk. To the Commons

101

York was popular because he supported their cry for governmental and financial reforms.

York's rival and enemy, Edmund Beaufort, the Duke of Somerset, was also on hand for the Parliament of 1450. Queen Margaret had hastily summoned Somerset back from France upon learning of York's return from Ireland. But at this Parliament, Somerset seemed like a man whose star was on the wane, York like one whose star was rising and growing ever brighter.

The early events of the Parliament contributed to this appearance. Supporters of York accused Somerset of criminal misgovernment. They insisted that York be named the first councilor of the king and that Somerset be arrested. On December 1 a band of Yorkists broke into Somerset's house, searching for him. The duke escaped, but his quarters were looted. King Henry, soon after, sent Somerset to the Tower of London. It was a move that seemed to satisfy both sides. To the Yorkists it appeared that Somerset had been imprisoned. To Queen Margaret, though, it was a protective measure, for Somerset was safe from harm behind the thick walls of the Tower.

York, though, was not yet skilled at this game of political intrigue. He allowed his initial advantage to trickle away. While his followers hesitated over their next moves, Queen Margaret and Somerset regained command. Suddenly the king, prodded by Margaret, declared Parliament adjourned until the following May. Once the troublesome legislators had gone their separate ways, Somerset was released from the Tower and given two posts of great prestige and power: Captain of Calais and Comptroller of the Royal Household. A combination of Margaret's guile and Henry's meekness had foiled York in his moment of seeming victory.

When Parliament returned in the spring of 1451, it was in an ugly mood. A lawyer named Thomas Young, who represented the town of Bristol, brought the issue of the succession to the throne into the open for the first time. An anonymous chronicler relates how Young "moved that because the king had no offspring, it would be for the security of the kingdom that it should be openly known who should be heir apparent. And he named the Duke of York."

No doubt York had suggested the idea himself, for Young had done legal work for the duke in the last few years. By trying to get from Parliament a formal declaration placing himself next in line for the crown, Richard of York simply was attempting to confirm a situation that should already have been self-evident. Age and warfare had taken their toll of many of the descendants of King Edward III's five sons. The line of the Black Prince had died out with the death of Richard II. The line of John of Gaunt now was represented only by the childless Henry VI, and by Somerset, who under law had no right to the throne. The line of Thomas of Gloucester still flourished in several families, but since Thomas had been Edward III's youngest son, his descendants were far from any claim to royalty. As for Richard of York, he combined in himself two lines of descent from the sons of Edward III. Through his mother, he was the sole heir of Lionel of Clarence, Edward's next to oldest son, and through his father he was the sole heir of Edmund of Langley, the next to youngest son. Leaving Somerset aside, Richard of York had clear title to succeed a childless Henry VI.

Queen Margaret, though, had no intention of surrendering so easily. She still hoped to give birth to an heir herself, although, after six barren years of marriage, that was begin-

THE YORKIST CLAIM

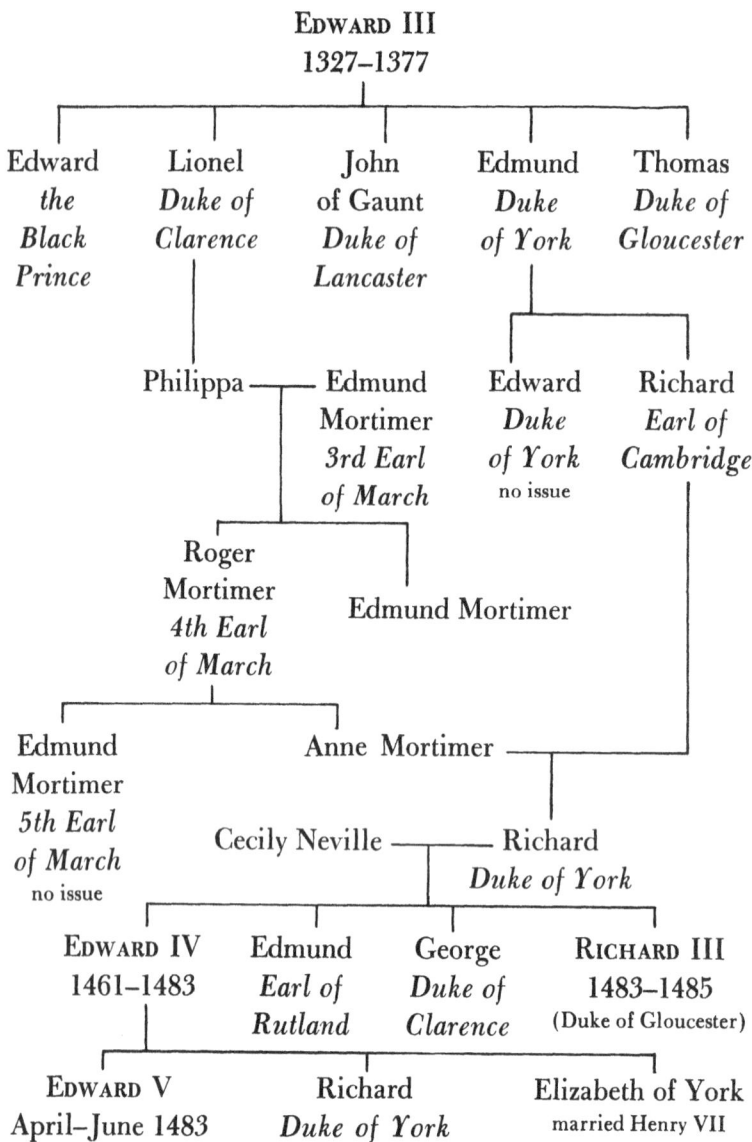

EDWARD III
1327–1377

Edward *the* **Black** **Prince**	Lionel *Duke of* *Clarence*	John *of Gaunt* *Duke of* *Lancaster*	Edmund *Duke* *of York*	Thomas *Duke of* *Gloucester*

Philippa —— Edmund Mortimer *3rd Earl of March*

Edward *Duke of York* no issue

Richard *Earl of Cambridge*

Roger Mortimer *4th Earl of March*

Edmund Mortimer

Edmund Mortimer *5th Earl of March* no issue

Anne Mortimer

Cecily Neville —— Richard *Duke of York*

EDWARD IV 1461–1483	Edmund *Earl of* *Rutland*	George *Duke of* *Clarence*	**RICHARD III** 1483–1485 (Duke of Gloucester)

EDWARD V April–June 1483

Richard *Duke of York*

Elizabeth of York married Henry VII

ning to look unlikely. Failing that, she wanted the throne
to pass to Somerset. What about the decree of Henry IV,
excluding the Beauforts from the succession? A simple
enough matter for Margaret. If one king could make such
a decree, a second king could overrule it. Henry VI was
perfectly free to name his kinsman of Somerset as his heir
if he chose. Did they not both spring from the stock of
John of Gaunt? Were they not both members of the House
of Lancaster?

When Thomas Young made his proposal to name York
the heir, then, he met an unexpectedly forceful response
from Henry VI. The king dissolved Parliament and whistled
the presumptuous Young off to the Tower as a prisoner.
York was astounded to realize that Somerset was still in
full control and that the power that had been his in autumn
had somehow slipped from his grasp by the spring. Angered
and discouraged, York retired to his castle on the borders
of Wales.

The realm remained in confusion. Soldiers were stream-
ing home from France steadily now, filling the land with a
brawling horde of archers and swordsmen accustomed to
bloodshed and angered by defeat. Many of these disgruntled
warriors drifted into the private armies of the great lords,
swelling them to ominous size and creating sources of potential trouble. York was among those who collected armed
followers at this time. Wily Somerset had kept the upper
hand in 1451, but York now was fully committed to Somerset's overthrow. The Beaufort family had to be ripped from
the government, York felt, like some stubborn weed that
had spread through valuable fields.

York's next move was made on February 3, 1452. He
released an open letter proclaiming his own loyalty and

Somerset's treason. York denounced Somerset for "laboring continually about the King's Highness for my undoing, and to corrupt my blood, and to disherit me and my heirs, and such persons as be about me, without any desert or cause done or attempted on my part or theirs." York therefore declared war on Somerset in these words:

I signify unto you that with the help and supportation of Almighty God . . . I, after long sufferance and delays, not my will or intent to displease my sovereign lord, seeing that the said duke [Somerset] ever prevaileth and ruleth about the king's person, that by this means the land is likely to be destroyed, am fully concluded to proceed in all haste against him, with the help of my kinsmen and friends.

Now York assembled his private army and led it toward London to seize Somerset. He chose a route that passed through Kent, the rebellious region that had spawned Jack Cade's uprising. York expected that those who had supported Cade would flock to his own banners. But most of the Kentishmen had had enough of rebellion for now; York was disappointed at the response. Still, he rode on to the capital at the head of a substantial force.

Queen Margaret and Somerset did not take lightly this naked threat against their power. Acting rapidly, Margaret brought together an army even larger than York's. Poor befuddled King Henry was thrust into his battle armor and clapped on a horse so that he might lead this army as a king should do. On February 16 the royal army marched for Blackheath to intercept York.

York had not come to wage war against his monarch, but only to capture his rival Somerset. When he learned that Henry VI was marching against him, York changed his path, avoiding a collision of the armies, and by a different route went on to London. London would not admit him. The city magistrates refused York permission to enter the city peacefully, but he held back once more from armed attack and withdrew a short distance to the south to make camp.

After some days of uncertainty York received a summons from King Henry, asking him to a parley at Blackheath. About noon on March 1 York with some forty knights rode into the king's camp. Thousands of royal soldiers stood assembled there. At a word from King Henry, York's life would have been forfeit. But Henry was not the man to give that word. As York, bareheaded and unarmed, entered the king's tent, Henry received him without anger.

What, the king asked, was the Duke of York's complaint.

York replied that he had come to arrest Somerset on charges of misgovernment. He insisted—as he had in Parliament fifteen months before—that Somerset be brought to trial. The king offered a vague promise that it would be done if York would only disband his army and cease to menace the peace of the kingdom.

Buoyed by that promise, York told his soldiers to go home. But at once he realized he had been cheated. The king was still a puppet; Queen Margaret and Somerset were still in control; all this had been no more than an elaborate charade, designed to trick him into releasing his troops. Once York's men had left, the duke himself was invited into London—as a virtual prisoner.

Though York was in their power, Margaret and Somerset did not dare to harm him. The duke was too popular in the land; and, besides, there were rumors that York's eldest son, Edward, the Earl of March, was waiting on the frontiers of Wales with a second army that would head for

London if York were in peril. The Earl of March was only ten years old, but in that era children often had high responsibilities, and the young earl was a big lad for his age, already skilled in generalship.

In London, though, the furious, helpless York was forced to yield to the wishes of his enemies. On March 10, 1452, he appeared in St. Paul's Cathedral before an assembly of high nobles and was compelled to swear an oath of allegiance to King Henry. He vowed to keep the peace, to raise no troops, and to obey the commands of the king. In case of misconduct in the future, York agreed, he would be subject to the penalties of treason, including the loss of all his property.

Baffled, outmaneuvered, York returned to his distant castle. More than ever he was committed now to the overthrow of Somerset, who had so publicly humiliated him. But for the moment there was little he could do except brood and sulk. York's sullen mood was brightened in the autumn of 1452 when Duchess Cicely presented him with a fourth son, who was named Richard after his father. The baby was small and sickly, though, and his body was poorly formed, with one shoulder higher than the other and the left arm crippled. This Richard clearly would never be a great warrior, such as his eldest brother Edward of March promised to be. Nor could any man predict that this feeble baby would one day wade through streams of blood to the throne of England.

In 1453 came three events that shook the realm and swerved the pattern of history.

A century of war between England and France ended in the summer. Since the disasters of 1449 and 1450 the

English had clung desperately to a dismal remnant of their French empire. Old John Talbot, an English general who had fought with distinction in France for thirty years, led the defense and early in 1453 even attempted a counter-offensive. Talbot had some brief success; for a few weeks it appeared that England might even regain the upper hand in the war. But in July he was defeated at Castillon. The French had called in engineers who designed the finest artillery in the world for them. Heavy catapults hurled gigantic stone balls into the walls of English castles, and booming cannon blew Talbot's men to bits. Talbot himself was killed, and the last English hopes collapsed. French gunpowder had blown the English out of France at last, leaving only the port of Calais in England's possession as the pitiful final outpost of overseas empire.

During these terrible months of final defeat the court was rocked by a second development: King Henry had gone mad. He had left London to pass the summer in Wiltshire, and there the news of Talbot's destruction reached him. Suddenly the world had come to be too much for the weary king. He placed himself beyond the reach of further bad tidings by slipping into a hopeless stupor, sitting with dull eyes turned toward the ground. He said nothing, recognized no one, understood nothing that was said to him. In much the same way Henry VI's grandfather, King Charles VI of France, had lost his reason years ago. Now that heritage of madness had reached the throne of England.

In the three decades since the death of Henry V, England had never had a strong king, but rather first a child and then a weak and simple young man. Now, though, there was no king at all, only the empty shell of Henry VI. And

in October of 1453 came the third great event of that year: Queen Margaret gave birth to a son. The prince was named Edward.

The House of Lancaster had its desired heir. Margaret brought the baby to King Henry, hoping that the sight of his son would jar him from his witlessness. But the king stared without comprehending. He did not speak. Unable to walk, to remember, to think, he gaped and driveled and laughed, more childish in his bearing than the newborn child itself.

A new atmosphere of crisis gathered over England. Everyone assumed—wrongly, as it turned out—that King Henry would soon die of his affliction. If that happened, would the throne pass once again to a baby, bringing on all the divisions and calamities that such an inheritance entailed? Or would Somerset illegally seize the crown by pushing the child's claim aside? Perhaps it was York who would be the usurper, some said.

Queen Margaret devoted all her fiery energy to protecting the interests of herself and her son. To her there was no question of the succession: Prince Edward was the rightful heir, and if the mindless king died, Prince Edward must have the throne. To assure that, the queen attempted to gain for herself the office of Protector of the Realm. When Parliament met in November of 1453, the queen proposed a bill making her the ruler of the land during her husband's madness, with the right to name all officers and to exercise the powers of the king. In a sense, Margaret had been the real ruler already, for generally King Henry had followed her wishes. But for Parliament to give its blessing to such an arrangement was an entirely different matter.

Parliament hesitated; and Richard of York made his move. For the third time in the past three years York grasped for power, this time successfully.

The high nobles of the realm feared and distrusted Margaret and Somerset. They drew back from delivering the kingdom into their hands. Instead they turned to York. The birth of Prince Edward destroyed any possibility that York might claim the throne upon King Henry's death; but with a good chance that an infant might soon be king, it seemed wise to grant great authority to the well-respected York. In December of 1453 Somerset was once more arrested and imprisoned in the Tower of London. Early in the new year York requested the title of Protector of the Realm as guardian for Prince Edward.

Everything was done by legal means. Parliament went through the motions of sending a delegation to Windsor Castle to consult with King Henry. A dozen lords and bishops visited the king and read him the terms of the agreement appointing York as protector. "To the which matters nor to any of them they could get no answer nor sign," wrote a contemporary chronicler, "for no prayer nor desire, lamentable cheer nor exhortation, nor any thing. . . ." Once more the document was read. The royal expression remained vacant. "They moved him and stirred him, by all the ways and means that they could think, to have answer of the matters aforesaid, but they could have none. . . ."

It was sufficient. On March 27, 1454, Parliament named Richard of York as Protector of the Realm. At the same time, the House of Lancaster received one sign of favor; the king's baby was awarded the title of Prince of Wales, the traditional title of the heir to the throne. If Henry VI died, Edward would be king. But York would hold the highest power in the land until young Edward came of age. Parliament cautiously spelled out limits to the duke's authority. He was not permitted to assume "the name of tutor, lieutenant, governor, nor of regent, nor no name that shall import authority of government of the land; but the said name of protector and defender, the which importeth a personal duty of intendance to the actual defense of this land, as well against the enemies outward, if case require, as against rebels inward. . . ."

Despite these clauses, York was now supreme, and it was Queen Margaret's turn to know despair and frustration.

Acting in the name of King Henry and his heir, Prince
Edward, York appointed his own ministers and took upon
himself the burdens of the realm. Somerset remained a
prisoner in the Tower. For the sake of keeping order in
the land, York could not risk the divisive step of bringing
Somerset to trial, but he would not release the powerful
duke under any circumstances.

For seven months York tasted the fruits of power. Then,
about Christmastime of 1454, Henry VI recovered his sanity
as suddenly as he had lost it.

An account of the king's miraculous recovery survives
in a letter written by a certain Edmund Clere to John Paston, who was a member of a wealthy landowning family of
the time. The Pastons saved virtually every letter written
to or by them, and their remarkable correspondence, full
of comment on current events, is one of our best sources for
information on the England of the fifteenth and sixteenth
centuries.

Under date of January 9, 1455, Clere wrote to John
Paston, "Blessed be God, the king is well amended, and
hath been since Christmas day. . . . And on the Monday
after noon the queen came to him and brought my lord
prince with her. And then he [King Henry] asked what the
prince's name was, and the queen told him Edward; and
then he held up his hands and thanked God thereof. And
he said he never knew till that time, nor wist not what was
said to him, nor wist not where he had be whilst he hath
be sick till now. . . . And he saith he is in charity with
all the world, and so he would all the lords were. . . ."

York, by terms of the decree of Parliament making him
protector, lost his special powers automatically the moment
the king returned to sanity. His protectorship came to an

abrupt and unexpected end. To his credit, he made no attempt to remain in office. He returned to his family lands once more. Somerset was released from the tower and Queen Margaret again held the key position in the realm.

Having been thrust from power once, Margaret and Somerset vowed that they would not let it happen to them a second time. In the spring of 1455 they summoned a council of great peers to meet at Leicester "for the purpose of providing the safety of the king's person against his enemies." The only nobles invited were those who were known to be loyal to the House of Lancaster. Any lord who had been associated with York during the months of his protectorship was excluded. The battle lines were forming in the war of Lancaster against York.

The Duke of York was well aware that this council of peers was meeting to plan strategy against him. Quickly he called his own kinsmen about him to discuss the best action to take. In the meeting of Yorkist nobles, one figure stood out as the most passionate advocate of armed resistance to Queen Margaret and Somerset. He was York's nephew, Richard Neville, the Earl of Warwick, later called "Warwick the Kingmaker."

Thus the central figure of the Wars of the Roses made his appearance on the scene. Richard Neville was twenty-seven years old in 1455. He was wealthy, proud, ambitious, fond of luxurious living, a man whose soul demanded that he must be at the heart of any enterprise, though he was somewhat lacking in personal physical courage. He belonged to one of the mightiest families in the realm, and by an intricate pattern of marriages in large families was related both to the houses of Lancaster and of York.

The power of the Neville family went back to the reign

of Richard II. Nevilles had been barons of a minor sort in England since the twelfth century, but Ralph Neville (1364–1425) did most to advance the fortunes of the house. Ralph was a supporter of Richard II in his struggle against the lords who attempted to overthrow him, and in 1397 was rewarded with the title of first Earl of Westmorland. To the traditional Neville lands Ralph added great tracts of land in northern England.

By then Ralph Neville already had a large family. While a very young man he had married Margaret Stafford, the daughter of the second Earl of Stafford, and she had given him nine children. Most of these married important members of the nobility. But Margaret died young, and in 1396 Ralph took as his second wife Joan Beaufort, the daughter of John of Gaunt. Joan produced fourteen more Nevilles for Ralph. Of his twenty-three children, seventeen lived to adulthood, and many reached great power.

Through his marriage to Joan Beaufort, Ralph Neville thus allied himself to the rising House of Lancaster. He was brother-in-law to the three Beaufort brothers who soon would be so prominent in the kingdom; and the Beauforts were half-brothers to Henry of Lancaster, the future King Henry IV. Although Ralph had won his great wealth through loyalty to Richard II, he quickly shifted support to Lancaster when Henry rebelled in 1399. It was largely with the aid of Ralph Neville, Earl of Westmorland, that Henry of Lancaster was able to depose Richard II and take the throne that year.

Ralph was suitably rewarded. During the reign of his wife's half-brother, King Henry IV, a steady flow of property passed into Ralph's hands as gifts from the king. And just as steadily, Ralph Neville saw to it that this vast collection of estates would pass permanently into the hands of his children. However, he made a point of favoring his second brood of children—Joan Beaufort's offspring—over the earlier family. Seven of his nine children by Margaret Stafford had lived into adulthood, and all were well taken care of financially; Ralph went to some lengths to cut them out of his inheritance and give the richest lands he owned to his younger group of heirs. This caused a great deal of bitterness in the Neville family, naturally, as the grown children of Ralph Neville watched their father transferring property to these upstart babes. He left little to his first family but the title of Earl of Westmorland itself, which remained for the descendants of his eldest son.

The second Neville family did remarkably well for it-self—not surprising, since the children were related through their mother to the King of England himself. One of Ralph's five adult daughters became a nun; the other four married noblemen. Catherine Neville wed John Mowbray, Duke of Norfolk. Eleanor Neville married Richard Lord Despenser. Ann Neville married Humphrey Stafford, Duke of Buckingham. Cicely Neville, the youngest of Ralph's army of children, married Richard Plantagenet, Duke of York.

Neville's second set of sons were as successful as their sisters. William Neville and Edward Neville each married the heiress to a noble title, and through their marriages became, respectively, Lord Fauconberg and Lord Aber-gavenny. George Neville inherited one of his father's titles and became Lord Latimer. Robert Neville, entering the church, rose to be Bishop of Salisbury. Richard, the eldest son of Ralph Neville by his second wife, married the daugh-ter of the Earl of Salisbury and inherited his father-in-law's title and estates. When Ralph Neville died in 1425, Richard, now Earl of Salisbury, emerged as the leader of the family.

There were furious disputes between Richard of Salisbury and his eldest living half-brother, Ralph II, over which branch of the family should hold more power. The children of Joan Beaufort prevailed, however, and the elder Nevilles retired from active life. Richard of Salisbury became one of the most important men in the kingdom during the reign of Henry VI. But he found himself caught between opposing factions. He was the nephew of old Cardinal Beaufort and the cousin of Edmund Beaufort, the Duke of Somerset, and that linked him to the "peace with France" party centering around the Beauforts, Suffolk, and Queen Margaret. On the other hand, his sister Cicely was the wife of the Duke of York, and that linked Richard of Salisbury to the "war with France" party centering around York and Duke Humphrey of Gloucester. These conflicting ties forced Salisbury to steer a careful course.

The Neville love for obtaining power through marriage descended to the next generation. Richard of Salisbury's eldest son and namesake, Richard Neville, married Anne Beauchamp, the only heiress to the title and possessions of Richard Beauchamp, thirteenth Earl of Warwick. Beauchamps had been Earls of Warwick since about 1090; but when Richard Beauchamp died in 1439, the title passed to his son Henry, who did not long outlive him. In 1450, the younger Richard Neville was made Earl of Warwick by virtue of his marriage to the only living member of the Beauchamp family. Thus, through his wife Anne, the future kingmaker was provided with his title.

At the meeting of the Yorkists in the spring of 1455, Richard of York received his strongest pledges of support from the two Richard Nevilles, father and son: the Earl of Salisbury and the Earl of Warwick, brother-in-law and nephew to York. With three thousand men, York, Salisbury, and Warwick moved south toward the place where the Lancastrian lords were gathered. It was not the first time that York, an army at his back, had marched out to gain power. The last time, he had been tricked into laying down his arms and meekly surrendering to the king. Now he would not hesitate to do battle against his foe Somerset if matters came to that.

the WARS of the ROSes

HEN OPEN warfare came to pass between Lancaster and York, it happened in a curiously haphazard way. The first battle in the Wars of the Roses was not really a battle at all, but rather an accidental collision between two armies.

It took place at the town of St. Albans, not far to the north of London. Most medieval towns and cities were ringed by sturdy walls, so that the citizens might shut out any band of invaders; but St. Albans was an open town, unprotected by stone and accessible to all. The Yorkist army was heading south toward London, and the Lancastrian army came north to meet it. The two forces met by chance at St. Albans on May 22, 1455.

The royal troops had reached St. Albans the day before. They numbered about two thousand men, chiefly the troops who were regarded as the king's own army. King Henry was with them, as were Somerset and several of the other leading Lancastrian lords. Early the next day the somewhat larger Yorkist army arrived and took up its position to the east of town.

Neither side was eager to give battle without first attempting negotiations. An account of the events written a few days later by an anonymous foreigner living in England declares: "Very early the king sent a herald to the Duke of York to know the cause for which he had come there with so many men. . . . It seemed to the king something quite new that he, the duke, should be rising against him, the king. The reply made was that he was not coming against him thus, he [York] was always ready to do him obedience, but he well intended in one way or another to have the traitors who were about him so that they should be punished, and that in case he could not have them with good will and fair consent, he intended in any case to have them by force."

York was asking specifically to have Somerset turned over to him. The Lancastrians refused, naturally. The king's herald went forth again to tell York that King Henry "was unaware that there were any traitors about him were it not for the Duke of York himself who had risen against his crown." The exchange of messages between the two angry camps might have continued all day but for the impatience of Warwick. It was quite clear to the young earl that the Lancastrians did not intend to hand Somerset over to his enemies. So while the negotiations still were going on, Warwick's troops burst into St. Albans shouting the earl's battle cry: "A Warwick! A Warwick! A Warwick!"

In the narrow, winding streets there was little room for the kind of fighting these armies had been trained to do. This was no encounter in open fields, where lines of men could batter and slam against one another. Thomas Lord Clifford, one of the most loyal of the Lancastrian nobles, set up a blockade across one important street. York led a frontal attack on the blockade with archers and cannon, while Warwick circled around to the rear of the city and forced an entry there.

For three hours there was savage fighting in close quarters. King Henry was at the center of the struggle, though not a combatant himself. Four members of the king's bodyguard were killed beside him by Yorkist archers; the king himself received a shallow wound in the shoulder from an arrow. Lord Clifford was slain. Somerset, the real object of York's attack, had been within an inn when the battle began. As Yorkist soldiers began to break down the doors, Somerset and his men came forth. Somerset killed four of the Yorkists, but then was struck down with an ax and perished. Another who died fighting for the Lancastrians that day was Humphrey Stafford, the son of the Duke of Buckingham. Buckingham himself was struck by three arrows but managed to escape from the field, seriously wounded. Here the struggle cut across family lines, for Buckingham, the husband of Ralph Neville's daughter Ann, was linked by that marriage both to York and to Warwick, yet fought against them on King Henry's side at St. Albans.

By early afternoon the battle was over. The naked bodies of Somerset and Clifford lay in the bloodied streets. Somerset's son, Henry Beaumont, the Earl of Dorset, had been wounded and was a prisoner of the Yorkists. Queen Margaret and her child had fled. King Henry, his royal robes stained with his royal blood, had taken refuge in a nearby abbey during the fighting, and there he was found by the Yorkists.

York took elaborate pains to show that his uprising had been aimed at overthrowing Somerset, not at injuring the saintly King Henry. Going to Henry at the abbey, York "went on his knees to him crying mercy," says the anonymous foreign observer, "for whatever way he might have offended and for the peril in which he had put his person." The duke uttered "many other good and humble words, showing him that he had not gone against him but against the traitors to his crown, and in the end before the Duke of York went away from there the king pardoned him everything and took him in his good grace."

The dazed king had no choice but to "pardon" York and to agree to accept the duke's homage. York spoke long and earnestly of his desire to be a loyal subject, but the plain fact was that Henry VI was his prisoner. York, Warwick, and Salisbury, the three victors of St. Albans, led the king back to London. With Somerset dead and Queen Margaret in flight, it seemed that no one stood between York and power. His would be the highest authority in the land once more, and the king would be his plaything.

Queen Margaret, though, was not the woman to concede defeat easily. First Suffolk and then Somerset, her two great confederates, had met violent dooms; but she still had the majesty, if not the power, of the throne as her weapon. She was the wife of the king, the mother of the royal prince. She could use those facts to rally support for the cause of Lancaster.

In truth, many influential Englishmen thought that the Duke of York had moved too fast and too far. They feared his vaulting ambitions now. As one priest who kept a chronicle of these events commented, King Henry's friends made York "to stink in the king's nostrils even unto death;

SCOTLAND

Bamborough 🏰
Alnwick 🏰

Newcastle •

- towns
🏰 castles
✕ battles
-·-·-·- boundaries

Barnard 🏰
Richmond 🏰

enGland 1399–1485

Lancaster 🏰

York •
Hull •
Towton ✕
Ravenspur
Pontefract 🏰
Sandal 🏰

Bolingbroke 🏰

Harlech 🏰

Derby •

Shrewsbury ✕
Much Wenlock •

Bosworth
✕ • Leicester

Norwich •

WALES

Ludlow •

Northampton •
Cambridge •

Milford Haven •

Tewkesbury ✕
Gloucester •

Oxford •

St. Albans ✕
✕ Barnet

London •

Salisbury •

Southampton •

Canterbury •
Dover •

Hastings •

Plymouth •

FRANCE

as they insisted that he was endeavoring to gain the kingdom into his own hands." Though weak and easily befuddled, King Henry VI was not altogether powerless. He still
could resist York in certain ways; and, once he came to see
that he was in real danger of being deposed, the king quietly
went about the business of gaining backers against York.

Parliament met for the first time since St. Albans on
July 9, 1455. York hoped for its blessing on his actions.
His plan was to have Parliament declare King Henry to
be insane once again, and to make him Protector of the
Realm a second time. But King Henry was clearly not
insane; Parliament refused to cooperate with York. He was
able to gain a pardon for the bloodshed at St. Albans, but
that was about all. He was recognized as the king's first
minister, with nothing said about the greater powers of a
protector. Then Parliament adjourned until the autumn.

During the summer the kingdom was swept by disorder.
The most terrible stories came out of Devonshire, in south-
western England, where law seemed to have broken down
entirely. Blood feuds had begun there; men murdered their
enemies in the streets, looted their homes, ran riot through
the towns. It was as if the violent collision of the realm's
greatest lords at St. Albans was the signal for any man with
a grudge to lift his sword against those he disliked. Such
lawlessness called for strong measures from the government.
To the Yorkists it seemed like a fine reason for making
Richard of York protector once more.

When Parliament convened again in November, a Yorkist member of Commons named William Burley proposed
just that. The violence in Devonshire, said Burley, required
extraordinary measures. If the king could not act for "the

protection and defense of this land," York must be summoned to act on his behalf.

Commons, always favorable to York, approved the measure. The Lords held back a while longer, until tales of wild atrocities came from Devonshire. The Lords gave way, and York resumed the protectorship he had surrendered at the end of 1454. One of his first acts was to place his nephew Warwick in command of Calais. The title of Captain of Calais was more than an honor; it was a key position in the government. The man who controlled Calais controlled the English Channel. Somerset, as Captain of Calais from 1450 until his death, had used the port greatly to the advantage of the Lancastrians. If a civil war were coming, it would be valuable to York to have Warwick in command there.

And civil war was very much in the air, everyone knew. What had merely been an uncertain jockeying for power over the past few years had exploded into violence in the spring of 1455, and violence, once abroad in the land, was not easily checked. Among the great families, battle lines were forming. In a realm where virtually every lord was the cousin of every other lord, the struggle between the White Rose of York and the Red Rose of Lancaster would be the most painful of all conflicts, a battle within a family. The ominous prelude to the Wars of the Roses had been sounded.

It should be remembered that no one in the fifteenth century thought of them as the Wars of the Roses. Nor did the rivalry between the House of Lancaster and the House of York have anything to do with the cities and counties of Lancaster and York. In fact, the city of York was for much of the time sympathetic to the Lancastrians, and the chief backing for the Yorkists came from southern England, far from the cities of York and Lancaster alike. What would be at war were noble families, not geographical areas. A grim feud of relatives would grind on for several generations. But what is most surprising about the Wars of the Roses is how remote they were from the lives of the English commoners. While earls and lords fought and sent each other to the headsman's block, peasants and merchants and townsfolk watched the carnage as though from a great distance, standing aloof while the nobility destroyed itself in an orgy of retribution.

York, Protector of the Realm in November of 1455, found himself out of office again within a few months. Queen Margaret had collected much powerful support for the Lancastrians. When the riots in Devonshire unexpectedly halted at the end of the year, York's pretext for remaining protector had vanished, and as soon as Parliament met again early in 1456 Margaret set about ridding her husband of the duke's unwanted services. On February 25 King Henry came in person to Parliament to announce that York had been dismissed from his protectorship.

York had grown accustomed, now, to having Margaret snatch power back from him each time he attained it. But by a gradual process the duke had moved more openly into a position of hostility to the Lancastrians. He had been drawn into prominence originally by his opposition to Suffolk and Somerset; they both were gone now, but in the course of removing them York had by easy stages reached a point where his logical next step was to demand the throne itself. Yet he could never bring himself to take that step. Both openly and privately he was loyal to Henry VI, the sanctified and anointed monarch. York's chief enemy now was Queen Margaret. His problem was to find some way to attack Margaret without seeming to attack the king. That problem was insoluble. Whenever he succeeded in obtaining influence over the king, Margaret found some way of canceling out his advantage and dismissing him from power.

Matters dragged along in an uneasy stalemate through the rest of 1456. Margaret had control of the king and most of the great lords; York was compelled to remain away from court, biding his time. York's chief encouragement lay in the support of the powerful Neville family. His chief advantage was that Warwick still kept control of Calais, which would be an excellent base from which to launch an invasion of England.

Attempts to mediate between the two factions failed. Riots broke out in the cities, for the government, paralyzed by the split in the nobility, could not enforce the laws. Yorkists and Lancastrians brawled in taverns. On the high seas, pirates freely raided the ships of English merchants, and the helpless government took no action. Other pirates—these English, and hired by unscrupulous English lords—attacked the merchant vessels of France and Portugal and Burgundy, leading to international friction. In 1457 came a French reprisal for English piracy: a French fleet commanded by Pierre de Brezé landed on the coast of England and burned the town of Sandwich. Brezé was a friend of Queen Margaret's, and Yorkists whispered that she had encouraged him to make the daring raid. The queen, it was noted, was of French birth. Yorkist rumors declared that she planned to hand the country over to the French. These tales did little to increase the popularity of the Lancastrians. In the spring of 1458 Warwick enhanced Yorkist prestige by launching a series of attacks on foreign shipping from Calais. These were little more than pirate raids, but to the average Englishman it seemed splendid that Warwick should be terrorizing the Spaniards and Burgundians this way. Everyone could plainly see that York and Warwick were strong men of action. Everyone could see just as plainly that Henry VI was an incompetent king and that Queen Margaret was an ambitious schemer. In private conversation many Englishmen admitted that it would be better for the land if York were king and the whole Lancastrian tribe out of power. Some even recalled that the Lancastrians were usurpers themselves. Had not Henry VI's grandfather, the Duke of Lancaster, overthrown the lawful King Richard II? The excuse then was that Richard was unfit to govern the realm. Perhaps it was time to give the wheel of fortune another turn, and cast down Lancaster as Lancaster had cast down Richard II.

But such words were treasonous and were never spoken in public. Henry VI remained on his throne, Queen Margaret beside him. And Prince Edward was growing swiftly, turning into a strong, active, healthy boy. The hopes of Lancaster resided in him. Perhaps if the nation could survive another ten years or so, until Prince Edward, at fourteen or fifteen, could replace his feeble father, all might yet be well for England and for Lancaster.

Ten years was a long time, though. For a full generation, since the death of Henry V, the structure of English government had been coming apart. Somehow it had survived the feud between Humphrey of Gloucester and Cardinal Beaufort in Henry VI's childhood; somehow it had outlasted the manipulations of Suffolk and Somerset. Now, however, the bitter undeclared war between Queen Margaret and Duke Richard of York threatened to destroy all.

In March of 1458 came a seeming end to that war. A spirit of mutual forgiveness enveloped the feuding Yorkists and Lancastrians, and they staged a touching public ceremony of reconciliation. An impressive procession wound through the streets of London from Westminster to St. Paul's. Hand in hand, two by two, came the former enemies. Richard of Salisbury marched beside young Henry Beaufort, who had become the new Duke of Somerset when his father was slain at St. Albans. Then walked the king, alone, in his crown and garments of state. Behind Henry came Warwick, accompanied by the Duke of Exeter, an important Lancastrian noble. At the rear were none other than Queen Margaret and the Duke of York, smiling, harmonious.

This gallant gesture, it seems, had been arranged by the gentle king. No one would deny Henry his whim of showing the land that all was whole again. But nothing was whole, and the sacred pledges of peace and friendship sworn that day in the cathedral meant nothing a day later. War was on its way.

The uneasy truce between York and Lancaster lasted only until the spring of 1459. Then both sides began actively and openly collecting troops for a direct confrontation.

Queen Margaret rode through the counties of Lancaster and Chester, urging the people to support the cause of good King Henry. Beside her was Prince Edward, not yet five years old but already sturdy and full of his mother's fighting spirit. By early summer a large royal army had gathered at the town of Coventry.

The Yorkists planned to meet force with force. All summer long messengers went back and forth across the lands of the House of York as pledges of backing arrived. Richard of York no longer would hesitate to fight for power. The full strength of the wealthy Richard of Salisbury was at his command, as were the troops of swashbuckling Richard of Warwick. And York took pride in his own two eldest boys, seventeen-year-old Edward, the Earl of March, and sixteen-year-old Edmund, the Earl of Rutland. Edward in particular had become a giant, six feet three inches tall, standing a head higher than any other man of his family. This broad-shouldered youth was a natural leader, loved and respected by the Yorkist troops. Edmund of Rutland, though slighter of build and more gentle of nature, was also a worthy son. York had the comforting knowledge that he had fathered a line of strong men.

Late in August Salisbury set out with his army to join York at the town of Ludlow, near the borders of Wales, where one of York's many castles was located. Queen Margaret sent royal troops from Coventry to cut off Salisbury and prevent him from reaching Ludlow. The armies met on September 23; Salisbury's archers used their weapons to deadly effect, and the Lancastrian troops were routed. One Lancastrian lord was killed, another captured. Salisbury continued his march, swinging wide around the main Lancastrian force at Coventry, and reached York's fortress at Ludlow safely two days later. Later that week Salisbury's son Warwick arrived. He had crossed the Channel from Calais at the head of a body of picked soldiers who had learned the arts of war while practicing piracy on the high seas. For long weeks York and his allies conferred, plotting strategy, muttering curses against the ferocious Queen Margaret whose ambitions had brought England to this pass.

At the beginning of October the Lancastrian army at

last began to move toward the Yorkists, marching westward from Coventry to the village of Ludlow. York still entertained the naïve hope that he could avoid the terrible bloodshed of civil war. He sent a petition to King Henry, expressing his loyalty and desire for peace. The petition was received by Queen Margaret, who scorned it; York, she argued, must be crushed at once. From the royal camp came word that the king offered a general pardon to any who would desert the Yorkist cause. Spreading its banners of war, the Lancastrian army continued to march toward Ludlow.

A second time York petitioned for peace, and a second time the royalists brushed his message aside. Now the Lancastrians were at Leominster, less than thirty miles from Ludlow, and moving swiftly upon the Yorkists. As the enemy approached, York arrayed his troops in a strategic position on the meadows south of Ludlow Castle. The meadows were bordered on the west by high ground, on the east by the River Teme. To the south—the direction from which the Lancastrians were coming—a high earthen wall blocked the valley and the road. To the north, behind the Yorkist troops, were the fortifications of Ludlow Castle. The Yorkists dug in behind the earthworks and waited for the Lancastrians to arrive.

On the afternoon of October 12, 1459, the banners of the royal army became visible down the valley. The distant sound of drums and trumpets could be heard. York, flanked by his allies and relatives Salisbury and Warwick, mounted the earthworks and studied the Lancastrian host unhappily. Queen Margaret's army outnumbered the Yorkists about two to one. But York had the advantage of position; the Lancastrians would have to fight their way up a narrow valley under a shower of arrows from Yorkists protected by

their earthen wall. With courage and determination the Lancastrians could be defeated.

As darkness fell, the royal troops pitched their camp about a mile from the Yorkists. Then, by cover of night, came sudden treachery. A pirate named Andrew Trollope, whom Warwick had brought from Calais, decided to accept the king's pardon and desert to the Lancastrian side. The whispered word spread through the ranks; Trollope gave a signal, and, as York and Warwick shouted in dismay, the heart of the Yorkist army rushed over the earthworks and scrambled down the valley to surrender to the Lancastrians.

York's hopes of victory were destroyed. His best trained and most reliable men had fled, and Trollope knew all the plans of the Yorkist generals. By the flickering light of torches York conferred grimly with Salisbury and Warwick in the great banquet hall of Ludlow Castle. To give battle now, they agreed, would be foolhardy to the point of suicide. They could do no more than flee and work to fight again some other day. Salisbury and Warwick would take refuge at Calais, accompanied by York's eldest son, Edward, the Earl of March. York himself, with his second son, Edmund of Rutland, would attempt to reach Ireland. The most painful problem was what to do about York's wife. The duchess was here at Ludlow, with her two youngest boys, ten-year-old George and seven-year-old Richard. If York tried to take his family with him as he fled, very likely they all would be captured before they were many miles from Ludlow.

It was a hard decision to make, but Duchess Cicely herself cast the deciding vote. She would remain behind at Ludlow Castle with George and Richard. If she fell into the hands of the Lancastrians, she would simply have to hope for their mercy. The risks were grave, but at the worst Queen Margaret would imprison the duchess and her two boys; there was no reason to fear any more deadly vengeance.

In the darkest hour of that dark night York bade farewell to his wife and his young sons. Then, with Salisbury, Warwick, Edward of March, Edmund of Rutland, and a hand-

ful of followers, York slipped from the castle and began
his flight.

Through back roads and down forest glades the escaping Yorkists rode. To avoid pursuit they smashed wooden
bridges as they crossed them. The fugitives slipped into
Wales and separated, according to plan.

York and Rutland continued westward to the coast,
hired a ship, and soon were in Ireland. The popularity the
duke had won there while governing the island in 1449–50
stood him in good stead now. York was received in Dublin,
one chronicler said, "as if he were a second Messiah." The
English settlers there pledged their support to the Yorkist
cause. Even the half-wild native Irish chieftains, who had
little reason to care which faction of the hated English ruled
their land, greeted York joyfully. The Irish Parliament declared that Ireland need no longer obey the commands of
King Henry but only those of the Duke of York.

Warwick, Salisbury, and March also reached safety,
though their journey was more complex. Riding wildly by
night, they struck southward to Devon and bought a small
ship for £73. When they put out to sea, bound for Calais,
they discovered that no member of the crew was skillful
enough to steer the ship. Warwick had to act as steersman
himself. After a stormy voyage they reached Calais, not
knowing whether the port had remained loyal to Warwick
or whether it had been taken over by the Lancastrians. To
their relief, when they landed on November 2 they found
Salisbury's brother, Lord Fauconberg, in command. As
soon as the Yorkist fugitives arrived, though, a Lancastrian
force under the young Duke of Somerset showed up with the
intention of arresting them. Warwick's men successfully defended Calais against the invaders.

While all this was going on, the Lancastrians at Ludlow were enjoying the pleasures of their unexpectedly easy victory. On the morning after the flight of the Yorkists, Queen Margaret's troops stormed into Ludlow without meeting resistance, and went on to take the Castle. Bravely Duchess Cicely awaited their coming, her two boys beside her. The royal troops sacked and pillaged the Yorkist stronghold as though it had been a French town, stealing everything that was movable and treating the citizens brutally. But the duchess and her sons were spared from harm. They were carried off and placed in the custody of the duchess' sister Ann, who was the Duchess of Buckingham. Buckingham, closely related both to the leading Yorkists and the leading Lancastrians, had attempted to remain neutral in the struggle. He agreed to keep his wife's sister as a prisoner on his estates.

The triumphant Lancastrians now proceeded to summon Parliament to a meeting at Coventry. The session, which began on November 20, 1459, was called at extremely short notice, and many members could not attend. By no coincidence, those that did attend were chiefly sympathetic to the Lancastrians—which led the Yorkists, in later days, to nickname the Parliament of 1459 "the Parliament of Devils." The first and main item of business was the passage of an act of attainder against the Yorkists.

An act of attainder was the highest punishment that could be inflicted on an English nobleman. It was a Parliamentary conviction of treason without judicial trial. An attainted noble was subject to a penalty of death and to the forfeiture of all his property. Most dreadful, attainder extended to the descendants of the guilty man; their blood was declared to be corrupted by their ancestor's crime, and they were prohibited from inheriting or transmitting property or titles of nobility.

In practice, acts of attainder were not nearly so terrible as they seemed. Each of the revolutionary upheavals in recent English history had seen many of the losing lords attainted; yet they or their descendants had generally managed to have the acts reversed during the next shift in the flow of power. For example, Richard of Cambridge had been attainted and put to death in 1415 for his conspiracy against the life of King Henry V; but his young son had been forgiven for his father's crime and had been allowed to inherit his father's estates. Now, forty-four years later, it was that same son—Richard, Duke of York—whose name came before Parliament in another act of attainder.

The vindictive Queen Margaret proposed to attaint York, Salisbury, Warwick, March, and nearly a dozen other key Yorkists. From Calais an angry Warwick sent a counterblast calling the charges against the Yorkists "matters falsely and untruly imagined," for which the Lancastrians would "answer afore Almighty God in the day of Doom." It was, he said, merely a conspiracy on the part of certain greedy Lancastrian lords, eager to destroy the Yorkists and to confiscate their rich estates. On the other side, an anonymous pamphlet written in fantastically elaborate prose listed all the sins of the Yorkists, accusing them "of a pure malice and longtime precogitate wickedness, the which after the first indulgence had relapse and recay in a greater and more pernicious offense than the first was . . . doing such deeds with such circumstance that no very true man can it ascribe to any other purpose but to the final destruction of this gracious king and to the irreparable subversion of all his true lovers. . . ."

Lengthy arguments of this sort were needless. The Parliament of Devils had no wish to thwart Queen Margaret. The Yorkists were duly attainted and would pay with their heads if they dared to set foot in England again. Once more the fierce queen could count herself the winner.

But it was an uncertain victory. She knew that the attainted lords were gathering strength in their exile—that Ireland supported York and that Calais was with Warwick. At any moment her enemies might invade England. There was talk in Kent, always a center of hostility to the Lancastrian reign, that Warwick might soon sail from Calais and lead the Kentishmen in open rebellion against the throne. To forestall this the queen sent troops to the Kentish port of Sandwich, just across the Channel from Calais. They were led by two loyal Lancastrians, Richard Lord Rivers and his son, Anthony Woodville. Lord Rivers was none other than that once-lowly squire, Richard Woodville, who in 1437 had startled the court by marrying Jacquetta, the widow of John, Duke of Bedford. He had been granted a title because it seemed unfit for the husband of King Henry VI's uncle's widow to be without one.

Rivers and his son were instructed to assemble a fleet at Sandwich, sail to Calais, and capture Warwick. Word of these intentions reached Warwick quickly; it was brought by the Kentish men-at-arms who each day were crossing the Channel to join Warwick's garrison. Early on the morning of January 7, 1460, Warwick staged one of his characteristically impudent coups. He sent a small detachment of men across into Sandwich, captured the royal fleet, and seized Lord Rivers and Anthony Woodville in their beds. Ships and captives were taken to Calais.

The amazing archives of the Paston family give us the

story. On January 28 William Paston, writing from London, told his mother: "As for tidings, my Lord Rivers was brought to Calais, and before the lords with eightscore torches, and there my Lord of Salisbury rated him, calling him knave's son, that he should be so rude to call him and these other lords traitors, for they shall be found the king's true liege men, when he should be found a traitor, etc. And my Lord of Warwick rated him, and said that his father was but a squire . . . and since then himself made by marriage, and also made lord, and that it was not his part to have such language of lords, being of the king's blood. And my Lord of March rated him in like wise."

Delighted by his quick humiliation of the shamefaced Lancastrian lords, Warwick now dared to sail to Ireland early in the spring of 1460 to hatch plans with York for an invasion of England. King Henry, watching peace dissolving into war, was fretful and concerned. "Civil dissension," declares Shakespeare's Henry VI, "is a viperous worm that gnaws the bowels of the commonwealth," and now that worm was gorging itself to the full. Queen Margaret, herself half numb with fear but still resolved to defend her son's birthright, made a second attempt to block the invasion. She put the Duke of Exeter in command of a large fleet and sent him out to seize Warwick between Calais and Ireland. Exeter's ships sailed from Sandwich, keeping close to England's southern coast, and got as far as the Devonshire port of Dartmouth. But the poverty of the inefficient, corrupt Lancastrian regime took its toll. Exeter had received so little money from the queen that he could not afford to pay his men or even to feed them properly. At Dartmouth Exeter's hungry, disgruntled crew dispersed, leaving him with no more than a skeleton force. And at that precise moment

Warwick appeared, returning to Calais after his conference with York in Ireland.

Exeter, with his shrunken forces, did not dare to give battle. On his part, Warwick had no wish to get involved in hostilities just now, and he went serenely past the Lancastrian fleet without difficulties. Soon after, Margaret ordered the young Duke of Somerset to attack Calais once more; but he was driven off easily, and the Yorkists raided Sandwich by way of revenge. Each Lancastrian move now was more ineffective than the last. The Lancastrians had begun to look absurd; bills and posters were plastered on the walls of buildings, carrying messages attacking the court, and ballad singers openly sang rhymes that praised the exiled Yorkists and prayed for their return. A full decade of incompetent Lancastrian rule since the uprisings of 1450 had weakened the country terribly. In 1450, with Jack Cade roistering through London, Richard of York had been forced to come from Ireland to put things to rights. York's rise to power had been baffled at every step. Now it was 1460, and things were worse than ever. King Henry, ten years older but not at all wiser, still was on the throne. Queen Margaret, her ferocity unchecked, ruled the land with her coterie of grasping friends. The country was divided and impoverished. The French empire was lost, and pirates thronged the seas about England. Within the realm, bandits turned even the shortest journey into terror. The people asked, "When will Richard of York return from Ireland again to save us?"

York and Warwick finished making their plans. Spring gave way to the rainiest summer in a century. And late in June the long-awaited Yorkist invasion at last began.

KING EDWARD IV

N JUNE 26, 1460, the Earls of Warwick, Salisbury, and March crossed from Calais with two thousand fighting men and landed at Sandwich. Traveling with them was an Italian bishop named Francesco Coppini, the Pope's representative in England. This was one sign of the international interest in the growing civil war in England. Bishop Coppini was no mere observer; he was also an active conspirator. He happened to be in the pay of Francesco Sforza, the Duke of Milan. Sforza ruled lands in Italy that were claimed by Queen Margaret's brother, John of Anjou. What the Italian duke feared was that Queen Margaret would conclude an alliance with France in support of her brother's claims. If Queen Margaret were overthrown or weakened, Sforza calculated, she would be unable to aid her brother against him. And so—through an involved maneuver having nothing to do with England—an Italian bishop was giving aid and comfort to the Yorkist earls.

Of course that left Bishop Coppini in an odd position relative to the existing English government. He felt compelled to write to Henry VI that he had begged the Yorkists to remain peaceful and obedient, and claimed that they "gave me a written pledge that they were disposed to devotion and obedience to your Majesty. . . . They desired to come to your Majesty and to be received into their former state and favor, from which they declare they have been ousted by the craft of their opponents, and begged me to cross the sea with them to interpose my efforts and prevent bloodshed."

At Sandwich the three Yorkist earls were greeted warmly by Thomas Bourchier, the Archbishop of Canterbury. The Bourchiers were of royal blood and thus related both to York and to Henry VI; Archbishop Bourchier was the great-grandson of King Edward III in the line of descent of his youngest son, Thomas of Gloucester. His brother had married the Duke of York's sister Isabel.

A medieval chronicler relates that "a great multitude of people" welcomed the Yorkists to Sandwich. The archbishop, "his cross before him, went forth with the said earls and their people toward London, and sent an herald to the city to know how they were disposed, and whether they would stand with them in their just quarrel, and grant them leave for to pass through the city." The Londoners were divided on the subject of the reception they should give the Yorkists, but finally agreed to open the gates and permit them free entry. On July 2 the three earls entered London. Those Lancastrian nobles who were in the capital barricaded themselves within the Tower.

The royal party had remained all this time at Coventry.

Upon hearing that the Yorkists had landed, the Lancastrian leaders moved their troops southeast, digging in at the town of Northampton. Queen Margaret and her son did not leave Coventry, but King Henry went with the army to Northampton. Warwick and young Edward of March led the Yorkist troops north from London to meet the Lancastrians. The Earl of Salisbury stayed behind in London to guard the city and to command the siege of the royalist lords in the Tower.

Once more battle was preceded by attempts at negotiation. Warwick sent a delegation of bishops ahead of his troops to try to arrange a reconciliation. They were met by the Duke of Buckingham, no longer neutral but now firmly on the Lancastrian side. "Ye come not as bishops for to treat for peace, but as men of arms," Buckingham declared, eyeing the well-armed soldiers who accompanied the delegation. The bishops explained that they wished to bring about a meeting between Warwick and King Henry. "Forsooth," said Buckingham, "the Earl of Warwick shall not come to the king's presence, and if he come he shall die."

Attempts at peacemaking having failed, Warwick prepared to make war. He faced a strong royal army, well entrenched behind earthen fortifications and equipped not only with longbows but with guns and heavy firearms. But Warwick himself had been in a similarly strong position at Ludlow the previous October, and still had been forced to flee when Andrew Trollope and his men deserted. Perhaps here, in the fury of battle, the courage of the Lancastrians would give way in like manner.

The battle of Northampton was the first true military encounter of the Wars of the Roses. The battle of St. Albans, in 1455, had been nothing but a wild skirmish in narrow streets. The battle of Ludlow, in the autumn of 1459, had never even taken place. Here, at last, a traditional fifteenth-century battle was to be fought.

The military tactics of the day had not changed much since Crécy and Poitiers and the other battles of the Hundred Years War, fought a century earlier. Each side drew up its front line of troops in a solid phalanx, leaving an aisle or two so that the men were grouped in two or three wings. The ordinary men-at-arms fought on foot, as did the archers; the great lords customarily arrived at the battlefield mounted on steeds of war but dismounted to fight. Occasionally mounted archers were employed. At the start of battle the archers remained at the flanks, with the men-at-arms and armored lords in the central wing, wielding swords, spears, or battle-axes. When hostilities commenced, the archers went into action, hoping to thin the ranks of the enemy and drive the survivors into a confused huddle. Then the men-at-arms would charge, flailing away with their weapons, and soon the neat battle lines would dissolve into chaotic masses of struggling men. The conflict generally lasted only an hour or two; as one of the lines began to give way under the assault of the other, the men-at-arms of the losing side would take to their heels, leaving the victors in full possession of the field.

Armor had evolved over the past several centuries, growing more massive, more cumbersome. William the Conqueror had won England in 1066 with troops clad in chain mail, a light, flexible armor of interlocking metal rings. Now, though, any man who could afford it encased himself in a solid metal shell. Wealthy lords wore armor of heavy steel plates, most of it fashioned by Italian craftsmen; ordinary men relied on thick leather coats covered with overlapping metal plates. Metal helmets with movable visors completed the outfit. Only archers, who needed great freedom of movement, were free from this burden; they wore padded leather tunics thickened with deerskins, which were good enough to deflect most blows and had the extra advantage of allowing their wearers to make speedy escapes. The archers on the losing side usually escaped; the common men-at-arms got away with more difficulty; while the nobles, turned into virtual walking tanks by their costly armor, were easy to capture.

The goal of any battle was to kill or capture the leaders of the opposition. As in chess, there was little advantage in going for pawns; one had to try to take the important pieces from the board. Pawns, in fact, had no strong allegiance and easily shifted sides, so that an archer or a common man-at-arms who was spared might fight for your side the next time. Warwick, as he rode into battle, always cried out, "Spare the commons! Kill the lords!" In the aftermath of victory, noble prisoners could expect quick execution; ordinary men rarely suffered.

Thus the chronicler notes: "On the Thursday the 10th day of July, the year of Our Lord 1460, at two hours after noon, the said Earls of March and Warwick let cry through the field, that no man should lay hand upon the king nor on the common people, but only on the lords, knights, and squires: then the trumpets blew up, and both hosts countered and fought together half an hour."

In the first surge of fighting the situation of Ludlow was reversed; a wing of the Lancastrian army suddenly changed sides and came scrambling across the fortifications to yield.

That left a great section of the Lancastrian earthworks un-
defended, and the Yorkists poured through the gap. At once
the royal men-at-arms fled, leaving only a few noblemen to
face the foe. The Duke of Buckingham, who had commanded the royal army, was killed. Such Lancastrian nota-
bles as the Earl of Shrewsbury and the lords Beaumont and
Egremont also fell. The superb Lancastrian artillery never
went into action, for, the chronicle relates, "That day was
so great rain, that the guns lay deep in the water, and so
were quenched and might not be shot."

King Henry VI, who had been captured by York at St.
Albans, now was taken prisoner in battle a second time.
Warwick handled the dazed monarch with consideration
and care, however. Once more the victors made a formal
apology to the defeated. Coming to the king in his tent,
Warwick said, "Most noble prince, displease you not, though
it have pleased God of His Grace to grant us the victory
of our mortal enemies, the which by their venomous malice
have untruly stirred and moved your highness to exile us
out of your land, and would us have put to final shame and
confusion. We come not to that intent for to inquiet nor to
grieve your said highness, but for to please your most noble
person, desiring most tenderly the high welfare and prosperity thereof, and of all your realm, and for to be your
true liegemen, while our lives shall endure."

Treated with all due respect for his royal nature,
Henry VI traveled with Warwick to London, arriving there
on July 16. Two days later the besieged lords in the Tower
surrendered, and the Yorkists held the capital without challenge. Warwick had cleared the way for the Duke of York
to come home from Ireland and take command.

The political situation in England had changed sharply since 1459. Then York could count on the support only of the two Nevilles, Salisbury and Warwick. Here, a year later, with the king in Warwick's custody and Queen Margaret a fugitive somewhere near Coventry, most of the great lords of the kingdom were shifting rapidly to the Yorkist side. At least a third of the sixty highest peers were Yorkists now; most of the others maintained a cautious neutrality, while only a few, for reasons of personal vengeance, continued to back the House of Lancaster.

Early in October, once he was certain that Warwick had gained for him the power he had so long desired, York crossed from Ireland. He marched slowly across England from west to east, preceded by trumpeters and waving banners, like a conqueror coming to take possession. On October 10, 1460, he reached London.

Warwick, Salisbury, and the rest of the Yorkists thought they knew what would happen next. York would appear in Parliament, proclaim his loyalty to King Henry, and accept the post of Protector of the Realm or some such title. Thenceforth York would make the decisions of the government, and pious King Henry would nod and give his royal blessing to anything York cared to do.

But York had plans of his own—plans that were a total surprise to everyone, including his own sons. Twice in the past he had forced King Henry to grant him a protector's powers, and each time Queen Margaret had taken the powers away. During his Irish exile in 1459 and 1460, York had resolved on a much more permanent step, one that would rid him of Margaret entirely. He intended to revive the old Mortimer claim and make himself King of England.

The genealogical background had nearly been forgotten by this time. In Part II of Shakespeare's *Henry VI*, York is shown explaining the situation to Warwick and Salisbury (who surely were familiar with it anyway), pointing out that Henry VI was the grandson of the usurping Henry IV, son of John of Gaunt, Edward III's fourth son, whereas he himself was descended from an older son of Edward III, Lionel of Clarence,

> *From whose line*
> *I claim the crown, [for he] had issue, Philippa, a daughter,*
> *Who married Edmund Mortimer, Earl of March:*
> *Edmund had issue Roger, Earl of March:*
> *Roger had issue Edmund, Anne, and Eleanor.*

As for this Anne Mortimer, York declares, she was

> *My mother, being heir unto the crown, [and]*
> *Married Richard, Earl of Cambridge, who was son*
> *To Edmund Langley, Edward the Third's fifth son.*
> *By her I claim the kingdom: she was heir*
> *To Roger, Earl of March; who was the son*
> *Of Edmund Mortimer; who married Philippa,*
> *Sole daughter unto Lionel, Duke of Clarence:*
> *So, if the issue of the eldest son*
> *Succeed before the younger, I am king.*

Shakespeare's Warwick replies, "What plain proceeding is more plain than this?" And indeed it was quite plain that York had title to the throne, but for one thing. For sixty years the Mortimer claim had lain dormant. York's uncle, Edmund Mortimer, had steadfastly refused to press the claim against Henry IV, Henry V, and Henry VI. York himself, inheriting the claim in 1425 upon Edmund Mortimer's death, had let a generation go by without bringing up the subject. For him to rise up and claim the throne now was something like pulling a rabbit from a hat.

He said not a word to his friends and family about his intentions. But when he reached London, he went at once to the royal palace at Westminster. Abbot Whethamstede of St. Albans, one of the chroniclers who wrote of the events of these times, describes, perhaps as an eyewitness, how when York entered the palace he "went straight through the great hall until he came to the usual room, where the king, with the commons, was accustomed to hold his Parliament. And coming there he walked straight on, until he came to the king's throne, upon the covering or cushion of which laying his hand, in this very act like a man about to take possession of his right, he held it upon it for a short time."

Then York took his hand from the throne and turned to face the audience of watchful, puzzled onlookers. Standing under the royal canopy of the throne room, he waited as though for someone to cry out and hail him as king.

Archbishop Bourchier stepped forward and asked if York would come now to see Henry VI. A look of fury crossed York's face, and he replied coldly, "I know of no one in the realm who would not more fitly come and see me than I should go and visit him." In crisp tones York explained that he had come to claim the throne by hereditary right.

Though a Yorkist himself, Archbishop Bourchier retreated, stunned, to report to King Henry. York strode from the throne room and took up lodging in the king's own chambers within the palace, smashing the bolts that kept the doors to the royal apartments locked. Through London ran the bewildering, incredible story that the Duke of York had demanded the crown.

The most bewildered man of all was Henry VI. Queen Margaret was keeping far away from Yorkist-occupied London, and Henry was lost without her. He told the lords who came to him, "Since my cradle, for forty years, I have been king. My father was king; his father was king. You have all sworn fealty to me on many occasions, as your fathers swore it to my father." He sounded mildly astonished at the notion that he might *not* be king. Had he ever since earliest childhood been anything else but king?

Henry VI might be mildly astonished, but Warwick and Salisbury were amazed and furious. The younger Neville, on learning that York had evicted the king from his own palace, rushed to Westminster to reason with the duke. Warwick asked if York intended to wreck all that they had accomplished thus far, by turning the country against him just as triumph was near. Power was his; there was no need for usurpation of the throne itself. Hot words were exchanged. York's sons, Edward of March and Edmund of Rutland, were there, and though themselves taken aback by their father's audacity, they tried to calm the situation. Turning to Warwick, Rutland said, "Fair cousin, you must not be angry, for you know that it is our right to have the crown, which belongs to my lord my father who is here, and he will keep it as anyone may see." But March, who had his own doubts about the wisdom of his father's action, said to Rutland, "My brother, be not despiteful to anyone, all will be well."

Nothing would swerve the suddenly obstinate York from his course. On October 16 he went before Parliament and asked to be made king. The House of Lancaster, he said, did not have rightful possession of the throne; what was even more damning, Henry VI of Lancaster had showed himself incapable of governing. Though York had stepped aside all these years, he now felt that the good of the nation required the crowning of the rightful branch of the family.

Confusion followed. The peers asked the king for his opinion; Henry told them to confer with the high judges of the realm. The judges quickly responded that this matter was too high and weighty for mere subjects to decide it; and furthermore they did not know what advice to give. The problem was passed upward and downward through the ranks of the governmental lawyers, but no one dared to offer a ruling. At last the matter came back to the lords themselves.

They were unwilling to give York the crown. York was a strong leader but a poor politician, and here as before he was undone by his timing. He was moving too rapidly, too awkwardly; the nation had looked to him to be a wise minister, and instead he had turned into a rash, arrogant usurper. After three weeks of debate Parliament produced a lame decision that, since the House of Lancaster had had the throne so long, it had somehow earned the true right to it. Old precedents and oaths of allegiance were cited; the fact that Richard of York had waited so many decades to raise the subject of his claim was held against him.

York replied that the old oaths were invalid because they had been made to usurping Lancastrian kings. "Though right for a time rest and be put to silence," he said, "yet it rotteth not nor shall not perish."

But it was no use. York had misjudged the temper of his allies, and they would not let him have the crown. Out of the muddled debate came a compromise late in 1460, modeled after the Treaty of Troyes that had made Henry V heir to the throne of France.

Henry VI would continue to reign. His son Prince Edward, though, would be disinherited, and York would be recognized as heir to the throne. In case York died before Henry VI, York's heirs and successors would inherit his rights. In short, harmless King Henry would be left on the throne for his lifetime, but after that the crown would pass from the House of Lancaster to the House of York. When this settlement was signed, the attainders passed by the Parliament of Devils against the Yorkists were canceled, and York, though he had not gained the crown himself, was content that he had gained a great deal for himself and his family.

The agreement was acceptable to Henry VI; at this stage in his troublesome reign almost anything was acceptable to the poor king, so long as he went unharmed. But it was hardly acceptable to his formidable wife, Queen Margaret. Scarcely would she permit her son, Prince Edward, to be disinherited this way by a stroke of a pen.

After the Lancastrian defeat at Northampton, Margaret and the prince had fled westward into Wales. Only a few loyal attendants rode with them, and their journey was a hazardous one; at one point brigands attacked and robbed her. She took refuge at length at Harlech Castle, near the Welsh coast. Harlech was a stronghold of Jasper Tudor, who was Henry VI's half-brother through the marriage of Henry's mother, Queen Katherine, to Owen Tudor. From Harlech, Margaret began to gather what remained of the might of Lancaster.

What remained was considerable. She could count on the backing of young Henry Beaufort, the Duke of Somerset, whose father had been killed by Yorkists at St. Albans. Young Lord Clifford, another who had gained his title through the death of his father in the same battle, also had a motive of vengeance in his loyalty to Margaret. Henry Percy, the second Earl of Northumberland, owed his rich estates to Lancastrian Henry V, and remained faithful to Lancastrian Henry VI. And there were others.

York, whose greatest fault was his tendency to overestimate his own strength and misjudge that of his opponents, was determined to crush this Lancastrian resurgence at once. On December 9, 1460, two small Yorkist armies left London. One was led by Edward, Earl of March, York's strapping giant of a son; it went westward toward Wales. The other, under York's command, headed north into Yorkshire, where Margaret's army was assembling. With this force went York's second son, Edmund, the Earl of Rutland, and Richard Neville, the Earl of Salisbury.

Two weeks later York halted at Sandal Castle, one of his properties, and learned that the Lancastrian army was camped at Pontefract, just ten miles away. For ten days the armies remained in their positions, neither willing to do battle during the Christmas season. But late on the afternoon of December 30 the Lancastrians suddenly appeared before Sandal Castle.

A small party of York's men had gone outside the castle walls to gather food in the countryside. These were immediately surrounded by the royal forces. In a noble but rash gesture York went to the rescue of his men. The Yorkist lords rushed from the castle and, near the town of Wakefield, engaged the Lancastrians in battle.

In the first heat of the fray the Lancastrians achieved their greatest goal. They closed in on Richard of York, fell upon him, and killed him. Sir Thomas Neville, a younger brother of Warwick, also died. With their leader

dead, the Yorkists were put to flight. Rutland, York's second oldest son, fled toward Wakefield, but was overtaken by Lord Clifford, whose father had died at St. Albans. Rutland asked for mercy; but Clifford cried fiercely, "By God's blood, thy father slew mine, and so will I do thee and all thy kin!" He slaughtered Rutland joyously. Old Richard Neville, the Earl of Salisbury, was captured alive early that evening, and taken to Pontefract Castle to be held for ransom. But the next day the urge for vengeance was too strong for the Lancastrians, and they had Salisbury beheaded.

On the first day of 1461 the heads of the Yorkist lords were mounted on the walls of the city of York. Richard of York had attained his crown at last, but it was only a mocking paper crown, placed on his bodiless head by the jeering Lancastrians in their moment of glorious victory. The heads of Rutland and Salisbury flanked that of the fallen duke.

The Yorkist cause seemed destroyed, and the forces of Queen Margaret now vented their pleasure in an orgy of looting and burning. The Lancastrian army, scarcely under control, swarmed southward toward London, leaving a trail of gutted villages in its wake. The hordes of drunken soldiers perpetrated terrible outrages on the innocent citizens, and frightening stories preceded the marchers, so that London was terror-stricken at the thought of the advancing marauders. One account of this devastation was set down by the Prior of Croyland Abbey, which lay in the path of the Lancastrian troops yet was spared from destruction by its island location:

> The duke [York] being thus removed from this world, the northmen, being sensible that the only impediment was now withdrawn, and that there was no one now who would care to resist their inroads, swept onwards like a whirlwind from the north, and in the impulse of their fury attempted to overrun the whole of England. At this period, too, fancying that everything tended to insure them freedom from molestation, paupers and beggars flocked forth . . . in infinite numbers, just like so many mice rushing forth from their holes, and universally devoted themselves to spoil and rapine, without regard of place or person. For, besides the vast quantities of property which they collected outside, they also irreverently rushed, in their unbridled and frantic rage, into churches and other sanctuaries of God, and most nefariously plundered them of their chalices, books, and vestments. . . . Thus did they proceed with impunity, spreading in vast multitudes over a space of thirty miles in breadth, and, covering the whole surface of the earth just like so many locusts, made their way almost to the very walls of London.

The looters, declared the Prior of Croyland, came within six miles of his abbey. Franctically the monks barricaded their doors and blocked all approaches to their isolated settlement, and their prayers were heeded. "Blessed be God," the chronicler wrote in relief, "who did not give us for a prey unto their teeth!"

While Queen Margaret vainly tried to halt this tide of anarchy that her own troops had let loose, the stunned Yorkists were beginning to recover from their shattering losses of Wakefield. The duke, the center of all their hopes, had incredibly been sent from the world just when power finally was his; but York's son Edward, the towering young Earl of March, still lived and was eager to avenge his father's death. Warwick, too, had a father to avenge; he had remained in London, guarding Henry VI, while Salisbury had been done to death at Wakefield. Now Edward and Warwick began to march against the Lancastrians.

Edward's army had been in Wales when York was killed. He swung around quickly to the east and on February 2, 1461, overtook a Lancastrian army led by the Earl of Wiltshire and Jasper Tudor, the Earl of Pembroke. At a place called Mortimer's Cross—the ancestral home of the Mortimer family—the stalwart Edward smashed the Lancastrians. Wiltshire escaped, as did the Earl of Pembroke, but Pembroke's father, Owen Tudor, was captured. He was an old man now and represented no threat to the Yorkists. But he was the stepfather of King Henry VI, and in this sort of war there was no mercy for the families of the contenders. Old Tudor was pushed forward toward the headsman's block. He could not believe that the Yorkists planned to execute him until the collar of his red velvet doublet was ripped off. Only then did he realize that his last hour had come, and he muttered a prayer and knelt to receive the fatal stroke of the sword.

Warwick, meanwhile, was marching north from London to attack the main body of the Lancastrian army. He took with him, as a sort of mascot, the helpless captive King Henry VI. On February 17 the Yorkists encountered the

Lancastrians for the second time at the town of St. Albans.

This battle was notable for the first serious use of fire-arms in the Wars of the Roses. Warwick had brought along a detachment of Burgundian troops armed with handguns that shot lead bullets or iron-tipped arrows. But the guns claimed more Burgundian lives than Lancastrian ones, for they tended to backfire or explode in the hands of those who wielded them.

The second battle of St. Albans, unlike the first, ended in victory for the Lancastrians. Warwick, a dashing, flamboyant leader but never an outstanding general, let himself be taken by surprise. Half his men were slaughtered in the first charge of Lancaster. Warwick himself barely managed to get away from the battlefield alive; with a few of his followers he fled westward to meet Edward of March.

King Henry VI had watched the battle from one side, standing under a large tree and laughing and talking to himself while two Yorkist knights saw to it that he came to no harm. When Warwick made his escape, he was unable to take the king with him. After the battle, the triumphant Lancastrians took possession of the monarch.

The next morning Queen Margaret had all the important Yorkist captives put to death. Among those who were in custody were the two knights who had guarded King Henry during the battle. They presented the bloodthirsty queen with a difficult problem, for the king said that he had asked the two Yorkists to remain by his side, and they had done so out of respect for him even though it cost them their chance to escape. Despite Henry's mild plea that they be spared, Margaret was determined to have the Yorkists destroyed without mercy. She turned to her son, seven-year-old Prince Edward, who had inherited all his mother's ferocity. "Fair son," she asked, "with what death shall these two knights die whom you see there?"

"Their heads should be cut off," was the boy's immediate reply.

Sir Thomas Kyriel, one of the doomed knights, exclaimed, "May the wrath of God fall on those who have taught a child to speak such words!" He was led away and executed.

Warwick's defeat at St. Albans, and the regaining of the person of the king by the Lancastrians, should have sealed the fate of the Yorkist faction. But the cruel ravages of the Lancastrian army had turned the countryside against Queen Margaret and her house. As the Lancastrians continued on toward London in late February they found the people sullen and hostile. London was paralyzed with fear that Margaret would bring her army of wild northerners into the city. An Italian eyewitness wrote, "The shops keep closed, and nothing is done either by the tradespeople or by the merchants, and men do not stand in the streets or go far away from home." Margaret sent messengers to London to assure the city that her men would do no harm. She asked to be admitted peacefully.

London remained fearful, and its gates remained shut. Queen Margaret realized that she could not enter London except as an invader. Already some of her soldiers were starting to slip away to their homes in the north, heavily laden with loot. And all the while young Edward of March

was proceeding toward London out of the west. Margaret hesitated. Another battle with the Yorkists at this point was out of the question, nor could she hope to gain anything by leading an army of conquest into London. Stymied, she moved her forces out of the hostile area just north of London and headed for the borders of Scotland. Up there, along England's northern frontier, the Lancastrians were in favor; down here they were hated.

Thus it was that the Lancastrians turned away from London and retreated northward as Edward of March approached the capital. On February 27, ten days after the Yorkist loss at St. Albans, Edward reached London and asked to be admitted. The gates were thrown open, and the Yorkists entered.

Edward now was Duke of York as well as Earl of March since his father's death two months earlier. But he sought a higher title. It was a time for swift action. Parliament was not in session; Edward depended wholly on popular support, not on the formality of the law, for what he intended now. Robert Fabyan's *The Great Chronicle of London,* a contemporary account, describes the events of March 1, 1461:

"The said earl caused to be mustered his people in St. John's Field, where unto that host were proclaimed and shewed certain articles and points that King Henry had offended in, whereupon it was demanded of the said people whether the said Henry were worthy to reign as king any longer or no. Whereunto the people cried hugely and said, Nay, Nay. And after it was asked of them whether they would have the Earl of March for their king and they cried with one voice, Yea, Yea."

Three days later Edward of March proceeded to St.

Paul's Cathedral for a religious ceremony and then was carried to the royal palace at Westminster. There he took his seat on the throne, grasped the scepter of office, and told a hushed crowd that he had come to take the crown of England, as his right by inheritance in the true line of descent from Edward III. Before him knelt such Yorkist lords as the Earl of Warwick, the Duke of Norfolk, and the Bishop of Exeter, who was Warwick's brother, George Neville.

For the third time in a hundred fifty years England had deposed her king. As the son of the Duke of York sat in regal majesty on the throne at Westminster, the cries rang out again and again: "Long live King Edward IV! Long live the king!"

the house of york triumphant

O F ALL those who celebrated the proclamation of King Edward IV that March day in 1461, perhaps no one was more surprised by it all than the new king himself. Less than six months before, his highest ambition had been to become Duke of York someday. He had had no inkling that his father planned to claim the throne, and certainly no notion that he would be sitting on that throne himself before the trees were green with the new leaves of spring.

The death of his father at Wakefield, though, had set him on this course, and there had been no turning back. Having seen York defeated so often by the mere fact that Lancaster possessed the mystic, sacred authority of the kingship, Edward had seized that authority for his own. He was nineteen years old, but his poise was impressive and his bearing was overwhelmingly regal. He had lived willingly enough in the shadow of his ambitious father since he had reached manhood, but Edward looked and thought much more like a king than had York.

160

At the moment, of course, he was king only in London; the old king still was recognized in the north. Parliament had not spoken on the subject. In London, where the citizens had ample opportunity to judge the incompetence of Henry VI at close range, there was general rejoicing. One chronicler notes that the people said, "Let us walk in a new vineyard, and let us make a gay garden in the month of March, with this fair white rose and herb, the Earl of March." But outside London what would be the reaction to the proclamation of the new king? Edward could not predict that. He was aware that he was virtually unknown to most of his subjects, since he had spent most of his life in Ireland and Wales. News traveled so slowly that here in March many Englishmen were unaware of the death of the Duke of York the previous December. Edward IV knew he would have to move warily until he was sure of his strength. And so, though he already had accepted the dignity of kingship, Edward postponed the formal ceremony of coronation until he had settled matters with the Lancastrians.

His position was precarious. Bishop Coppini, the agent of the Duke of Milan, wrote his master to say, "Just now, although matters in England have undergone several fluctuations, yet in the end my lord of Warwick has come off the best and has made a new king of the son of the Duke of York." A story was circulating that Queen Margaret had poisoned Henry VI and planned to marry the Duke of Somerset, putting her own Prince Edward up as a rival claimant to the throne of the usurping Edward IV. But actually Henry VI was very much alive, and Edward IV's strength was alarmingly thin.

He could count, as always, on Warwick the Kingmaker and on most of the other Nevilles. He also had the support of the Bourchier family; his uncle Thomas Bourchier, as Archbishop of Canterbury, was the most powerful churchman in the realm, and the archbishop's brother Henry, the Earl of Essex, was a dependable adviser to the new king. Beyond them, though, Edward IV had relatively few strong men in his faction.

His two living brothers, George and Richard, were still children. The marriages of his sisters had not brought him any useful allies; Ann had married the Duke of Exeter, a Lancastrian, and Elizabeth was the bride of John de la Pole, who had been Duke of Suffolk since his father's murder in 1450. The younger Suffolk had no reason to be fond of the Yorkists. Edward's third sister, Margaret of York, was still unmarried.

There were numerous Lancastrian foes to contend with, most of them arrayed on the northern and western frontiers of England. In the west was Jasper Tudor, burning to avenge his father's execution. In the north, sheltering Queen Margaret and King Henry, was Henry Percy, the second Earl of Northumberland. The Beauforts still existed; their leader now was Henry Beaufort, the young Duke of Somerset, grandson of John of Gaunt's eldest Beaufort son. He had two brothers, sworn to defend the Lancastrian cause, at his side.

These three Beauforts also had a cousin, Margaret Beaufort, whose role in the tangled dynastic story would be important later on. Born in 1443, Margaret had been wed while still a child to Edmund Tudor, Earl of Richmond—the eldest son of Owen Tudor. Edmund Tudor had died in 1456—of natural causes—leaving his thirteen-year-old wife pregnant, and the following January she had given birth to a child named Henry Tudor, the new Earl of Richmond, for whom a royal future was waiting. By her marriage Margaret had linked the two great Lancastrian families of Tudor and Beaufort. As her second husband she took Henry Stafford, the second son of the Duke of Buckingham who had died for the Lancastrians at Northampton in 1460; thus she bound the Staffords more tightly into the Lancastrian camp. So long as these powerful families remained unbroken, Edward IV was little more than king in name only.

On March 29, 1461—Palm Sunday—King Edward settled accounts with the Lancastrians at the village of Towton, near the city of York. He had marched north from London with some ten thousand men who hated the cruel Queen Margaret and were willing to give their lives to see her overthrown at last. Edward IV, Warwick, and Warwick's uncle Lord Fauconberg each led a separate force to the scene. Some twenty thousand Lancastrian troops were waiting for them, asssembled on a narrow plain bounded by a stream swollen with late winter floods.

Warwick, leading the Yorkist advance guard, had arrived the day before the others, on Saturday, March 28. His men clashed with a Lancastrian detachment under Lord Clifford at a town called Ferry Bridge. Clifford, who had uttered that savage vow to avenge his father's death on all Yorkists, fought desperately to keep his enemies from crossing the bridge that gave the town its name. Warwick was wounded, and the Yorkists were thrown back; but then reinforcements arrived and seized the bridge. Clifford was slain and the Yorkists passed over to await the armies of Edward and Fauconberg.

On the next day was fought the bloodiest battle of the Wars of the Roses, and perhaps the most savage ever fought on English soil. Heavy snow began to fall as the outnumbered Yorkists rushed toward the Lancastrians. The wind whipped the white flakes into swirling patterns, blinding the men-at-arms so that they wandered bewildered over the field. The wind favored the Yorkist archers, whose merciless onslaught cut down hundreds of the enemy. The same wind caught the Lancastrian arrows and hurled them back from their Yorkist targets. Under cover of the blinding snow, Yorkist spearsmen moved up the slope and fell savagely upon Queen Margaret's troops. Hour after hour the battle raged; here was Edward IV like a giant in the midst of his foes, sword ringing against the armor of Lancaster; here was Warwick, fighting with all his might; the drifting banks of snow were stained red with the blood of the fallen.

Night came early on that wintry day, and as darkness fell the Lancastrians, routed and shattered, began to flee in the direction of the town of Tadcaster, eight miles from York. Now a fresh contingent of Yorkist troops under the Duke of Norfolk, arriving late at the scene, fell upon the Lancastrians, turning their retreat into a massacre. Thousands of men in full armor tried all at once to rush across the narrow wooden bridge that led to Tadcaster. The bridge was jammed by the fugitives, and the Lancastrians plunged into the stream instead. So many of them drowned that bridges were formed of the corpses, and some soldiers were able to make good their escape by crossing the stream on the bodies of their fallen comrades.

Many of the Lancastrian nobles were killed, including the Earl of Northumberland, the Earl of Devon, and the Earl of Wiltshire. Queen Margaret and King Henry, accompanied by the Dukes of Somerset and Exeter, escaped with Prince Edward. They headed for Scotland, where Margaret had earlier arranged to take refuge in case of defeat.

But the battle of Towton had been no mere slaughter of earls. Thousands of common soldiers had given their lives that day for Lancaster or for York—most of them for Lancaster. Of those who had begun the battle that day, one man out of four was dead by nightfall. In the pale dawn of the morning following, the scene of blood and death was frightful; men lay crumpled everywhere on the snow. Bishop Coppini, writing to the Duke of Milan, declared, "Anyone who reflects at all upon the wretchedness of that Queen [Margaret] and the ruins of those killed, and considers the ferocity of the country and the state of mind of the victors, should indeed, it seems to me, pray to God for the dead, and not less for the living." George Neville, the Bishop of Exeter, had sent word of the battle to Coppini. Bishop Neville himself, though grateful for this victory of his brother Warwick and the other Yorkists, commented somberly, "If it had been fought under some capable and experienced captain against the Turks, the enemies of the Christian name, it would have been a great stroke and blow. But to tell the truth, our riches are beginning to give out, and we are shedding our own blood copiously among ourselves. . . ."

Lancaster was crushed. The heads of the Lancastrian earls replaced those of York, Salisbury, and Rutland atop the walls of the city of York, where they had remained in grisly display since December. The overthrown Henry VI and his queen were fugitives in Scotland. Young King Edward IV returned in royal pomp and state to London. An Italian observer wrote to a friend in his native country:

King Edward has become master and governor of the whole realm. Words fail me to relate how well the commons love and adore him, as if he were their God. The entire kingdom keeps holiday for the event, which seems a boon from above. Thus far he appears to be a just prince who intends to amend and organize matters otherwise than has been done hitherto.

When Henry IV had usurped the throne in 1399, his deed left him plagued with terrible guilt that stained his soul and shortened his life. But Edward IV felt no guilt, and did not think of himself as a usurper. He was convinced of his own hereditary right to govern. More important, he and most of the nation felt that—matters of genealogy aside —the House of Lancaster had shown itself unfit to rule. Edward IV had been able to take the throne because

Henry VI was incapable of performing the duties of a king. The new monarch presided over a nearly bankrupt land.

On June 28, 1461, Edward was crowned king at Westminster in a ceremony as splendid as the rather frayed royal purse could afford. During the festivities the king named his twelve-year-old brother George as Duke of Clarence. A few months later King Edward's remaining brother, nine-year-old Richard, was named Duke of Gloucester, withered arm, crooked shoulders and all.

Very belatedly Parliament met on November 4 to confirm all that had happened since February. A lengthy act of Parliament traced the course of English history since the "most vile, heinous, and lamentable death" of Richard II and the usurpation of the throne by Henry of Lancaster. The old tale of the Mortimer-York claim to the throne was set forth once more, and Edward IV's "right and title of the said crown and lordship" was flatly asserted. As for "Henry, late called King Henry VI," he was considered removed "from the occupation, usurpation, intrusion, reign and governance of the same realm of England."

Briskly Parliament moved on to the next item on the agenda: the most severe and wide-ranging act of attainder in English history. The attainted Lancastrians were 113 in number: Margaret, Henry, and their son; the Dukes of Somerset and Exeter; the Earls of Devonshire, Northumberland, Pembroke, and Wiltshire; Lord Clifford, and many more of the lesser nobility. One third of the estates in London changed hands. Among the properties confiscated were the huge holdings of the House of Lancaster. Henry VI, as king, had also been hereditary Duke of Lancaster, but now the estates of that duchy were forfeited to the government.

All acts of attainder against Yorkists still on the books were reversed; Parliament even reached all the way back to 1415 to cancel the verdict of treason against Richard, Earl of Cambridge, King Edward IV's grandfather.

New ministers moved into positions of authority. Most of them were Nevilles; Warwick had not made Edward king for nothing. George Neville, the Bishop of Exeter, became chancellor—a rough equivalent to the modern office of prime minister. He shortly was granted the rank of Archbishop of York. His brother Warwick took control of the royal army and gained the chief voice in England's foreign policy as well. A third brother, John Neville, Lord Montagu, was given the earldom of Northumberland that had been stripped from the attainted Percy family, and thus became the master of northern England.

Though shorn of their possessions, many Lancastrians remained at large, menacing the security of the new rulers. Queen Margaret, unconquerable even in defeat, never rested in her efforts to restore her husband to the throne. She found support in Scotland, which was then an independent kingdom that had been at war with England, on and off, for two centuries; the Scots feared the strength of Edward IV and preferred to see the foolish Henry VI back in power. Margaret also had strong influence in her native land, France. King Louis XI, who had succeeded his father Charles VII in 1461, was her kinsman and was willing to listen to her proposals. If restored to the throne, she said, she would give Calais to the French and the English border town of Berwick to the Scots. After lengthy negotiations Louis XI agreed to place French troops at her disposal.

While Margaret was pulling these strings abroad, conspiracies against the Yorkists were sprouting in England too. John de Vere, the twelfth Earl of Oxford, planned to assassinate Edward IV while the king toured Northumberland early in 1462. The plot was discovered; Oxford and his eldest son lost their heads. A second scheme, supposedly centering around Henry Beaufort, the Duke of Somerset, never materialized.

In November of 1462, though, Queen Margaret came from France with a small army and fleet commanded by her old friend, Pierre de Brezé. The invaders landed in the north. By prearrangement, Lancastrian loyalists within the three strongest northern castles, Bamburgh, Alnwick, and Dunstanburgh, surrendered those fortresses to Margaret. In five days Edward IV and Warwick were on their way north to meet this threat. They were ready for it; Warwick had spent most of the summer recruiting an army in Yorkshire.

When Margaret learned of the size of the force marching against her, she "broke her field and fled," according to one contemporary account. She and Brezé and Prince Edward put out to sea in a ship, taking with them their possessions; but a storm came up, wrecking the vessel, and they barely managed to escape. Continuing on in a fisherman's boat, the three fugitives journeyed along the coast to Berwick. Most of Margaret's men remained hemmed up in the castles they had taken.

The Yorkists laid siege to the castles. Edward fell ill with measles late in the year, and Warwick directed the triple siege in his place, to such good effect that by January of 1463 all three fortresses had surrendered. Among the important Lancastrians captured were the Duke of Somerset and Sir Ralph Percy, a member of the great Northumberland family.

Edward IV now showed his desire to end the letting of

blood. Somerset and Percy, instead of having their heads lopped off instantly, were pardoned and restored to their estates, in return for swearing allegiance to the king. Percy was quick to betray Edward's trust in him. Margaret slipped away to France and returned with more soldiers; at once Percy turned Bamburgh Castle over to them, and another officer surrendered Alnwick. Only Somerset, of those pardoned by Edward, kept his vows. So in 1463 the Yorkists had to repeat their campaign of 1462. Once more the northern castles were besieged; Warwick's artillerymen blew great chunks out of their masonry; the Lancastrians were beaten, and Margaret took to flight.

The adventures of the former queen before she finally reached safety in Burgundy were truly lamentable. George Chastellain, a chronicler in the service of the Duke of Burgundy, heard the story from Margaret the following year and set it down. Margaret told him "that it happened, for the space of five days, that her husband the king, her son, and she had for their three selves only one herring, and not one day's supply of bread; and that on a holy day she found herself at mass without a brass farthing to offer; wherefore, in her beggary and need, she prayed a Scottish archer to lend her something, who, half loth and regretfully drew a Scots groat * from his purse and lent it to her. She also related how, at her last unfortunate discomfiture, she was robbed and despoiled of all she had, of her royal jewels and dresses, of her plate and treasures, with which she thought to escape into Scotland; and when all this had been taken from her, she herself was seized upon, villainously reviled, run upon with a drawn sworn, caught hold of by

* a coin of little value

her headgear to have her neck severed, menaced with divers torments and cruelties, while she, on her knees and with clasped hands, wailing and weeping, prayed that, for the sake of divine and human pity, they would have mercy upon her. Withall she perseveringly called upon God's mercy; and Heaven heard her appeal; for speedily there arose such a discord and dissension among her captors about the booty, that furiously slaughtering each other like madmen, they concerned themselves no more about the dolorous queen. . . ."

At length a Yorkist squire took pity on Margaret and rescued her from the brigands. After much further hardship she reached the coast and was reunited with some of her followers. Henry VI remained in Scotland; Margaret sailed for Burgundy, accompanied by seven ladies-in-waiting, six knights, the Duke of Exeter, and Pierre de Brezé. They arrived with no possessions other than the clothes they wore. Eighteen years earlier, as a beautiful girl of sixteen, Margaret of Anjou had sailed to England to become a queen. Now she was an exile, a wanderer, and into her face were carved lines of anguish and frustration.

Alnwick and Bamburgh still held out against King Edward, but with fiery Margaret in flight there seemed little hope for the Lancastrian cause. In a leisurely way Edward went about the business of retaking the two defiant castles. One of his closest comrades in this campaign of 1463 was the Duke of Somerset—an astounding development, in view of the terrible enmity between their fathers, Edmund Beaufort and Richard of York. Yet the high-spirited young Somerset, having pledged his allegiance to Edward, was the king's boon companion that summer. "The king made full much of him," says *Gregory's Chronicle,* "in so much that he lodged with the king in his own bed many nights, and some time rode a hunting behind the king. . . . And for a great love the king made a great jousts at Westminster, that he should see some manner of sport of chivalry after his great labor and heaviness." But, the chronicler notes, Somerset "thought treason under fair cheer and words, as it appeared."

In the autumn of 1463 Edward went north to wage war against the stubborn Lancastrian castles, and Somerset was at his side. At Christmastime, though, Somerset deserted to the Lancastrians. With Edward far from London, he entertained some thought of killing the king and destroying the Yorkist regime. But Edward—accompanied by Warwick and Warwick's brother John Neville—struck back quickly. On April 25, 1464, John Neville defeated a Lancastrian army at Hedgeley Moor, near Alnwick. Among those killed was the treacherous Sir Ralph Percy. A few weeks later Neville won a second battle, this time killing or capturing most of the remaining Lancastrian leaders. Somerset was taken and speedily beheaded.

The victory of Towton in 1461 now was made complete. Through the length and breadth of England scarcely any Lancastrians survived except in isolated outposts. Jasper Tudor was still on the loose in Wales, although his nephew of Beaufort blood, little Henry Tudor, Earl of Richmond, was a Yorkist prisoner. Henry VI still lived, wandering somewhere in the north of England. Margaret and her son Edward were living in poverty in France, having met little support in Burgundy. Nearly all the rest were dead. The other nations of Europe acknowledged Edward IV as lawful

King of England. Even Louis XI of France, Margaret's friend and protector, did not attempt to deny that Edward was king; in his crafty way Louis saw advantages in keeping the good wishes of England's powerful young monarch, who might some day think of making war against France if offended at this point.

The final triumph of the House of York came in the summer of 1465. Henry VI had been drifting aimlessly through northern England and Scotland for two years, his clouded mind scarcely aware of what had befallen him. Half a dozen ragged attendants traveled with him as the ghost of his royal court. At a place called Bungerly Hippingstones, in the county of Lancaster, the deposed king was discovered by Yorkists and captured. He was taken on horseback to London, his legs bound to the stirrups, and rode through the streets of the capital while silent citizens beheld the sad spectacle of a ruined monarch. Henry was given lodgings in the Tower of London; at the orders of Edward IV he was provided with attendants, treated with care and respect, and allowed to receive visitors. For the House of Lancaster the game had come down to check and mate.

Edward IV as king was surprisingly skillful at drawing the country back from the brink of the abyss to which it had come under Henry VI. In Henry's reign, or rather non-reign, England had lacked direction, force, thrust. A governmental system based on a king must have an active king in order to succeed; when government is left to a council of ministers, their private feuds and greeds obstruct the progress of the realm. England's economic ills actually went back fifty years, to the reign of Henry V; for that gal-

lant, romantic king had poured the national resources almost entirely into the ultimately useless expenditure of the
war with France.

King Edward IV revived the concept of a king who
personally exercised the powers of the monarchy. And he
directed those powers toward improving trade, enforcing
the law, reducing taxation, and reforming the machinery
of government. Henry VI had been incapable of such activities; Henry V, the warrior-king, had had no time for them;
Henry IV had had a hard enough time simply maintaining
his uncertain grip on the throne. Nor had Richard II been
a successful monarch; one had to look back more than a
century, to the great Edward III, to see the kingdom in
such strong, able hands. What was surprising was the depth
of Edward IV's skill. He was still a very young man, and
his background was that of a man of action, not that of a
serious thinker. The transformation of this brawny warrior
into an outstanding king was the great revelation of the
Wars of the Roses.

He believed in the idea that the king "should live of his
own"—that is, should be able to meet the expenses of the
government out of the revenues of the royal lands, without
needing to place direct taxes on his people. Inheriting a
monstrous load of Lancastrian debts, Edward paid them off
by recapturing possession of huge estates that once had belonged to the king, but which had been given to or taken
by the various court favorites under Henry VI. With the
rental income and farm revenues from this land again
coming into the royal treasury, Edward was able most of
the time to pay the government's bills out of his personal
and hereditary income, while avoiding the taxation of his
subjects. The most modern methods of land management

helped to boost the income from the royal properties, in addition. Edward surrounded himself with financial experts who helped him get the realm on a sound economic basis at last.

New gold and silver coins went into circulation, giving fresh confidence to merchants who had come to despair over the shrinking value of English currency. Edward encouraged the merchants in every way; with great shrewdness he saw that England's path to prosperity lay in an expansion of foreign trade. English ships once more traveled seas that again were safe. They carried wool and cloth overseas to be sold in Europe at good profits. The king himself became a merchant as early as 1463; he owned ships for his private account, and his agents went abroad with cargoes of merchandise destined for Italy, Spain, Portugal, and other lands. A typical commercial enterprise of this unusual king is recorded under date of November, 1466: Edward hired one Alan de Monteferrato to convey through the straits of Gibraltar 6,000 sacks of wool, 20,000 woolen cloths, dyed and undyed, 10,000 blocks of tin, and 10,000 barrels of vessels of pewter or tin. He was becoming the King of England, Incorporated.

Not that all was business and toil for Edward IV. Far from it. He was a high-spirited, luxury-loving king, fond of hunting, feasting, and music, and perhaps too fond of good wine and beautiful women. As England emerged from the dark shadow of the 1450's into the bright prosperity of the 1460's, a taste for elegance returned to the royal court. Both lords and ladies now affected gorgeous costumes of satin and velvet. The women wore tall linen-covered headdresses; the men decked themselves out with shoes whose tips had points so long that they were hooked at the knee

with golden chains. The Pope himself protested against these long points, or "pikes," calling them a disturbing sign of worldliness. But, the chronicler Gregory reports, "Some men said that they would wear long pikes whether Pope will or nill, for they said the Pope's curse would not kill a fly."

Gay draperies hung in the royal chambers. The floors were strewn with fresh-cut rushes; flowers of many hues enhanced the lively atmosphere. Minstrels strummed lutes for the king's amusement, and on occasions of state great orchestras sounded forth with the music of viols and rebecs and sackbuts and other instruments of the time. The warm sunlight of the Renaissance, already in full blaze in Italy, had at last reached the cloudy, rainy isle of England in the handsome person of Edward IV. When his responsibilities pressed, though, Edward could leave the music, the wine bowl, and the venison roast, transforming himself instantly into the serious, dedicated monarch who exercised such close control over the government he had established.

But England's time of troubles was not yet over. New storms were brewing; more blood would be shed. Once more the realm would turn inward on itself in a self-devouring civil war, and kings would fall from their thrones, and proud heads would roll in the dust.

The seeds of catastrophe were planted innocently enough, in 1464—when King Edward took a wife.

Kingmaker Warwick had begun to insist as soon as the Yorkists had triumphed that Edward should marry. One king did not a dynasty make; Edward needed a son, and the sooner the better. So long as he was wifeless and childless, the heir to the throne was his brother George of Clarence. But Clarence, now a boy in his teens, was showing himself to be flighty, irresponsible, talkative, altogether too light-hearted to be a king. Beyond Clarence the heir was Richard of Gloucester, still a child, and set apart from men by his deformities. So Warwick started to stir up marriage plans. Always the cunning schemer, the kingmaker had fastened on the idea of allying England and France by marrying Edward to Lady Bona, the sister of the Queen of France. In the spring of 1464 Warwick journeyed to France to discuss the matter with crafty King Louis XI.

Louis was willing, even enthusiastic, to bestow his wife's sister upon Edward. For several weeks Warwick was wined and dined at the city of Tours while the marriage arrangements were completed. Then, quite pleased with his work, Warwick returned to England to give the good news to Edward.

Edward seemed strangely cool to the idea of the French marriage. He raised a few objections to it; and when Warwick answered them, the king found a few objections more. All summer long this odd courtship of Edward by Warwick continued. The king was evasive, remote, coy. Warwick grew impatient. It embarrassed him to have to report to Louis XI that the king was undecided. Why was Edward stalling this way? A brilliant royal marriage had been devised; it was poor diplomacy to mock the French like this by avoiding a decision. At a meeting of the royal councilors on September 28, 1464, Warwick forced a showdown. He demanded to know, before the other great lords of the realm, why Edward was fending off the subject of marriage.

Warwick received an explosive, incredible, demolishing reply. Edward explained that he was already married, and had been these five months past! Secretly, on the first of May, he had exchanged wedding vows with the fair Elizabeth Woodville Grey, widow of a Lancastrian knight! Even while Warwick had been devoting all his energy to the complex task of negotiating a marriage between two royal houses, Edward had made himself ineligible for Lady Bona's hand.

Riding southward from the battle of Towton in the spring of 1461, King Edward had seen Elizabeth Woodville for the first time. She was an attractive woman; Raphael Holinshed, the sixteenth-century chronicler, says she was "both of such beauty and favor that with her sober demeanor, sweet looks, and comely smiling (neither too wanton, nor too bashful), besides her pleasant tongue and

trim wit, she so allured and made
subject unto her the heart of that
great prince that . . . he finally
resolved with himself to marry
her."

Marriage was probably not on
Edward's mind when he met the fair
Elizabeth in 1461. He was not yet
twenty years old and too newly settled on his throne to think much of
dynastic problems. Furthermore, she came from a Lancastrian family. Her mother was Jacquetta of Bedford, the
widow of Henry VI's uncle John. Her father was Sir Richard Woodville, formerly a member of John of Bedford's
household staff, now dignified with the title of Lord Rivers.
Both Lord Rivers and his son, Anthony Woodville, had
been active on the Lancastrian side in the war. (They had
been so embarrassingly captured by Warwick at Sandwich
in 1460, it will be recalled.) Anthony Woodville had fought
for Henry VI at Towton.

More than that, Elizabeth was the widow of Sir John
Grey, a knight who had died fighting on the Lancastrian
side at the second battle of St. Albans, in February of 1461.
She had borne two sons for Sir John, Thomas and Richard.
When Edward met her some weeks later, she was living at
Lord Rivers' manor at Grafton Regis, a new widow who
scarcely would consider marrying the great enemy of her
family.

Yet Edward pursued her. Within a few days both Lord
Rivers and Anthony Woodville received pardons from the
king for their Lancastrian activities. When he could, Edward slipped away secretly to visit Elizabeth at Grafton

Regis. Slowly she weakened; motivated more by ambition than by love, perhaps, she agreed to become his queen.

Late in April of 1464, while on his way to meet the army besieging the Lancastrian castles in the north, Edward stopped for the night at a village called Stony Stratford. The next morning—it was the first day of May—he told his men he was going hunting and rode off in the direction of Grafton Regis. When he returned, three hours later, he was a married man; but no one knew that except Elizabeth Woodville, her mother, two gentlewomen who served as witnesses, the priest who had performed the ceremony, and a young choirboy who sang the wedding hymns. For the next five months Edward kept the marriage a secret. One wonders how much longer he would have hidden the truth if Warwick had not forced him to reveal it over the matter of the French marriage.

But now the news was out. In France the jilted Lady Bona wept, and the astonished, insulted King Louis XI vowed to have revenge on the impudent English king. In England proud Warwick's face was dark with fury, for he had been made to look like a fool, and in public. Elizabeth Woodville, clad now in the radiant robes of a queen, sat enthroned beside her husband, and on the surface all seemed well. But one did not humiliate a Warwick without feeling the consequences, even if one were a king. Warwick, whom Shakespeare's Edward IV calls "thou setter up and plucker down of kings," had placed Edward on his throne. By marrying for love and rejecting Warwick's counsel, Edward all unknowingly had invited the haughty earl to tear him from that throne and put another man there. Slowly, by imperceptible stages, Warwick began to move along the course that led once more to civil war.

One reason for Warwick's gathering enmity toward Edward was the sudden and dizzying rise of the Woodville family. Elizabeth had a father, five brothers, seven sisters, and two sons. Through royal decrees Edward raised all these Woodvilles to the highest ranks of the nobility and moved them into positions of influence. It was the same process by which the large family of Ralph Neville had come to power a generation earlier. Now there were Nevilles entrenched everywhere, led by Warwick and his brothers George and John. The Nevilles would not make way gladly as these upstart Woodvilles began to challenge them.

At a time when there were only sixty English noblemen, Edward IV created eight new titles of peerage for the Woodvilles. The queen's father, Lord Rivers, was only a baron—the lowest noble rank—but Edward raised him to the title of Earl Rivers, and by 1466 gave him the high office of Constable of England. Her brother Anthony Woodville became Lord Scales. Her older son, Thomas Grey, was named Marquis of Dorset. Five of Elizabeth's sisters were married to high lords: Margaret to the heir of the Earl of Arundel; Catherine to the young Duke of Buckingham; Anne to the son of the Earl of Essex; Elinor to the son of the Earl of Kent; and Mary to Lord Dunster.

Elizabeth's four other brothers also enjoyed the royal favor. Lionel, who was in holy orders, quickly became Bishop of Salisbury. Edward was knighted and made an admiral. John was also knighted, and though only a boy was married to the wealthy widowed Duchess of Norfolk—a marriage that caused a scandal, for the duchess was close to eighty years old. Richard, the youngest Woodville brother, was knighted, and would receive greater honors later on.

The sight of all these Woodvilles flooding into high places infuriated Warwick even more than the humiliation he had suffered over his matchmaking in France. Edward could not or would not see that the Nevilles were becoming hostile to him. He went so far as to arrange a wedding between Queen Elizabeth's son, Sir Thomas Grey, and the heiress of the exiled Duke of Exeter, even though the girl had previously been promised to Warwick's nephew, the son of John Neville, third Earl of Northumberland. The greed and vanity of these new Woodville nobles unbalanced the delicate political structure of the realm. There had been a vacuum, caused by the butchery of the English aristocracy between 1455 and 1464, but no one had ever expected to find that vacuum filled with former commoners suddenly raised to high places.

Hiding his feelings of outrage, Warwick remained active in the royal government and worked to recover some of his former influence. His particular sphere of interest, now that the civil wars had ended, lay in foreign policy; he believed that England's best hope for security lay in an alliance with France, and though his attempt to engineer that alliance through King Edward's marriage had failed, he continued to maneuver toward such a goal. France, England's closest neighbor, had grown strong under Louis XI, and there seemed little question of reviving the Hundred Years War and trying to regain the territories lost in the disastrous reign of Henry VI. Since France could not be defeated, Warwick reasoned, it was best to guarantee peace with her. That would have the incidental effect of frustrating the schemings of former Queen Margaret, now living as a pauper in France with her son Prince Edward. Margaret was surrounded by a shadowy court of exiled and attainted Lan-

castrian nobles, as penniless as herself: the Dukes of Somerset and Exeter, several younger Beauforts, and about a
dozen knights and squires. These miserable refugees spent
their time trying to persuade either Louis XI of France or
Duke Philip of Burgundy to support an invasion that would
rescue King Henry VI from captivity and put him back on
the throne.

Margaret had met with no success, only with regretful
sympathy, first in Burgundy and then in France. But she
might yet win the backing of one or the other of these states,
Warwick thought. His instinct told him that England
should ally itself with the stronger state—France—so that
together France and England could check the ambitions of
Burgundy and the dreams of former Queen Margaret. Warwick proposed to create this alliance in the traditional way,
through a royal marriage between King Edward's only unmarried sister, Margaret of York, and some leading French
prince.

Edward IV, though, had a much deeper understanding
of international politics. He grasped the essential fact that
in a situation involving England and two other strong states,
England should ally herself with the weaker of the other
two. England allied with France would have no control
over France; but England allied with less powerful Burgundy would not only be able to control Burgundy, but
together with her ally would be strong enough to keep
France in bounds.

By the autumn of 1466 Edward was discussing alliance
with Charles of Charolais, the heir to the duchy of Burgundy. These talks were secret, for Edward knew Warwick's
hostility toward a Burgundian pact. The following spring
Charles' younger brother Antoine came to London, sup-

posedly to compete in a tournament of arms against Anthony Woodville, but really to negotiate a matrimonial alliance. Quietly Edward IV and the Burgundian agreed on the marriage of Margaret of York to Charles of Charolais.

It was always Warwick's fate to be in France while Edward was concocting a secret agreement of marriage. This time the kingmaker was a guest once more at the court of Louis XI, spinning a web of intrigue and wedlock.

Louis XI was in the middle of what was, for him, a highly interesting situation. He had already been approached by John of Anjou, the brother of former Queen Margaret, on behalf of the Lancastrians. John was trying to get Louis to lend troops to restore Henry VI to the throne, and had dangled the bait of a marriage between Louis' daughter and the Lancastrian Prince Edward. "This boy, though only thirteen years of age," an Italian observer wrote that year, "already talks of nothing but of cutting off heads or making war, as if he had everything in his hands or was the god of battle."

Louis was tempted by an offer that could make him father-in-law to a grateful Lancastrian King of England, after the death of Henry VI. But then, in the spring of 1467, came the Earl of Warwick with an even more attractive suggestion.

Warwick had drawn King Edward's brother, George of Clarence, into his web. Clarence, ambitious and idle at the same time, was dissatisfied with his place in his brother's kingdom, and had come to hate the Woodville upstarts as much as Warwick did. Warwick had won Clarence's support by offering to let him marry his elder daughter Isabel; but when Edward IV learned of the match in the summer of 1466, he vetoed it, fearing the dangers of an alliance between his untrustworthy brother and his too-powerful cousin of Warwick. Nevertheless, Warwick and Clarence continued to make plans together.

What Warwick proposed to Louis XI in early 1467 was a military alliance of England and France, dedicated to the destruction of Burgundy. The two allies would invade Burgundy, wipe out its troublesome ducal house, and divide its territory. The Burgundian possessions that lay in France would go to Louis; the Burgundian lands in what today are Belgium and the Netherlands would be made the dowry of Louis' younger daughter and would pass to her husband. That husband, according to the scheme, would be Richard of Gloucester, youngest of the three living Yorkist brothers. (Richard was almost certainly unaware of his part in this plan.) Two other marriages were included in the package: King Edward's sister Margaret would marry a French prince, and Clarence would marry Warwick's daughter Isabel.

A second time Warwick returned from France with an agreement of alliance in his pocket, and a second time he met with a stinging rebuff from King Edward. Warwick learned of the betrothal of Margaret of York to Charles of Charolais, who by then had succeeded his father as Duke of Burgundy. All hope of a French marriage was lost. Warwick, fuming, was ripe to commit treason. He had had enough of being mocked, enough of the Woodvilles, enough of Edward IV himself. Though still avoiding an open break with the king, Warwick was resolved now to destroy the Yorkist monarchy he had labored so hard to create.

a tale of two kings

THE GREATEST subject in the land had become the enemy of the king. Warwick was a man who saw himself in a vivid, dramatic way, as the hero of an exciting theatrical piece that he had written himself; and from 1468 on he set about giving the script a strange and unpredictable twist.

He was a man who loved magnificence. Energetic, generous, charming, vain, Warwick conducted himself after the manner of a king. When in the spring of 1466 Edward IV entertained a group of visiting knights from Bohemia with a fifty-course dinner, Warwick felt it necessary to give them a dinner of sixty courses not long after. He surrounded himself with courtiers; at his mansion in London it was not uncommon for six oxen to be roasted for breakfast, and he kept open house at which any man who entered was free to carry away as much meat as he could hold on a long dagger. He loved nothing better than high intrigue, playing the role of the master statesman who could juggle kings and kingdoms with ease, and he moved through England with such pride and pomp that he seemed somehow more kingly than the king himself. Yet Warwick had serious flaws that kept him from real greatness, as distinct from the mere splendid show of greatness. His pride was easily wounded; he could not imagine that King Edward could ever fail to show gratitude to the man who had made him king, even when Warwick's interests did not coincide with those of the nation. He was a poor strategist, whose delight in complex plots all too often left him snarled in his own web; and he had shown an unfortunate tendency on the battlefield to flee too quickly to safety when things went poorly for his side.

Through most of 1467 Warwick remained at his castle of Middleham in northern England, sulking over Edward IV's new alliance with Burgundy. Unable to halt the course of events, Warwick watched in growing displeasure as Edward cemented the alliance with a series of treaties that seemed to be leading to a war by England and Burgundy against France. In January of 1468 Warwick returned to Edward's court, hiding his anger as best he could, and the following July the wedding of Margaret of York to the Duke of Burgundy took place in the Burgundian city of Bruges. A member of the Paston family wrote that the wedding guests were "as richly beseen . . . as cloth of gold, and silk and silver, and goldsmith's work, might make them; for of such gear, and gold, and pearl, and stones, they of the duke's court, neither gentlemen nor gentlewomen, they want none; for . . . by my troth, I heard never of so great plenty as there is [here.]"

The rumor of a split among the great Yorkists brought a few Lancastrians from hiding. Jasper Tudor emerged and invaded Wales, but was quickly driven off. Bothered by several Lancastrian conspiracies and uprisings in 1468, Edward IV did not have the opportunity to notice that Warwick and Clarence were plotting against him, with the vague intention of overthrowing Edward and making George of Clarence king in his place.

In the spring of 1469 Warwick went to Caláis. That was no occasion for surprise, since Warwick for many years had been Captain of Calais. Then, in July, Warwick's brother George Neville, the Archbishop of York, arrived at the French port. He brought with him Warwick's daughter Isabel and George of Clarence. Five days later, in a quiet wedding on July 11, Clarence and Isabel were married by the Archbishop. By the time Edward IV learned of the wedding it was far too late for him to do anything about it, and in any event he had more serious problems to deal with.

Earlier that spring had come an uprising in northern England—carefully staged by Warwick and Clarence. An agitator calling himself Robin of Redesdale gathered a horde of angry peasants dissatisfied with the Yorkist government and led them on a wild march south toward London. Warwick's brother John Neville, the Earl of Northumberland, immediately called out his army to put the rising down. He was still loyal to Edward IV and had no sympathy for Warwick's conspiracy. John Neville's troops quelled the rioting, but Robin of Redesdale escaped. Shortly there were other local rebellions, and Robin seemed to be stirring up trouble everywhere at once. Matters grew so disorderly that King Edward was forced to go north himself to quiet them.

Having only a small army at his disposal just then, Edward asked the leading nobles of the kingdom to come to his aid with their own troops. Warwick and Clarence, having slipped off to Calais to celebrate Clarence's marriage, did not receive the summons. Edward's chief support came from the new nobles he had created, most notably, of course, the Woodvilles. His father-in-law, Earl Rivers, offered assistance, as did his brothers-in-law Anthony Woodville (Lord Scales) and Sir John Woodville. Backing came, too, from certain men who had recently risen to prominence in the kingdom, such as William Herbert, the new Earl of Pembroke; Humphrey Stafford, the new Earl of Devon; and William Hastings, King Edward's dearest friend since youth, now Lord Hastings.

At the beginning of July, 1469, King Edward advanced as far north as Nottingham and waited there for the troops of Pembroke and Devon to reach him. Shortly he learned that the mysterious Robin of Redesdale was marching south with a huge army. A proclamation issued by Robin fell into the king's hands. It denounced the Woodvilles, Pembroke, Devon, Hastings, and other recent royal favorites as parasites and enemies of England. It accused the king of having given preference to these men while ignoring the lords of his own blood—meaning Warwick and Clarence. Most ominously, the proclamation compared Edward IV to Edward II, Richard II, and Henry VI—all of them monarchs who had been deposed.

At last it dawned upon the king that Warwick had turned against him and meant to overthrow him. Somewhat uneasily, now, Edward continued to wait at Nottingham for his reinforcements. Suspicion turned to certainty in the middle of July when Warwick and Clarence crossed the Channel from Calais at the head of a strong army. Warwick published a manifesto supporting the northern rebels, whom he called "the king's true subjects." Enrolling thousands of Kentishmen in his army, he began to march north, reaching London on July 20 and proceeding onward to challenge the king at Nottingham. Edward now was caught in a pincers, with Warwick coming on him from the south and Robin of Redesdale advancing from the north. It now was known that "Robin" was actually Sir John Conyers, a relative of Warwick's by marriage.

The situation looked desperate, and Edward allowed his wife's relatives to seek safety. Lord Scales fled to his estates in Norfolk; Earl Rivers and his other son, Sir John Woodville, rode toward the west. Nothing could save the king now except the arrival of the Earls of Pembroke and Devon. But on July 26 the armies of these earls were intercepted by Sir John Conyers and the rebels at Banbury, south of Nottingham. The rebels had sidestepped Nottingham to deal with the reinforcements before dealing with the person of the king.

Pembroke's army was ambushed and defeated. Pembroke and his brother, captured, were taken before Warwick, who had them beheaded at once. The Earl of Devon tried to escape but was seized shortly afterward and beheaded as well.

Edward still remained at Nottingham, accompanied by his brother Richard of Gloucester and by Lord Hastings. Ignorant of the fate of Pembroke and Devon, they decided finally to move southward with a small armed escort in the hope of reaching London. Soon the royal party met stragglers from the troops of Pembroke and Devon, who informed the king of their defeat and warned that Warwick and Clarence were on their way with a mighty army.

The king, always a realist, knew it was suicidal to do battle under such circumstances. He had been outmaneuvered and outgeneraled by Warwick, and his only hope for survival now lay in the possibility of outwitting the earl somehow. Edward dismissed his few faithful soldiers and waited with his brother and Hastings for what might befall. Soon Warwick's brother, the Archbishop of York, galloped up at the head of a party of cavalry. The archbishop, a warlike man like many church leaders of his time, was clad in full armor. But he spoke politely as he suggested that King Edward accompany him. Just as courteously the king accepted the invitation, which meant accepting the fact that he was Warwick's prisoner.

On August 2, 1469, Edward came before Warwick and Clarence at the town of Coventry. A tone of bland amiability marked the occasion, for neither side wished to stress the point that a civil war had ended with the defeat of the King of England. Gently Warwick suggested that Edward should withdraw from the active leadership of the country, allowing his brother Clarence and his cousin Warwick a greater role in making official decisions. Gently Edward indicated that he would abide by any requests Warwick and Clarence cared to make. The air of friendly agreement endured until King Edward had disappeared behind the gray, ten-foot-thick stone walls of Warwick's Middleham Castle, north of the city of York.

Now Warwick was master of the realm. The kingmaker was in a unique position, for he had both rival kings of England in his possession—Henry VI a prisoner in the Tower of London, Edward IV a prisoner at Middleham. And now things were not so amiable as Warwick's vengeance fell upon his remaining enemies. Earl Rivers and Sir John Woodville, Edward IV's father-in-law and brother-in-law, were captured and beheaded without a trial. Thus did Warwick pay the Woodvilles back for their fame. Several of Edward's other allies met the same terrible fate.

In the middle of August the Duke of Clarence and the Archbishop of York came to London to take control of the government, supposedly in the name of Edward IV, but in reality in the name of Warwick.

Now, finally, the news of the summer's deeds spread through the kingdom. Handsome, popular King Edward a prisoner? Warwick the master? False-tongued Clarence lording it in London? Shock and dismay were the universal reactions. The Duke of Burgundy, who had become Edward IV's brother-in-law, threatened to punish any who harmed the imprisoned king. John Neville, the Earl of Northumberland, wholly refused to support his brothers Warwick and the archbishop. In London knots of tense men gathered in the streets, ready to burst into riot on the slightest provocation. The entire land hovered at the edge of chaos.

It was an opportune moment for the Lancastrians to start trouble. Far to the north, on the border with Scotland, a certain Humphrey Neville, a distant kinsman of Warwick's, launched a pro-Lancastrian uprising. But Warwick had no wish to see the Lancastrians returning to harass him. At the beginning of September, 1469, Warwick went to Yorkshire to raise an army that would quell the disturbance.

Very much to his embarrassment he was unable to collect any troops. The men of Yorkshire simply refused to serve until King Edward was at liberty. Nothing Warwick said could shake their resolve. The country would not respond to his control. Edward, only Edward, was the ruler of England.

Warwick conferred with his brother the archbishop. They admitted to one another that they simply could not carry on the government with Edward imprisoned. In great distress they were forced to set the king free. Edward emerged from Middleham Castle and asked his people to take up arms against the Lancastrian rebels. Instantly soldiers came forward; Warwick, chagrined, went north and defeated the rioters. Humphrey Neville was captured and beheaded at York on September 29.

Once free, Edward could not be put back in his cage—especially since Richard of Gloucester and Lord Hastings had quietly gathered an army. While the Nevilles debated ways of regaining command, these soldiers went to Edward's side and escorted him toward London. Edward was king again.

He showed great restraint in dealing with the men who had imprisoned him. Outwardly he took a friendly attitude toward the Nevilles, as though Warwick and the archbishop had committed no more than a boyish prank. He forgave his brother Clarence too, making allowances for Clarence's unstable nature. In the autumn of 1469 a sweet atmosphere of harmony existed in England. Edward had outfoxed the conspirators by refusing to resist them. Bowing to their wishes in all ways, the king had shown them that England was his.

Warwick and Clarence could not accept this defeat, which was all the more painful to them because it had been so suavely administered. Soon they were conspiring again. In March of 1470 came word of a popular uprising in Lincolnshire, a northeastern county. At once King Edward raised a substantial army and marched against the rebels. He met them in battle near the town of Stamford and defeated them handily. As the routed rebels fled, they shed their heavy jackets so they might run faster; the engagement was afterward known as the battle of Losecoat Field.

Incriminating papers were found on the body of a servant of the Duke of Clarence after the battle. Then Sir Robert Welles, a leader of the uprising, was captured and confessed that Warwick and Clarence were behind the entire plot. Welles admitted that their goal was to put Clarence on the throne in place of his brother.

King Edward cautiously led his army toward Warwick and Clarence, who were some thirty-five miles away. They retreated warily. He ordered the two "great rebels" to come before him. With growing fear Warwick and Clarence edged away from the king's army, though all the while sending messengers to Edward to proclaim their loyalty and love for the monarch. As Edward closed in they took to flight, heading for Calais. Once more their scheming had backfired; but this time instead of merely losing control of the country, they had actually been driven from England by the resourcefulness and cleverness of Edward IV.

At Calais the "great rebels" met a cool reception. The port had been left under the command of one of Warwick's henchmen, Lord Wenlock; but Wenlock refused to admit the fleeing earl and duke. As the ships bearing the refugees neared Calais, Wenlock had the guns of the port fired to warn them away. Privately Wenlock sent word to Warwick that it would be wise of him to land somewhere else, for he could not guarantee Warwick's safety in Calais now; the town was too loyal to King Edward. So far as outward appearances went, it looked as if Wenlock had broken with Warwick and given his support to Edward IV, and the king rewarded him well for this seeming show of loyalty.

Leaving Calais, Warwick and Clarence proceeded to land along the coast of the French province of Normandy. They sent word to King Louis XI of France that they sought sanctuary with him. The French king was embarrassed and disturbed to have these treasonous Englishmen come to him; but after a little thought, he concluded that they might be useful to his plans, and he gave them refuge for the moment in the town of Honfleur.

Edward IV watched this maneuver with distinct uneasiness. He could not predict what schemes Warwick and Louis XI might spawn against him, and the best he could do was patrol his kingdom and wait for trouble to break out. Borrowing ships and sailors from his brother-in-law, the Duke of Burgundy, Edward blockaded the French coast to guard against an invasion. He put his wife's eldest brother, Anthony Woodville—now the second Earl Rivers—in command of a fleet watching over the English Channel. In northern England, where anti-Yorkist disorder was rising again, King Edward asked the ruling earls to raise troops and keep a close check on the situation.

It was with these northern earls that Edward made a grave miscalculation. Traditionally the earldom of Northumberland had belonged to the Percy family. But the second Earl of Northumberland, Henry Percy, had been a Lancastrian killed at Towton. One of Edward IV's early acts had been to take Northumberland away from the Percies and give it to Warwick's brother John Neville, Lord Montagu. Such a princely gift had kept John Neville loyal to Edward even after Warwick had rebelled against him; but it had angered the men of the north, who still regarded the Percy family as their lords. Much of the unruliness in the northern counties of Yorkshire and Northumberland resulted from the fall of the Percies, and in the spring of 1470, for the sake of appeasing the northerners, Edward IV restored the earldom of Northumberland to the current Henry Percy. John Neville's shabby consolation was the title of Marquis of Montagu, not nearly so exalted as that of earl or duke, though he still retained great estates in the north.

By this exchange, Edward had won the firm support of the important Percy family; but he had angered John Neville. To the new Marquis of Montagu the loss of Northumberland seemed like a poor reward for his loyalty. From that moment, Montagu turned away from Edward IV and toward the cause he had earlier rejected, that of his brothers Warwick and the Archbishop of York. Edward had forfeited the aid of the only Neville who had remained on his side.

In the middle of the summer of 1470 King Edward received word of a new revolt in Yorkshire—something he had feared and expected for months. Percy, the Earl of Northumberland, reported that the uprising was too strong for him to put down. The other northern lord, Montagu, was ominously silent. Early in August Edward ventured north himself with a small army. His brother Richard of Gloucester once more accompanied him, as did his friend Lord Hastings. The sight of the royal banners quickly caused the revolt to collapse; but Edward decided to remain in Yorkshire for a while anyway, until he saw which way the currents were flowing. There was a disturbing amount of talk about a forthcoming invasion of England by Warwick and Clarence.

Warwick, indeed, had become entangled in a fantastic new conspiracy initiated by Louis XI. The cunning king had done nothing less than forge an alliance between Warwick and the Lancastrian exiles in France!

If Queen Margaret and the other banished Lancastrians hated any one man as the cause of their downfall, that man was Warwick. Warwick, the loathed kingmaker, had stood beside Richard of York to help topple Henry VI from his throne; after York's death, Warwick had thrust young Edward of March forward and proclaimed him to be King Edward IV. To the Lancastrians, Warwick was a demon who had tormented their house for twenty years. Now this same Warwick, a fugitive like themselves from Edward IV, had turned up in France, looking for help. But how could the Lancastrians link themselves to their archenemy?

King Louis sent for Margaret and set about the seemingly impossible task of reconciling her with Warwick. She blazed up in all her old fury at the mere mention of Warwick's name. Pardon him for his sins against her family? Never! Join forces with him? Inconceivable! Unthinkable!

The French king persisted. Wheedling, cajoling, intriguing, he painted a glowing picture for Margaret: her husband restored to his throne, her son once more the heir to the crown, her exiled and attainted friends again in possession of their lands. And all this could come to them if only she would forgive Warwick! Would she consent to see the great earl and accept his apology for all he had done to her house and line? Grudgingly Margaret agreed. She would see Warwick; but she did not guarantee that anything would come of the meeting.

On July 22, 1470, King Louis brought Margaret and Warwick together. Warwick entered the room and found

himself confronted by the grim ex-queen and her son Edward, now a strong, fierce boy of sixteen. There was a frosty silence. The memory of old crimes was like a wall between them. For decades they had been enemies. Margaret's executioners had claimed the heads of Warwick's father Salisbury, of his uncle York, of his cousin Rutland. Warwick's victims had included two Dukes of Somerset, father and son, and many of Margaret's dearest friends and comrades; and this same Warwick had thrust a lanky boy onto the throne of Henry VI. How could they make common cause now? Each had attainted the other with treason. Each had called down the vengeance of heaven on the other. And now—

Louis XI, who was managing this meeting as though he were directing a play, made an imperceptible signal and proud Warwick sank to his knees before Margaret and her son. Though it went against the grain for Warwick to grovel to anyone, these were unusual times for the earl. Margaret left him on his knees for fifteen minutes while he begged for her pardon. A contemporary account relates that Warwick "confessed well that by his conduct . . . the King Henry and she were put out of the realm of England; but, for an excuse and justification thereof, he showed that the King Henry and she by their false counsel had enterprised the destruction of him and his friends in body and in goods, which he had never deserved against them. . . . Also he said over that, and well confessed that he was causer of the upsetting [creating] of the King of England that now is, but now, seeing the evil terms that the king hath kept him, and cast him out of the realm . . . now he will be as far contrary and enemy unto him hereafter."

Warwick beseeched the "queen and said prince that they would . . . forgive him that in time passed he had done and attempted against him: offering himself to be bound, by all manner wise, to be their true and faithful subject in time to come."

Louis XI spoke up now, guaranteeing the honesty and faith of all that Warwick had said. At last, enjoying her triumph to the fullest, Margaret bade Warwick rise and forgave him for the injuries she had suffered at his hands.

At once the French king presented all the details of the proposed alliance. Warwick's younger daughter Anne Neville, now fourteen, would marry Prince Edward, Margaret's son. Warwick would use his strength and influence to restore King Henry VI to the throne. France and England would ally themselves against France's enemy, Burgundy. All the Lancastrian exiles would receive their old possessions again.

Warwick would hold a powerful place in Lancastrian England until Prince Edward came of age or succeeded his father as king.

This neat arrangement had just one loose end: George of Clarence. The glib, easily swayed Clarence had been branded as a traitor by his royal brother Edward IV; some place had to be found for him in the new plan. As Warwick's son-in-law and co-conspirator he could hardly be shunted aside, although Lancastrian Margaret was not eager to give much of a place in her schemes to a son of Richard of York. A last-minute compromise was patched together: Clarence, all agreed, would succeed to the throne if Anne Neville bore no heir to Prince Edward. That was something less than satisfactory to Clarence—no more than a conditional grasp on a hypothetical crown—but he had little choice in the matter.

On July 25 all these terms were solemnly vowed in a majestic ceremony at the Cathedral of Angers. Margaret and Warwick touched a piece of wood said to be part of the True Cross on which Christ had died, and swore their mutual loyalty. Anne Neville and Prince Edward were betrothed that same day. Immediately the conspirators began to organize their invasion of England. For Margaret, presented with her first solid hope of revenge since she had fled to France seven years before, Warwick seemed the savior of her family. For Warwick, motivated mainly by injured pride, the astonishing pact was more cynical and opportunistic. But they were allies now.

The invasion plans moved swiftly, Warwick summoning the ships and soldiers loyal to him, King Louis lending other ships to Margaret. Early in September of 1470 a storm scattered the Burgundian fleet patroling the French coast, allowing the invaders to cross the Channel. On September 13 the Lancastrian forces landed at the ports of Dartmouth and Plymouth, along England's southwestern shore. They marched eastward through Devon, gathering surprising support as they went.

King Edward was still in the north when the Lancastrians landed. Though warned by the Duke of Burgundy that an invasion was coming, the king had not taken the threat seriously enough. Now, though, he felt only slight alarm. What he would do would be to return to London, the master city of the realm, and rally his people against the outcast Lancastrians. With a small force of some three thousand men Edward began to march south. He sent a message to the Marquis of Montagu—John Neville—asking him to join him with his much larger army.

While Edward was camped for the night at the town of Doncaster, one of the royal minstrels burst into his bedroom crying that enemies were "coming for to take him." Still calm, Edward went out to discover his men in an uproar and an army approaching his camp. Scouts reported that the enemy was the Marquis of Montagu. John Neville had openly changed sides now; instead of coming as asked to Edward's aid, he was here to seize the king and present him to Warwick a captive.

Once more—as when he had been pocketed by Warwick at Nottingham in the summer of 1469—Edward recognized the futility of doing battle against overwhelming odds. Then he had merely allowed Warwick to take him into custody, relying on his popularity in the kingdom to win him his freedom without a struggle. Now, though, matters were different. Messengers arrived with the news that Devon and Kent were up in arms against the government and that

Warwick was marching with the Lancastrians toward London. In the north the treachery of John Neville had deprived Edward of power. After nine years as king Edward IV saw his authority collapsing in a single day as the Lancastrians enveloped him. The men of his own army were crying out, "God save King Henry!"

Edward ordered his horse saddled. He rode off into the night, accompanied by his brother Richard of Gloucester, his brother-in-law Earl Rivers, and Lord Hastings, with a few followers. The sea was nearby. The fugitives seized a couple of small boats and pushed off down the coast. On Sunday, September 30, they arrived at the port of Lynn, where several fishing ships lay in the harbor. It took several days to get the ships ready for an ocean voyage. On October 2 they sailed for Flanders (Belgium), which was still under the rule of Edward's brother-in-law, Charles of Burgundy. Philippe de Comines, a diplomat at the Burgundian court who wrote an account of these events, told how "thus fled King Edward the year 1470 with two hulks and a little boat of his own country . . . having none other apparel than they wore in the wars, utterly unfurnished of money, and hardly knowing whither they went. Strange it was to see this poor king . . . to fly after this sort pursued by his own servants, and the rather, for that he had by the space of twelve or thirteen years lived in greater pleasures and delicacies than any prince in his time: for he had wholly given himself to dames, hunting, hawking, and banqueting."

The voyage of the fleeing king was a perilous one. Some of the Dutch towns were independent of Burgundy, and their ships preyed on all vessels that came their way. The king's little crafts were pursued and barely escaped seizure, but at last they reached Burgundian Flanders safely.

While the Yorkist King Edward thus was rudely thrust from his kingdom, the Lancastrian army on the same day was entering London, led by Warwick. On October 3 Warwick sent the Bishop of Winchester to the Tower of London to bring forth King Henry VI, who had been jailed there, out of sight and forgotten by nearly everyone, for some six years. *Warkworth's Chronicle,* one of the many medieval records of English history, says that the bishop found Henry "not worshipfully arrayed as a prince, and not so cleanly kept as should seem such a prince; they had him out, and new arrayed him, and did to him great reverence, and brought him to the palace of Westminster, and so he was restored to the crown again, and wrote in all his letters, writs, and other records, the year of his reign, *In the year of the reign of King Henry VI the 49th, and of his readeption to royal power the first.*"

The "readeption" of Henry VI astonished everyone, perhaps including the Lancastrians. Here, trotted forth from the Tower like a sack of sawdust, was the dim old king, scarcely comprehending what had taken place. There, a penniless fugitive in Burgundy, was the glorious young King Edward, an outcast from the realm. York had fallen, and Lancaster had returned to the heights of power. It had all happened so swiftly. And, once again, Warwick had played the kingmaker's role; but who would ever have dreamed he would lead a Lancastrian to the throne?

the destruction of lancaster

HE WHEEL had come full circle. Henry VI was king again, although, as Philippe de Comines of Burgundy said, he was "no more than a crowned calf, a shadow on a wall." That was enough. Now the exiled Lancastrians flooded home to claim their estates.

On November 26, 1470, Parliament was summoned in the name of King Henry VI. There had been few sessions of Parliament in the nine Yorkist years; Edward IV had felt little need of calling the legislators, and since the land had prospered under his strong reign there was no agitation for more frequent meetings. His first Parliament, in 1461, had been called mainly for the purpose of passing an act of attainder against the Lancastrians; there had been brief Parliaments in 1464 and 1467 but none since. Now Lords and Commons gathered to reverse the Yorkist attainders and welcome the Lancastrians back to power.

All winter long the exiles returned: Edmund Beaufort, the Duke of Somerset; Lord John of Somerset, his younger brother; Jasper Tudor, again Earl of Pembroke; Henry Holland, Duke of Exeter; John de Vere, thirteenth Earl of Oxford; and all the rest. No longer under act of attainder, these Lancastrians returned to their ancestral lands. George Neville, Archbishop of York, received from his brother Warwick the high office of chancellor, which Edward IV had taken from him in 1467. One who did not return at this time was Queen Margaret. She was expected to sail for England momentarily, but, hesitating, she remained in France, the land of her birth, as though she could not really believe that the Lancastrian revival could last. It was the only time in her life when she hesitated to move boldly; Margaret in England could have been winning new support for Lancaster by her fiery spirit, but Margaret in France was of no value to her family's cause.

It was a hard winter for Yorkists. Some of Edward IV's courtiers humbly begged the triumphant Lancastrians for pardon and were pardoned. Others were seized and put to death after brief trials. Most of the leading lords of the overthrown regime fled the country or rushed into sanctuary. The Woodvilles managed to avoid the fury of the Lancastrians in this way. The greatest Woodville of them all, Queen Elizabeth, took refuge in Westminster Abbey, where she was safe from arrest. There, on November 2, 1470, she complicated the dynastic picture by giving birth to Edward IV's first son, after several daughters. The infant, heir to the throne his father had lost, was named Edward.

Edward IV, among the Burgundians, was sparing no effort to regain his throne. He pointed out to Duke Charles the likelihood of an Anglo-French alliance against Burgundy, perhaps even an imminent invasion; and the duke agreed. For his own safety he would back his brother-in-law Edward. He put up a substantial sum of money with which Edward hired ships and men in Burgundy and Flanders. By February of 1471 Richard of Gloucester, Lord Hastings, and Earl Rivers were directing the outfitting of a Yorkist invasion force at a Burgundian port.

On March 11, 1471, Edward set sail at the head of this fleet. The story of his adventures is told in a little book called *The Arrivall of Edward IV*, written "by a servant of the king's that presently saw in effect a great part of his exploits, and the residue knew by true relation of them that were present at every time." According to the *Arrivall*, "Upon the morn, Wednesday, and Thursday, the 14th day of March, fell great storms, winds, and tempests upon the sea." On the fourteenth, Edward landed on the Yorkshire coast "in great torment." His "other ships were disseevered from him, and every from other, so that, of necessity, they were driven to land, every far from other."

The king's ship, carrying several hundred troops, landed on the Yorkshire coast at the port of Ravenspur, which no longer exists, the shore at that point having long ago been engulfed by the sea. Despite the storm, Edward had landed at precisely the proper place. Through no accident, he had come to the same port where Henry of Bolingbroke had landed in 1399 when he returned to England to overthrow Richard II.

The scattered Yorkists regrouped their forces while storm winds howled over the gray, wintry sea. Lord Hastings had been in Edward's ship. Richard of Gloucester and three hundred men had been driven ashore four miles from Ravenspur. Earl Rivers, with two hundred men, had landed another ten miles farther on. By morning of March 15 the troops were assembled. They marched through a countryside of sullen, hostile farmers toward the city of York.

This was Lancastrian territory. Once, a century ago, all this land had belonged to John of Gaunt, and the people who dwelled here remained stubbornly loyal to John of Gaunt's great-grandson, King Henry VI. Edward had to move cautiously and tactfully here. Having imitated the route of Henry of Bolingbroke, Edward now imitated Bolingbroke's strategy as well. In 1399 Bolingbroke had announced merely that he had come back to England to claim his rightful title of Duke of Lancaster, with no mentions of his plan to become King Henry IV. Here in 1471 Edward announced merely that he had come back to England to claim his family title of Duke of York, with nothing said of his intention to remain King Edward IV.

The people of Yorkshire did not want Edward as their king, but they had no objections if he had come to regain his private estates. The *Arrivall* says:

The people were sore induced to be contrary to him, and not to receive, nor accept him, as for their king; notwithstanding, for the love and favor that before they had borne to the prince of full noble memory, his father, Duke of York, the people bore him right great favor to be also Duke of York. . . . And, upon this opinion, the people of the country, which in great number and in divers places were gathered, ready to resist him in challenging of the realm and the crown, were disposed to content themselves, and in no wise to annoy him.

Marching northwestward toward the city of York, Edward met a frosty reception at the town of Kingston-upon-Hull, which slammed its gates in his face. But the next town,

Beverley, received him willingly if not enthusiastically. He came then to York and found the gates locked there. Only through great personal courage and shrewdness did Edward gain admittance to York. With just a handful of men, the king and his brother Richard approached the locked gate and spoke to city officials within. Edward explained humbly that he meant no harm to King Henry and accepted his own fall from power. He was here only as Duke of York, and uttered a few cheers for the House of Lancaster to prove it. The officials of York were convinced; they opened the gates and allowed Edward and his men to find lodgings and refreshment in the city.

In the morning the Yorkists began their southward march toward distant London. Edward took stock of his situation. He learned that Montagu—John Neville—lay in wait for him at nearby Pontefract with an army larger than his own. Another possible source of danger was the strong army of Henry Percy, the Earl of Northumberland. Edward had restored Percy to his earldom, but Northumberland also had Lancastrian ties. Which loyalty would prove stronger? If Percy had marched against Edward just then, Edward would have been doomed; but Henry Percy solved his own conflict of loyalties by remaining on his ancestral estates, offering aid neither to Lancaster nor to York.

With Percy thus neutral, Edward was able to slip around Pontefract, avoiding a clash with Montagu, and come safely to his family stronghold of Sandal Castle. It was there, nearly a decade ago, that his father Richard of York had died in the battle of Wakefield. Now, loyal followers of York flocked to Edward's support. The tides were shifting once more.

Warwick, in London, had beheld the events of March with mounting dismay. All winter long, fearing Edward's return, he had begged Queen Margaret to come to England and inspire the Lancastrians with her presence. But Margaret remained in France, and now Edward was marching toward London. An uneasy Warwick mustered his forces to crush the Yorkists while it could still be done. He himself went to Coventry to raise an army. Clarence began collecting troops in Devonshire. A Lancastrian fleet occupied the English Channel. The Duke of Exeter and the Earl of Oxford led a Lancastrian army that was camped east of the Yorkists. Montagu was north of them.

The moment was ripe for a triple hammerblow against Edward: Warwick coming upon him from the south, Montagu from the north, Exeter and Oxford from the east, with Clarence held in reserve to the west. The moment was allowed to pass. Montagu, torn between his loyalty to his brother and his still lingering respect for Edward IV, could not bring himself to attack the Yorkists, and held back unhappily at Pontefract. Clarence was on his way, but too slowly. Warwick did not trust the reliability of his own army. That left only the troops of Exeter and Oxford to carry the assault.

While the Lancastrians dithered, Edward moved. He feinted to the east so convincingly that he compelled the Earl of Oxford to retreat. Then, still managing to give the impression that he led an enormous army, Edward swung around and marched on Coventry. Warwick immediately shut himself up within the city.

On March 29 Edward proclaimed himself king again. He sent an ultimatum to Warwick, still bottled up in Coventry: surrender and be pardoned, or else come forth and do battle. Warwick did neither, but continued to stew unhappily behind Coventry's walls. His hope now was that his brother Montagu would appear and shatter Edward's army —or that Clarence finally would arrive and save the day.

Montagu sat tight at Pontefract. Clarence, though, indeed was drawing near. Leading a strong army pledged to the support of Henry VI, the brother of Edward IV reached the town of Banbury on April 3 and the next morning left Banbury for Coventry, supposedly to rescue the besieged Warwick.

But Clarence—"false, fleeting, perjured Clarence," Shakespeare calls him—was about to change sides. He had had ample time to weigh his loyalties, and it now seemed to him that his brother Edward IV had more to offer him than his father-in-law Warwick. The deal with Queen Margaret and Louis XI, restoring the Lancastrians to the throne and giving Clarence only a faint hope of becoming king himself, had not been to his liking. So while pretending to be coming to Warwick's assistance, Clarence had secretly sent word to Edward that he planned to deliver his troops to the Yorkists.

Edward and Clarence met on the road between Banbury and Coventry. Brother embraced brother warmly; Clarence dropped to his knees, and the king instantly raised him and kissed him. All of Clarence's treachery seemed to be forgiven in an instant. Clarence spoke to his army and Edward's with the eloquence for which he was famed, urging them to fight on for the House of York. The next day Edward allowed Clarence to try to persuade Warwick to surrender and accept a royal pardon. Warwick stiffly refused

and remained secluded in Coventry. Oxford and Montagu had now arrived with their armies, but, like Warwick, chose to shun battle.

Ignoring this large but immobile force at his back, Edward proceeded on the morning of April 5 toward London. On Wednesday, April 10, Edward was at St. Albans, just a short march north of the capital. He sent word ahead to the city officials of London to arrest King Henry and keep him in custody until his arrival.

It was a day of frantic confusion in London. George Neville, the Archbishop of York, had been placed in charge of the city by Warwick. Word had come that Queen Margaret had left France at last, and her landing on English soil was expected momentarily. The Duke of Somerset and the Earl of Devon* had gone to the coast to meet her, two days earlier. Within the city, Lancastrians still seemed to be in control, and the tower was full of Yorkist prisoners. Yet the citizens wavered between one king and the other. With Edward IV's army almost upon them, was it wise to continue to back Henry VI?

George Neville attempted to rally the city to Lancaster by making a public show of Henry VI. It was a futile, pathetic parade. The king was trundled through the streets on Thursday morning, April 11, with the archbishop tightly grasping his hand and an aged nobleman, Lord Zouche, struggling beneath the weight of the king's sword. A knight on horseback led the procession, carrying a pole with two foxtails fastened to it—a sign of defiance, only the ragged foxtails drooped as feebly as did the befuddled Lancastrian monarch himself. Henry wore a long gown of blue velvet, patched and frayed, his only remaining ceremonial robe. The foolish display aroused pity, perhaps, but no support for the Lancastrians. And before King Henry had completed his entire route, the advance guard of King Edward's army was at the gates of London.

Deserted by his attendants, King Henry stood in confusion as the gates were thrown open and Edward IV entered the capital to the joyous sound of trumpets. Richard of Gloucester rode at his brother's side. There was no question of resistance. George Neville, who had been given the

---

* This was John Courtenay, whose father, as Earl of Devon, had been attainted by the Yorkists. Edward IV had named a member of the Stafford family to that title; he was beheaded by Warwick in 1469, and when the Lancastrians were restored the following year the earldom returned to the Courtenays.

responsibility of barring Edward from London, rushed to the king and in slippery fashion begged for pardon. The city belonged to York.

In this bloodless moment of victory Edward had Henry VI and Archbishop Neville quickly packed off to custody in the tower, then went to St. Paul's Cathedral to make an offering of thanksgiving. He rode then to Westminster Abbey. The Archbishop of Canterbury was there to place the crown once more on Edward's brow; and, safe in the sanctuary of the abbey, Queen Elizabeth and her six-month-old prince waited for the king. Edward had never yet seen his son and namesake and heir.

The curious "readeption" of Henry VI was at its end. Once again the sorrowful king was a prisoner; once again Edward IV was on the English throne. And now matters moved toward their climax, for the Lancastrian army had left Coventry and was heading toward London to settle the dynastic issue for good.

Warwick drew up the Lancastrian forces on a high plateau outside the town of Barnet, ten miles north of London, on Saturday, April 13. That same afternoon King Edward led his troops up from London to meet the attackers, and under cover of darkness brought them virtually on top of the Lancastrians. The next day was Easter Sunday, not normally a day for warfare; but Edward's troops were so close to Warwick's that black Saturday night that a collision in the morning was inevitable.

Both sides had cannon, but Warwick's were far more numerous and greater in range. During the night he made use of this seeming advantage by carrying on a steady bombardment of the Yorkists, without realizing how close they actually were. *The Arrivall of Edward IV* relates: "It so fortuned that they [Warwick's artillery] always overshot the king's host, and hurted them nothing, and the cause was the king's host lay much nearer them than they deemed. And, with that also, the king and his host kept passing great silence all night, and made . . . no noise, whereby they might not know the very place where they lay. And, for that they should not know it, the king suffered no guns to be shot on his side, all that night. . . ."

A thick blanket of fog covered both armies as dawn approached. Edward, as he drew up his battle lines, was unable to see Warwick's army at all, although they were face to face. He assembled his troops in three wings. The king himself led the center wing, assisted by Clarence—which allowed Edward to keep an eye on his tricky brother. Richard of Gloucester commanded the right wing of the Yorkists, and the faithful Lord Hastings led the left.

The mixed army of Lancastrians and Nevilles that faced them also was arrayed in three wings. Warwick's brother Montagu commanded the central wing, the Earl of Oxford the right, the Duke of Exeter the left. Warwick, leading a reserve force, was well to the rear. But the fog created such confusion that the lines of battle were awry, with the armies actually at angles to each other; the Lancastrian right wing, which should have been opposite the Yorkist left wing, was in fact far to one side of it, and the other two wings of each army were likewise displaced so that they overlapped at the ends.

The *Arrivall* tells us that between four and five in the morning, despite the fog that made everything invisible, King Edward decided to open the conflict: "He committed his cause and quarrel to Almighty God, advanced banners, did blow up trumpets, and set upon them."

Instantly the field was in chaos as the armies rushed upon one another and became disarrayed. Oxford, on the Lancastrian right, discovered that the displacement of the armies allowed him to outflank the Yorkist left. His troops burst upon those of Hastings and smashed through them. Hastings' men gave way in panic, scattering and fleeing. The soldiers of the Lancastrian right wing gleefully stormed through the fog, giving pursuit, and very shortly found themselves beyond the battlefield and in the town of Barnet itself. There the Lancastrian soldiers forgot all about the war and started to loot houses and shops. Hastings' soldiers, meanwhile, found horses and sped off toward London, crying that King Edward and his two brothers were slain and all was lost for the House of York.

During this chaotic episode at one end of the field, Richard of Gloucester was discovering that his Yorkist right wing had accidentally outflanked the Lancastrian left. But Gloucester did not gain the same advantage that Oxford had obtained; for, over here, a deep, marshy ravine separated the armies, and the Yorkists had no opportunity to fall upon their foes in a sudden ambush. Instead Richard led his men around the ravine, a route that took them behind the Lancastrian lines. This brought the Yorkist right wing onto the flank of the rear guard of the Lancastrians, commanded by Warwick, and put the Lancastrian front left wing into bewilderment. The muddled armies hacked and slashed at each other while desperately trying to form lines once again.

In the center of the field the fighting was more orthodox: a direct impact between the Yorkists under Edward and Clarence and the Lancastrians under Montagu. King Edward was in the midst of the battle, says the *Arrivall,*

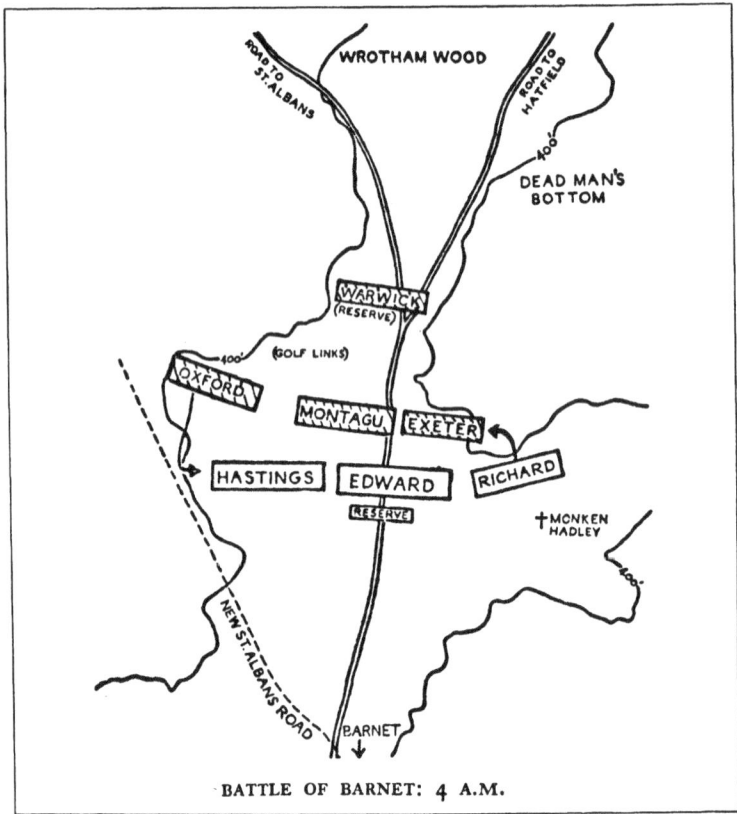

BATTLE OF BARNET: 4 A.M.

"where he with great violence, beat and bore down afore him all that stood in his way."

Hastings now had reassembled the remnants of the Yorkist left wing and was pressing Montagu on the flank. Warwick and Exeter had restored order on the Lancastrian left and were driving Richard of Gloucester's troops toward the ravine. Messengers moved back and forth in the ghostly mist. King Edward was holding his own in the center, but the Yorkists were already badly weakened on the left and seemed to be in trouble on the right.

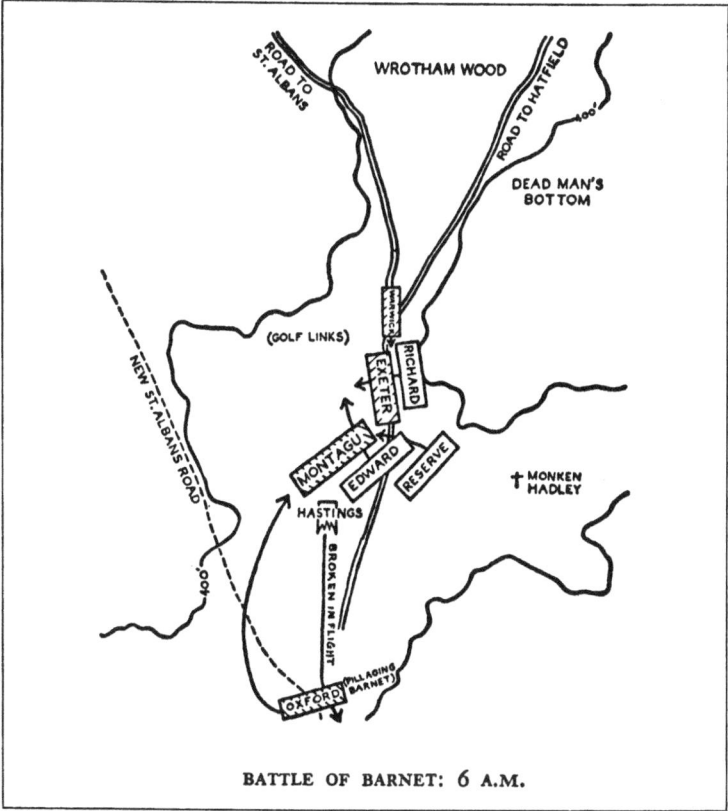

BATTLE OF BARNET: 6 A.M.

Then a cry went up from the Lancastrian side: "Treason! Treason!" And abruptly the confusion was doubled. An army appeared from nowhere and fell on Montagu's forces from the rear.

They were the soldiers of the Earl of Oxford, who had chased escaping Yorkists all the way into Barnet. With some difficulty, Oxford had collected his men and had persuaded them to return to the battlefield. They had circled around to the left of the Yorkist line, intending to attack King Edward from the rear. But in the fog the armies had shifted, and what had been east-west battle lines now were north-south lines. Oxford collided with Montagu's men. Oxford's banner, showing a glowing star, seemed in the dimness to be that of Edward, showing a blazing sun, adding to the disorder. A moment later the Lancastrians were fighting among themselves.

These Lancastrians, though, were of two groups. Montagu's men owed loyalty not to the House of Lancaster but to the family of Neville, and were fighting against York only because the Nevilles had ordered them to do so. The idea spread that the Nevilles had changed sides and were supporting King Edward again. Instantly the true Lancastrian loyalists set up the shout of "Treason!" and left the field. The Earl of Oxford rushed to his horse and rode off toward Scotland.

Now came King Edward's chance. Cutting through the panicky center line of Montagu's army, he smashed directly into the rear guard under Warwick. The giant figure of the king loomed like a colossus on the battlefield. He joined his forces with those of his brother Richard. Montagu was killed about seven in the morning, in the third hour of the battle.

The dismal tidings were brought to Warwick. The king-maker, stung by earlier accusations that he was a coward, had fought fiercely all morning, but now he saw certain defeat at hand. His brother John was dead; Oxford had taken flight; the Lancastrian army had crumbled. Moving slowly in his heavy armor, Warwick lumbered from the field, heading for a nearby forest where his horses were tethered. Yorkist soldiers came upon him before he reached his steed. King Edward would have spared Warwick's life, but his troops were not so merciful. They threw him to the ground and slew him. In early afternoon Edward rode in triumph back to London, and the next morning the bloody corpses of Warwick and Montagu were put on public display at St. Paul's Cathedral to show everyone that the House of Neville had been destroyed.

Edward took little pleasure in the death of these two adversaries, for they had served him well in bygone times, and he had never lost hope of winning them back to his side. Yet the thing was done, and it remained now only to close the account with the few surviving Lancastrians. On the same day the battle of Barnet had been fought, Queen Margaret and Prince Edward finally had landed in England, bringing with them a contingent of Lancastrian exiles. Edward's scouts reported that Margaret was moving through southern England toward London, winning pledges of support from the men of Devon and Cornwall.

The king prepared to meet this head-on thrust, though he and his men were wearied by the ferocity of the conflict at fog-swept Barnet. Now, though, came later word: Margaret had changed her route and was heading to the northwest, toward Wales, where Jasper Tudor was gathering a Lancastrian army. If Margaret's army joined forces with Tudor's men, the combined power might be too much for the Yorkists, Edward knew. He had to head Margaret off before she could reach Wales.

With a swiftness the Lancastrians did not expect, the king and his troops hurried westward and overtook them. Both armies moved with fierce energy, and in their final march each force covered forty miles in a single day. To enter Wales, Margaret had to cross the Severn River. There was a bridge across the Severn at the city of Gloucester; but King Edward sent a message ahead to the authorities at Gloucester, ordering them to keep the Lancastrians out at all costs. When Margaret's forces came there at ten in the morning on Friday, May 3, 1471, the gates of the city were barred and soldiers patrolled the walls. The Lancastrians could not enter and could not reach the bridge. And Edward's army was coming up rapidly behind them.

Though near exhaustion, the Lancastrians had to move on. The next bridge over the Severn was at Tewkesbury, some miles to the north. The day was hot; the road was dusty; the infantrymen limped along, and the weary horses moved in terrible fatigue. The only hope of the Lancastrians was to cross the Tewkesbury bridge, destroy it, and regain their strength by resting on the other side. So they pushed onward in this grim race, marching, the *Arrivall* tells us, "in a foul country, all in lanes and stony ways, betwixt woods, without any good refreshing."

At four that afternoon the Lancastrians reached the outskirts of Tewkesbury. But they could go no further. The foot soldiers dropped to the ground and lay there gasping for breath. Ahead lay the bridge; but they would have to fight their way across it, for the townsfolk barred the way, and just now fighting was impossible. Margaret urged her men to rouse themselves and hurry forward, but the officers told her it could not be done. Neither men nor horses could go another step. They would have to camp at Tewkesbury for the night and defend themselves against Edward in the morning.

The royal army drew near. Edward had taken much the same route as the Lancastrians, on "which his people might not find, in all the way, horse-meat, nor man's-meat, nor so much as drink for their horses, save in one little brook, where was full little relief. . . ." But the Yorkists felt the scent of victory in the air, and that gave them renewed strength. By late afternoon they were at the town of Cheltenham, nine miles from Tewkesbury. There, says the *Arrivall,* King Edward "comforted himself, and his people, with such meat and drink as he had done to be carried with him, for victualling of his host." Then he moved his army forward until it was within three miles of the Lancastrians and made camp for the night.

In the morning—Saturday, May 4—Edward drew up his battle lines, adjusting them to the strength of the Lancastrian position. Margaret's troops were well arrayed for defense. They occupied a line of high ground with a stream to their left and a wooded ridge to their right. The town of Tewkesbury lay to their rear. In front of them—the ground that Edward's attacking men had to cross—"were so evil lanes, and deep dykes, so many hedges, trees, and bushes, that it was right hard to approach them near." Edward took command of his central wing, with Hastings commanding the right wing and Richard of Gloucester the left. For the Lancastrians, the center of the line was under the command of Henry VI's warlike son, seventeen-year-old Prince Edward, assisted by Lord Wenlock, he who had been rewarded by Edward IV for turning Warwick away from Calais. The Lancastrian right was commanded by young Edmund Beaufort, Duke of Somerset, who had succeeded to that title upon the beheading of his brother Henry by the Yorkists in 1464. The Earl of Devon led the left wing of the Lancastrians.

Edward IV, says the *Arrivall*, "displayed his banners; did blow up the trumpets; committed his cause and quarrel to Almighty God, to our most blessed lady his mother, Virgin Mary, the glorious martyr Saint George, and all the saints; and advanced directly upon his enemies." Since the Lancastrian position was "full difficult to be assailed," Margaret's proper strategy was to hold her ground and force the Yorkists to attack. So the battle began; Richard of Gloucester led his men into the "evil lanes and deep dykes," but found that the heavy underbrush kept him from reaching the Lancastrians. After a sharp exchange of arrows and some cannon fire, the Yorkists pulled back.

Then the Duke of Somerset committed a basic tactical error. Seeing the Yorkists hesitate, he ordered a quick attack on their left wing, counting on the hedges and thickets to conceal his men until the last moment. The Lancastrians stole around onto the slope of the wooded ridge and charged the soldiers of the Duke of Gloucester. Though caught off balance, Richard rallied his men and held the line. His brother Edward had stationed a corps of spearsmen atop the ridge for just such a moment; now these warriors rushed down, falling upon the rear of the Lancastrian right wing. Thinking they were caught between two full-sized armies, Somerset's men broke into flight and were pursued and slaughtered.

By leaving the safety of the underbrush so rashly, Somerset had thrown the Lancastrians wide open to attack. Now Edward led his wing forward into the Lancastrian center, while Richard finished destroying the Lancastrian right wing and fell upon the right flank of the enemy center. The Lancastrian Prince Edward found himself surrounded by furious Yorkist soldiers. In that same moment Somerset

rode up to Lord Wenlock and
accused him of treachery because he had not supported
Somerset's charge against the
Yorkist left wing. There was a
brief dispute; then Somerset
lifted his battle-axe and smashed
Wenlock's skull. Seeing their
leaders fighting among themselves, the Lancastrians were
thrown into chaos.

They rushed off in every direction. Many were forced
into the nearby river and drowned; some took refuge in
Tewkesbury; most were spitted on Yorkist swords as they
tried to escape. Prince Edward, the hope and inspiration of
the Lancastrians, was slain on the battlefield. Some accounts say that he was killed by Clarence, who was eager
to show his newly rediscovered loyalty to Edward IV. The
Earl of Devon lost his life. Somerset rushed into Tewkesbury Abbey to take sanctuary, and Queen Margaret hid in
a nearby house. Two days later Edward's troops dragged
Somerset and about a dozen other Lancastrians from the
holy place over the objections of the abbot, tried them for
treason, and beheaded them in the marketplace of Tewkesbury. Queen Margaret was captured; the fire seemed to leave
her when she learned of the death of her son, and she accepted the destruction of her house with the numb passivity
of one who has lost everything. All the Lancastrian lords
who had fought at Tewkesbury were dead. The Beauforts
had been obliterated at last, and the dangerous Prince Edward had gone to his death, eliminating Queen Margaret's
only hold on the future.

Except one. Her husband's half-brother Jasper Tudor still lived, and so did Jasper's nephew, Henry Tudor, a boy of fourteen. The blood of Lancaster flowed in Henry Tudor's veins, for his mother, Margaret Beaufort, was the great-granddaughter of John of Gaunt. Upon word of the Lancastrian disaster at Tewkesbury, Jasper Tudor hurriedly left Wales and set sail for France, taking the boy Henry with him. They landed in Brittany and were granted refuge there. Edward IV regretted their escape, but the survival of a pair of unimportant Lancastrians like the Tudors meant no threat to his reign.

On Tuesday, May 21, 1471, King Edward entered London in triumph. Flags and banners streamed in the breeze, trumpets blasted shrill cries of glory, citizens shouted in praise of their victorious king. Duke Richard of Gloucester was given the honor of leading the parade, with Lord Hastings behind him, then King Edward, followed by Clarence, and the dejected, shattered Queen Margaret seated in a chariot at the rear.

The long civil war was over, but an extra king still remained. Not, however, for long. That Tuesday evening, in the musty darkness of the Tower of London, the troubled life of Henry VI came to its end. *The Arrivall of Edward IV* reports that Henry died "of pure displeasure and melancholy" upon being told of the defeat at Tewkesbury. But it seems far more likely that the unhappy monarch was sent from the world by an executioner, on the express command of Edward IV. According to some accounts, Richard of Gloucester himself supervised the murder of the deposed king. In any event, it was a merciful dispatch. Henry VI had outlived his own reign, had seen his supporters thrust into early graves, and had descended into a gray mist of insanity. The babe born in the bright radiance of Henry V's victories had become a dismal old man who seemed far older than his forty-nine years when the end came. He was at last at peace.

And Edward IV could declare, as he does in Shakespeare's play:

> *Once more we sit in England's royal throne,*
> *Re-purchas'd with the blood of enemies.*
> *What valiant foemen like to autumn's corn,*
> *Have we mow'd down, in tops of all their pride!*
> *Three Dukes of Somerset, threefold renown'd*
> *For hardy and undoubted champions;*
> *Two Cliffords, as the father and the son,*
> *And two Northumberlands: two braver men*
> *Ne'er spurr'd their coursers at the trumpet's sound;*
> *With them, the two brave bears, Warwick and Montagu,*
> *That in their chains fetter'd the kingly lion,*
> *And made the forest tremble when they roar'd.*
> *Thus have we swept suspicion from our seat,*
> *And made our footstool of security.*

KING
RICHARD
III

A DECADE and a half of bitter war had made England a land of mourning widows, but now in 1471 there was peace—the peace of exhaustion. The Lancastrians were broken, the proud Beauforts extinct, the Nevilles destroyed, Queen Margaret a prisoner. Without rivals, without challenges, King Edward IV settled down comfortably to enjoy the power he had won so dearly.

As before, he was an efficient monarch who kept close personal control over his government. He strengthened commerce, fattened the royal treasury, and maintained law and order throughout the land. About him were the men who had stood faithfully by his side in the troubled years. Lord Hastings, as Chamberlain of the Household and Captain of Calais, played an important role in the government,

as did Anthony Woodville, Earl Rivers. Richard of Gloucester, despite his withered arm and frail body, had been a
source of strength and comfort for his brother Edward in
the wars and now held the high post of Admiral of England.
These and other court nobles were enriched with gifts of
land that had belonged to dead or exiled Lancastrians and
Nevilles. A second son was born to the king in 1474—
Richard, to whom he gave the title of Duke of York.

Where it was prudent to do so, Edward IV pardoned
his few surviving enemies. Between 1472 and 1475 he reversed thirty of the attainders against his opponents. However, the Earl of Oxford remained safe in Scotland, and
Jasper and Henry Tudor stayed in Brittany. Edward tried
to gain possession of these potentially dangerous foes but
could not secure them.

George Neville, the Archbishop of York, was one who
believed he had won King Edward's favor, but the king had
a surprise in store for Warwick's only surviving brother.
Warkworth's Chronicle relates how Archbishop Neville
"was with King Edward at Windsor, and hunted, and had
there right good cheer." Sometimes the king would visit the
archbishop at the latter's handsome manor, where he had
prudently hidden a great deal of treasure at the time of the
downfall of the Lancastrians. But one day, the chronicler
reports, "the king sent a gentleman to the said archbishop,
and commanded him to come to Windsor to him; and as
soon as he came he was arrested and appeached of high
treason." The archbishop was accused of conspiring with
the Earl of Oxford against King Edward, and was placed
in custody. His treasure was confiscated—"Such goods as
were gathered with sin," said the chronicler, "were lost with

sorrow." The archbishop remained a prisoner for two and a half years; released late in 1475 in ill health, he died a few months later. As for the Earl of Oxford, he and his two brothers were captured in 1473 and were imprisoned near Calais, where they remained under guard for more than a decade.

Edward now was free to indulge his taste for luxury, for the realm was at peace and the royal wealth was multiplying. The Prior of Croyland's chronicle shows us King Edward at his palace at Westminster, "frequently appearing clad in a great variety of most costly garments, of quite a different cut to those which had been usually seen hitherto in our kingdom. The sleeves of the robes were very full and hanging, greatly resembling a monk's frock, and so lined within with most costly furs, and rolled over the shoulders, as to give that prince a new and distinguished air to beholders, he being a person of most elegant appearance, and remarkable beyond all others for the attractions of his person. You might have seen, in those days, the royal court presenting no other appearance than such as fully befits a most mighty kingdom, filled with riches and with people of almost all nations. . . ."

It was a time of consolidating, a time of rebuilding. Edward IV, a crafty monarch as well as a glamorous one, employed many techniques to draw his nation together. One sure way to unify England, he knew, was to promote a foreign war. He had merely to speak of conquest in France, and patriotism would cause every man to pledge his support.

So in November of 1472, at the first session of the first Parliament since his restoration, Edward began to speak of war. Sounding very much like Henry V reborn, he called for the recapture of England's ancient empire in France, and in stirring warlike phrases envisioned new deeds of heroism. War, of course, would cost money. Despite his promise "to live of his own," Edward asked Parliament to levy a special tax to pay for the invasion.

Parliament granted an income tax of 10 per cent on all revenue from rents, in order to equip thirteen thousand archers. The king's subjects failed to respond with enthusiasm. Many refused to pay the tax at all; others paid grudgingly. Some of the tax collectors pocketed the receipts. Funds dribbled in, and the proposed invasion of France had to be postponed several times.

Since it was proving impossible to raise money for the war through taxes, the king tried a different tactic: begging, cajoling, or bullying the richer citizens into making "voluntary" financial contributions, the so-called benevolences. Traveling from town to town, Edward called landowners, knights, mayors, aldermen, and anyone else who was worth a few pounds into his presence and openly asked each "what he would of his free will" contribute toward the war fund. *The Great Chronicle of London* reports "that as he passed by a town in Suffolk and called before him among others a rich widow and asked of her what her good will should be toward his great charge, and she liberally had granted to him £10, he thanked her and afterward took her to him and kissed her, the which kiss she accepted so kindly, that for that great bounty and kind deed, he should have £20 [instead of] his £10."

Extracting these notorious "benevolences" by kisses, threats, and any other means that seemed appropriate, Edward raised a large sum of money. A treaty of alliance

against France was negotiated with Charles, Duke of Burgundy, and the invasion force assembled. Late in June,
1475, the largest and best-equipped army that England had
ever sent against France began to cross the Channel from
Dover to Calais. Edward himself made the crossing on
July 4.

King Louis XI of France, no warrior at all, was terrified
by this invasion. It was just such an event that he had hoped
to forestall by restoring Henry VI to the throne. That
attempt had failed, and now here was Edward on his door-
step with a formidable host of well-trained, well-armed
troops. Louis wished to avoid this war at any cost.

But Edward IV was not Henry V reborn at all. Edward
had fought all the wars he planned to fight, and had never
had any intention of injuring France. All these military
preparations had been nothing more than a cunning pag-
eant, designed to frighten Louis XI and strengthen Edward's
own financial position. When Louis, in panic, offered to buy
peace, Edward instantly agreed to discuss terms.

The meeting of the monarchs took place at Picquigny,
a castle near the city of Amiens. As the huge English army
arrived King Louis sent three hundred cartloads of fine
French wines to the men as a preliminary gift and staged a
magnificent feast to keep everyone in a pleasant frame of
mind. Soon the English were slumbering in cheerful repose,
well fed and none too sober. It would have been easy for
the French army to fall upon them and destroy them, but
Louis XI was no man for such bloodthirsty tactics.

A special bridge had been constructed as the site of the
royal negotiations. The Burgundian diplomat Philippe de
Comines wrote: "In the midst of the bridge there was con-

trived a strong wooden lattice, such as the lions' cages are made with, the hole between every bar being no wider than to thrust in a man's arm; the top was covered only with boards to keep off the rain, and the body of it was big enough to contain ten or twelve men of a side, with the bars running across to both sides of the bridge, to hinder any person from passing over it either to the one side or the other. . . .

"On the next day, which was the 29th August, 1475, the two kings appeared. The King of France came first, attended by about 800 men-at-arms; on the King of England's side, his whole army was drawn up in order of battle; and though we could not discover their whole force, yet we saw such a vast number both of horse and foot, that the body of troops that were with us seemed very inconsiderable in comparison with them."

Each king entered the cage accompanied by a dozen courtiers. With Edward were Clarence, Lord Hastings, and the Earl of Northumberland. All were dressed in cloth of gold, and Edward wore a black velvet cap adorned with precious stones. Philippe de Comines says he "was a prince of a noble and majestic presence," but inclining to become a trifle fat by this time; he had looked much more handsome, notes the Burgundian, when he had come as a refugee to Burgundy in 1470. Edward advanced to the bars of the cage and made a low bow to Louis; then the two kings thrust their arms through the bars to embrace, and began to parley.

They agreed on a nine-year peace treaty, to be sealed by a marriage between Louis' son and Edward's eldest daughter Elizabeth. (It was a marriage destined never to take place.) Edward would take his army from France at once.

To buy peace, Louis was to pay 75,000 crowns in gold as a down payment, with a yearly tribute of 50,000 crowns besides. As a final transaction, Edward sold his prisoner, former Queen Margaret, to her kinsman King Louis for another 50,000 crowns. Edward had no further need to keep Margaret in custody, and the price was a good one; she was released to the French in 1476 and spent the remaining six years of her sorrow-darkened life in poverty and neglect in Anjou.

Not everyone was pleased by this quick, inglorious end to Edward IV's invasion of France. The Burgundians, infuriated, assailed Edward as a coward and a traitor. Edward's own troops grumbled, for they had been looking forward to a joyful career of looting and ransacking. For them it was a wasted trip. But Edward did not care. He felt no hunger for glory. Ignoring the insults hurled his way, the king returned to England richer by 125,000 crowns of Louis XI's gold coinage. For the next seven years the French tribute of 50,000 crowns a year duly arrived on schedule—nearly enough to balance Edward's budget and make him independent of Parliament. He also kept most of the unspent money that had been raised in England to fight the war, so all in all he did quite well for his two months' visit to France.

King Edward's chief problem in the happy years after Tewkesbury lay in his own family: the ambitions of his brother George, Duke of Clarence. This restless, unpredictable man, the black sheep of the Yorkist family, had been heir to Edward's throne until the birth of Edward's first son, and coming so close to supreme power had made him giddy with greed. That was why he had allied himself with his father-in-law Warwick in 1469 and 1470 against Edward; and, still seeking power, that was why he had abandoned Warwick for Edward in 1471.

Upon Warwick's death that year, Clarence expected to inherit the kingmaker's vast possessions by virtue of his marriage to Warwick's older daughter, Isabel. But he did not reckon with the cleverness of his younger brother, Richard of Gloucester. Nineteen-year-old Richard saw another Warwick heiress available for marriage: Anne Neville, younger daughter of the kingmaker. It is incredible to think that this newly widowed girl would marry a Yorkist duke, for these Yorkists had in the space of one month killed her husband, Prince Edward; her father, Warwick; and her father-in-law, Henry VI. Yet Richard wooed her and, amazingly, won her. Having married Anne Neville, Richard had an equal claim with his brother to the Warwick estates.

Much feuding followed, and Clarence, who had been unable to prevent this marriage from taking place, now was equally unable to keep Richard from taking possession of half the Warwick land. That left Clarence bitter and disgruntled; and Edward, who had experienced his brother's treachery once, began to keep close watch on him.

In 1476 Clarence's wife Isabel died. Soon after, Charles of Burgundy also died, leaving as his heir a daughter, Mary. This girl was Clarence's niece, since his sister Margaret had been the wife of Duke Charles. Although marriage with one's niece was forbidden by law and custom, Clarence began to agitate for the hand of Mary of Burgundy—in order to make himself duke of that rich land. Edward IV would not tolerate having such power pass to his unreliable brother and prevented the match. Eventually Mary married an Austrian prince.

Once more Clarence had been thwarted. Once more he sulked and began to scheme against Edward. The Prior of Croyland's chronicle says that Clarence "now seemed gradually more and more to estrange himself from the king's presence, hardly ever to utter a word in council, and not without reluctance to eat or drink in the king's abode." The estrangement grew to an open break. King Edward came to suspect that Clarence was plotting to overthrow him. It may or may not have been true; but in any event Clarence had grown unruly and full of spite. Edward feared him.

It is never healthy to be feared by a strong king. In January of 1478 Edward had Clarence arrested and imprisoned in the Tower on charges of "committing acts violating the laws of the realm." A few days later Edward asked Parliament to pass an act of attainder against the duke, accusing Clarence of "more unnatural and loathly treason than had been found at any time previously during the reign." No one dared speak in Clarence's favor, and a sentence of death was voted. On February 18, 1478, the sentence was carried out. A famous legend, which many historians accept as true, says that Clarence was executed by being drowned in a barrel of Malmsey wine. More of a nuisance than a danger to Edward, Clarence was the victim of his own unstable nature. His death left the king feeling the guilt of one who has murdered his brother, and the deed shadowed Edward's days to the end of his life.

That end was not far off, though Edward IV was still a young man. With the kingdom in good order, Edward gave himself over more and more to feasting and revelry, and grew fleshy as he entered middle age. He still cut a handsome figure, but now, as Philippe de Comines said, he had become "marvellous gross." He hunted less, ate more; according to one tale, he fell into the habit of purging his body with a drug after he had eaten, so that he could gorge himself again at once. He became eager beyond necessity for money, too, piling up wealth in a kind of feverish avarice. Slowly he lost his grip on the affairs of the kingdom as this orgy of self-indulgence came to preoccupy him.

But he had been a strong king when England had needed a strong king, and, no matter how fat and greedy he became now, his people loved him for the great achievements of his youth. It was unhappy news, then, when Edward fell ill in the spring of 1483, and it was a stunning shock for England to learn, on April 9 of that year, that the king was dead after an illness of ten days' time. He had not yet reached the age of forty-one. Some said that his sudden, wholly unexpected death was God's punishment upon the king for his gluttony. But it appears more likely that Edward was a victim of appendicitis.

A dazed nation mourned its lost king. Once again, as at the death of Edward III and the death of Henry V, the heir to the throne was a boy. But the situation did not appear dangerous. Edward IV was the first king in two hundred years to die a rich man, free of debt. His twelve-year-old son, the new King Edward V, inherited not merely a considerable fortune but a strong nation and an able staff of devoted advisers. It seemed certain, that mournful spring of 1483, that the House of York would remain in secure control of England and that the land would prosper while Edward V was growing toward manhood.

Fate had prepared a final convulsion for this tragic era, however. Edward V would never truly be king, and in two more years York would be cast down as Lancaster had been, with a new dynasty taking the throne.

The new leader of England, by far the most powerful man in the realm, was the young king's uncle, Richard, Duke of Gloucester. As the youngest son of Richard of York, and a sickly, ill-formed child as well, Richard of Gloucester had not seemed destined for power. But his brother Rutland had died honorably in battle, and his brother Clarence had died dishonorably in the Tower, leaving only Richard as the survivor of the Yorkist clan. During all the years of Edward IV's varying fortunes Richard had been a loyal shadow to his brother, ever at his side, fighting in his battles, supplying with force of personality what he could not supply in force of body. Never had Richard been tempted into treason against his royal brother. Certainly now he seemed a worthy guardian for his brother's children. The old title of Protector of the Realm would have to be revived, and that protector must surely be Richard of Gloucester. Though he was only thirty, Richard was the senior member of the royal family now, except for the old Archbishop of Canterbury, Thomas Bourchier, a great-grandson of King Edward III.

The youthful new king, though, had another uncle: his mother's brother, Anthony Woodville, the second Earl Rivers. At the time of Edward IV's death Prince Edward and his nine-year-old brother, Prince Richard, had been staying with Rivers at Ludlow Castle, far from London. There was an unvoiced conflict between Edward V's two uncles; though all remained peaceful on the surface, a tug of war was developing for possession of the new king. Richard of Gloucester was resolved to keep the Woodville side of the family from gaining influence over the boy; Rivers, as the head of the Woodvilles, sought to check the power of Richard.

For three weeks both parties parleyed, and at last it was agreed that Edward V, guarded by an escort of two thousand horsemen, should come to London to be crowned. The boy was to be escorted by Earl Rivers and by his half-brother Sir Richard Grey, Queen Elizabeth's son by her first marriage. Another in the royal party was Sir Thomas Vaughan, a household official of the Woodvilles.

The cavalcade rode southward toward London. It passed through the town of Northampton and halted at the nearby town of Stony Stratford. There, Rivers received word that another important party was traveling to London: Richard of Gloucester, who was returning from Yorkshire. In friendly fashion Rivers and Grey left the procession, turning back to Northampton to greet Richard.

Richard arrived in Northampton in the company of his kinsman Henry Stafford, the Duke of Buckingham, a man a year or two younger than himself. Buckingham occupied an odd position in the England of 1483. He was of royal blood, the great-great-great-grandson of Edward III, but he had no reason to feel affection toward the Yorkists. His father, Humphrey Stafford, Earl of Stafford, had been killed fighting for the Lancastrians at St. Albans in 1455. His grandfather, Humphrey Stafford the elder, first Duke of Buckingham, had died for Lancaster at Northampton in 1460. Henry Stafford's mother had been a Beaufort, a daughter of the first Duke of Somerset—making him a grandson of Somerset, York's most hated foe until his death in 1455 at St. Albans.

Despite all these strong Lancastrian ties, Henry Stafford had managed to survive the triumph of York. In 1465, at the age of eleven, he received from Edward IV his family title and became the second Duke of Buckingham, succeeding his grandfather. The following year he was married to Catherine Woodville, one of Queen Elizabeth's sisters. This marriage was somewhat against his will, for the Woodvilles were commoners, and young Buckingham was not merely noble but of royal blood; but it tied him effectively to the Yorkists. It was Buckingham who had the duty of pronouncing the sentence of death upon Clarence in 1478.

When Edward IV died, Buckingham found himself being approached by Richard of Gloucester. What passed between these two dukes is unknown, but it would seem that they had formed some sort of alliance to wrest power away from Earl Rivers and the other Woodvilles. This was carefully concealed when Richard and Buckingham met with Rivers and Grey at Northampton at the end of April, 1483. The four men had a friendly dinner at a Northampton inn, discussing the future course of the government. But in the morning Rivers awoke to find the doors of the inn locked. He went to the two dukes to ask what was happening.

Richard and Buckingham were cold and brusque. According to an account written thirty years later by Sir Thomas More, "they began to quarrel with him and say that he intended to set distance between the king and them and to bring them to confusion; but it should not lie in his power." Rivers realized in dismay that he was trapped. Through a sudden stroke, Richard and Buckingham had gained control of him while feigning hospitality. Rivers and Grey were made prisoners.

Later that day, April 30, Richard and Buckingham rode to Stony Stratford, where Edward V and his escort of two thousand horsemen had camped to await Rivers' return. Buckingham calmed the soldiers, and then he and Richard went before the young king, kneeling in proper obeisance.

Richard informed his nephew that he had discovered a plot on the part of Earl Rivers and the other Woodvilles to seize the government. "I dare well answer . . . that they be innocent of any such matters," replied the boy, who had been raised with his mother's family and favored the Woodvilles over Richard.

"Yea, my liege," said Buckingham, "they have kept their dealings in these matters far from the knowledge of your good grace."

Sir Thomas Vaughan, the Woodville official who was

with the king, was arrested also. He, Rivers, and Grey were sent to castles in the north. Edward V realized that his uncle Richard had staged a speedy coup against his mother's family. Frightened now, the young king wept. Richard assured him that all would be well, that he was acting purely for his nephew's own good.

Dismissing the military escort, Richard and Buckingham continued toward London with Edward V in their custody. The boy would be crowned, Richard said; as for himself, he desired only the office of Protector of the Realm.

There was consternation among the Woodvilles. Queen Elizabeth rushed into sanctuary at Westminster Abbey, taking with her her other royal son, Prince Richard, and her daughters. They settled down there, prepared to remain secluded for many months if necessary. Her older son by her first marriage, Thomas Grey, Marquis of Dorset, fled to France. No one knew the fate of Edward V; Queen Elizabeth feared that Richard might try to depose him and even to slay him. Thomas Rotheram, who had become Archbishop of York in 1480 and had been Chancellor of England for many years, offered what he thought was comforting advice to Elizabeth, but his words were the foolish ones of an old man: "Madam, be ye of good cheer. For I assure you if they crown any other king than your son [Edward V], whom they now have with them, we shall on the morrow crown his brother, whom you have here with you."

Amid great distress and commotion Duke Richard arrived in London on May 4, King Edward V at his side. He ordered preparations made for the boy's coronation, and on May 13 sent out a summons for Parliament to meet late in June. The question immediately arose as to where King

Edward should take up lodgings until the coronation. Richard suggested that the boy should live in the Tower of London, where he would be safe from any disorder that might occur at this time. No one cared to oppose the protector's wish, and Edward entered the Tower—but whether as king or as his uncle's prisoner, it was hard to say.

Nor is it easy for us to say at which point Duke Richard came to the idea of making himself king in place of Edward V. Nothing in his conduct during the life of Edward IV indicates that Richard had such criminal ambitions. Even in the maneuvers by which he took possession of his nephew and arrested Rivers, Grey, and Vaughan, it could be argued that he was merely trying to keep the Woodvilles from ruling the country in the boy's name. Surely Richard, by right of blood and service, was entitled to hold power until Edward V was a man. By thwarting the Woodvilles, he seemed simply to be protecting the House of York.

But then, subtly, Richard ceased to be a protector and began to be a usurper. His actions between 1483 and 1485 are matters of historical record; what remains mysterious is the motive that led this once-loyal duke to stain his name with treachery. To this day Richard seems an enigmatic, controversial figure. Shakespeare's *Richard III* shows him as a darkly sinister villain, a demonic monster. But Shakespeare, writing a century after the fact, relied mainly on the biography of Richard published in 1513 by Sir Thomas More; and More had political reasons for depicting Richard as a villain, as we will see. More recently some historians have tried to correct the account by pronouncing Richard not guilty of some or all of his alleged crimes. Shakespeare —and More—accuse Richard of the murders of Henry VI and Clarence, as well as many later misdeeds. Richard's defenders rightly absolve him of those deaths, and also attempt to show that he was merely acting for the good of the nation when he usurped the throne.

Perhaps so; but the Richard most familiar to us is the devilish Richard of Shakespeare and More. More tells us that Richard was "little of stature, ill featured of limbs, crook-backed, his left shoulder much higher than his right," and says he was "close and secret, a deep dissimulator, lowly of countenance, arrogant of heart, outwardly companionable where he inwardly hated." Polydore Vergil, an Italian historian who wrote an account of Richard's reign early in the sixteenth century, adds, "The while he was thinking of any matter, he did continually bite his lower lip, as though that cruel nature of his did so rage against itself in that little carcase."

Richard's "cruel nature" revealed itself openly for the first time on June 13, when he brought about the death of his old comrade-in-arms, Lord Hastings. Hastings, the childhood friend and closest adviser of Edward IV, was loyal to the new king and had watched uneasily as Richard moved toward taking power. Though he had backed Richard against the Woodvilles in April, Hastings began to draw back from the protector's actions in May. Since he owned a large private army, he represented a potential threat to Richard; but Hastings seems to have been unaware that Richard planned to eliminate him until the final moments of his life.

There are several versions of Hastings' death. All agree that on June 13 Richard summoned him to a meeting of the council of nobles at the Tower. In one story, Richard cried out by prearrangement that he was being attacked, whereupon his bodyguard burst into the room and cut Hastings down. Sir Thomas More's account is more dramatic. More gives us an angry Richard confronting Hastings and demanding, "What punishment do they deserve who conspire against the life of one so nearly related to the king as myself, and entrusted with the government of the realm?"

The punishment of traitors, Hastings replied. But whom did Richard mean?

"That sorceress my brother's wife," cried Richard, "and others with her—see how they have wasted my body with sorcery and witchcraft!" He bared his withered arm, his crooked shoulder.

Hastings said, "Certainly if they have done so heinously they are worth a heinous punishment."

Richard shouted at the unsuspecting Hastings, "What? Dost thou serve me with 'ifs' and 'ands'? I tell thee they have done it, and that I will make good upon thy body, traitor!" Striking the council table with his fist, Richard cried, "Treason!" Soldiers rushed in and arrested Hastings. Richard told him to prepare to die. "I will not dine until I have his head," the duke declared. Taken into the yard of the Tower, Hastings was hurriedly beheaded. The reign of terror had begun.

Now Richard's own troops were marching from his northern strongholds, led by one of the duke's lieutenants, Sir Richard Ratcliffe. On his way south to London Ratcliffe collected Earl Rivers, Sir Thomas Vaughan, and Sir Richard Grey from the castles at which they had been jailed and took them to Pontefract, where they were executed. Once again the earldom of Rivers had proven fatal to a

Woodville; it passed now to Anthony Woodville's youngest brother, Richard.

Richard of Gloucester's next move was to gain possession of his other nephew, Prince Richard. He was with his mother in Westminster Abbey. Richard surrounded the sanctuary with troops and prepared to invade it if necessary. Reluctantly Queen Elizabeth surrendered her nine-year-old son after the Archbishop of Canterbury, venerable Thomas Bourchier, promised her that no harm would come to him. Prince Richard went to join his brother Edward V in the Tower. There was still one lad of royal blood at large: ten-year-old Edward, the only son of the dead Duke of Clarence. This boy, who had inherited his grandfather's title of Earl of Warwick, had originally stood ahead of Richard in the line of succession to the throne, although he was under an act of attainder as a result of Clarence's "treason." Richard imprisoned him.

Little lay in Richard's path now. Dominic Mancini, an Italian who was in London during these events, shows us the sad picture of twelve-year-old King Edward V in the Tower: "He and his brother were withdrawn into the inner apartments of the Tower proper, and day by day began to be seen more rarely behind the bars and windows, till at length they ceased to appear altogether. . . . The young king, like a victim prepared for sacrifice, sought remission of his sins by daily confession and penance, because he believed that death was facing him." This gentle, scholarly boy, mature beyond his years, had been carefully groomed to inherit the kingdom; but his uncle Richard had intervened.

A few days after Hastings' death, a preacher named

Ralph Shaw delivered an astonishing sermon in London. This man—hired by Richard—declared that Edward IV had been illegitimate and no true son of Richard of York! Shaw argued that "in shape of body" Edward IV had been nothing like Richard his supposed father, "for he was high of stature, the other very little; he of large face, the other short and round." But Duke Richard of Gloucester, said Shaw, was a true son of Richard of York—the only legitimate son of York now alive, and thus entitled to the throne. For if Edward IV were illegitimate, Edward V could not be king.

Having shown himself willing to slander his own mother to have the crown, Richard tried to fortify his position with a second line of argument. Whether or not Edward IV's birth had been proper, Edward IV's children certainly were illegitimate, Shaw claimed. This, he said, was because Edward IV had entered into a contract of marriage with a certain Lady Eleanor Butler—long since dead—before he ever met Elizabeth Woodville. By law Edward had not been free to marry Elizabeth; his marriage to her was bigamous, and her children were outside the law. With Clarence dead and his son attainted, that left Richard of Gloucester as the rightful king.

As Londoners mulled these fanciful charges, Richard appeared publicly and waited for the people to cry, "Long live King Richard!" But the cry did not sound forth. A couple of days later Buckingham made a speech telling London that Richard was their true king, and again the response to the idea was cool. Nevertheless the usurpation proceeded to its climax. On June 26 Buckingham and a group of carefully picked citizens paid a call on Richard and invited him to be king. Richard modestly refused the high honor. Buckingham repeated the invitation, more eloquently; and with a great show of reluctance, Richard overcame his scruples and accepted. By nightfall he had taken his seat on the marble throne at Westminster as King Richard III.

His coronation took place on July 6. With Warwick's daughter beside him as Queen Anne, Richard sat enthroned in splendor while Archbishop Bourchier anointed him with oil and performed the rites of kingship. By that time a cooperative Parliament had declared Edward IV's two sons to be illegitimate and had ratified Richard's seizure of the throne. Edward had not been in his grave three months yet, and his brother had usurped the crown.

Former Queen Elizabeth and her daughters had remained walled up in sanctuary at Westminster Abbey even while the coronation ceremony was taking place in another part of the building. Nor did they come forth now. The unhappy woman knew that her brother Rivers and one of her sons, Richard Grey, were dead, and she had no hope for the two princes in the Tower.

The fate of those princes was a cruel one. They were last seen by visitors to the Tower in the fall of 1483. By the spring of 1484 they were dead, or at least had vanished so thoroughly that no one ever saw them again. The usual assumption is that Richard III had them murdered, and many years later a certain Sir James Tyrell confessed to having done the crime at Richard's order. But Tyrell was a scoundrel whose word was worthless, and his "confession" is open to serious suspicion. The grim story of the smothered princes that Shakespeare dramatized may be no more than a fable. In 1644 the bones of two boys were found walled up in a chamber of the Tower; thirty years later a second set of bones was discovered in a different place. Both times, the bones were said to be the remains of King Edward V and his brother Richard. The verdict of history remains in doubt. It seems likely that Richard III did have the two princes murdered, but the evidence is not such that would lead any fair court to convict him.

At any rate, the boys presumably were dead, and Richard III ruled England. He was hardly popular. King Richard bought the favor of the high nobles through the distribution of wealth that traditionally followed a usurpation of the throne. Buckingham, his chief henchman, gained large properties in Wales. Henry Percy, Earl of Northumberland, was given some of Richard's own holdings in northern England. A friend of Richard's, Francis Lovell, became a key member of the government, as did that other lieutenant, Sir Richard Ratcliffe, and much power flowed to another of Richard's men, Sir William Catesby. Despite all these appointments, Richard III had little support in the land. The rise to power of Lovell, Ratcliffe, and Catesby produced a seditious jingle:

> *The cat, the rat, and Lovell our dog*
> *Rule all England, under a hog.*

The second line was a reference to Richard III's personal banner, which showed a white boar as his emblem.

At the beginning of August, 1483, Richard undertook a tour of his new kingdom. The people of the north, remembering him as a just and wise administrator as Duke of Gloucester, greeted him with cheers. But in the south the faces that lined his route were stony with hatred. It was hard for many to believe that good Duke Richard had transformed himself overnight into evil King Richard, but so it had befallen, and now Richard was an object of dread.

Late in August the king named his only son, ten-year-old Edward, Earl of Salisbury, as Prince of Wales. Thus he formally recognized the boy as heir to the throne. Richard also sent an envoy to the Duke of Brittany to ask that Henry Tudor be handed over to him for "safer custody." Tudor, thanks to his Beaufort ancestry, was the only surviving Lancastrian, and no matter how flimsy his claim to the throne might be, Richard wanted to see him safely out of the way. But Henry remained in Brittany, out of Richard's reach.

By October Richard felt that his power was well established. Though no one was cheerful about his presence on the throne, and many whispering enemies accused him of the foul murder of the two princes, he seemed secure. He had already taken certain steps to reform the government, hoping to win favor with the common people. Then, unexpectedly, came word of a revolt. His own most loyal associate, the Duke of Buckingham, had turned against him and was leading a rebellion designed to place Henry Tudor on the throne!

BOSWORth fielD

NLY A few months before, Buckingham had helped Richard of Gloucester to become King Richard III. Now suddenly Buckingham had renounced his allegiance to Richard. What had caused the swift change of heart?

One possibility is that Buckingham had felt short-changed in the handing out of rewards when Richard took the throne. Another is that the duke, shocked and repelled by the death of the two princes, felt that his conscience would let him back Richard no longer. There is a third theory, which seems to fit most closely with what we know of Buckingham's character: that the duke had planned a double-cross all along. Secretly Lancastrian in sympathy, Buckingham had encouraged Richard to destroy the children of Edward IV and now was conspiring to destroy Richard himself. That way the whole House of York would be swept away, permitting Buckingham to bring the Lancastrian Henry Tudor home from exile and make him king.

Buckingham's plan called for a general uprising to begin on October 18. He would lead the revolt in south-western England. At the same time, Henry Tudor, the Earl of Richmond, would land in Wales with five thousand men and march toward London. They would seize and slay King Richard; Henry would be crowned; and, to link Lancaster with York at last, the new king would marry Elizabeth, the daughter of Edward IV.

Everything went wrong, though. Buckingham tried to rouse the populace to anger by revealing that the princes in the Tower were dead, and succeeded so well that the revolt began ten days early in Kent, Sussex, and Devonshire. That gave Richard time to get his army ready to meet trouble. Henry Tudor, setting sail from Brittany on October 12, met with storms and his fleet was scattered. And when Buckingham massed his own troops near the borders of Wales, a flood on the Severn River cut him off from moving eastward into England.

The royal troops put down the uprisings in the south. Henry Tudor landed at the English port of Plymouth with only two ships, learned that the rebellion was a fiasco, and hastily returned to Brittany. Buckingham's army melted away, and the duke himself was captured on November 2 in the town of Salisbury. Without a moment's delay Richard had Buckingham beheaded in the public marketplace of Salisbury the day he was taken prisoner.

Order had been restored, virtually without fighting, and Richard now continued his attempt to win popularity in the kingdom. He staged magnificent pageants, offered pardons to former opponents, gave handsome gifts to the church, and even declared Edward IV's favorite tactic of raising money through "benevolences" to be illegal. He restored power to Parliament, which Edward IV had practically ignored. In many ways Richard III was an excellent monarch, with an enlightened knowledge of government. But no one could forgive him for the way he had come to the throne.

If we can rely on Sir Thomas More's biography, Richard himself was tormented by guilt. "I have heard by creditable report," More says, "that . . . he never had quiet in his mind, he never thought himself sure. Where he went abroad, his eyes whirled about, his body privily fenced, his hand ever on his dagger, his countenance and manner like one always ready to strike again. He took ill rest at nights, lay long waking and musing; sore wearied with care and watch, he rather slumbered than slept. Troubled with fearful dreams, suddenly sometimes started he up, leapt out of his bed and ran about the chamber. So was his restless heart continually tossed and tumbled with the tedious impression and stormy remembrance of his most abominable deed."

In the spring of 1484 the foundations of Richard's dynastic dreams abruptly collapsed. His son Edward, the Prince of Wales, died at Middleham Castle, leaving the heartbroken usurper without an heir. It was a catastrophe that crushed Richard's spirit and took from him the dynamic ambition that had propelled him so abruptly into the throne. From this point on he moved uncertainly, often seeming hardly to care what befell him.

With the prince's death, the heir to the throne now was another boy named Edward—the Earl of Warwick, Clarence's son. Richard had this boy in custody. The next heir beyond that was twenty-year-old John, Earl of Lincoln. He was the son of Richard III's sister Elizabeth, whose husband was John de la Pole, Duke of Suffolk. The ironies of these tangled family relationships were gathering fast. Richard could not bear to see Clarence's son succeed him; but the other heir was the grandson of that long-dead Suffolk whom the Yorkists had hated beyond all others!

Richard III had no hope that his wife Queen Anne, Warwick's daughter, could present him with another son. Anne's health was shattered, and her death was near. While his queen was sinking toward the grave, Richard showed a flash of his old demonic shrewdness: somehow, against all probability, he won the friendship of former Queen Elizabeth.

Elizabeth Woodville—Dame Elizabeth Grey, as Richard called her—had remained in the sanctuary of Westminster Abbey for more than a year, her daughters beside her. Now the man whom everyone suspected of having murdered her sons tempted her out with kindly offers. He solemnly promised "on his honor as a king" to treat her with generosity and to marry her daughters to suitable gentlemen. Elizabeth came forth and was warmly received at Richard's court. He loaded her and her girls with gifts, and paid special attention to his eighteen-year-old niece Elizabeth.

Richard's motives in all this were transparent. He needed a queen; and he feared that young Elizabeth might marry Henry Tudor and thus strengthen Tudor's shaky claim to the throne. When Queen Anne finally died in March of 1485, rumors circulated that King Richard was going to ask the Pope for the necessary permission, so that he could marry his sister-in-law's daughter.

But Richard hesitated. Perhaps he felt that such a marriage was useless after all; perhaps he remembered that in 1483 he had had all of Elizabeth Woodville's children by Edward IV declared illegitimate. Or possibly he had come to a state of inner paralysis of the will that prevented him from taking any action. His enemies were gathering against him; an invasion of England seemed imminent. In a mood of dull despair Richard ignored his niece and waited for the worst.

Henry Tudor, Earl of Richmond, would soon be on his way from Brittany to take the crown.

Of all those who claimed the English throne in the fifteenth century, Henry Tudor's right to it was the most feeble. On his father's side he had no royal blood at all, unless one was willing to accept the claim that the Tudors were descended from the legendary ancient kings of pre-Saxon Britain, among them King Arthur. And on his mother's side he was royal only by virtue of some winking at the laws. His mother, Margaret Beaufort, was the granddaughter of John of Gaunt's son John Beaufort. But the Beauforts all were illegitimate, and had been made legitimate merely through a decree long after the fact. Moreover, Parliament had specifically ruled, at Henry IV's request, that the Beauforts were ineligible to inherit the throne. So, although he could truthfully say that he was the great-great-great-grandson of King Edward III, Henry Tudor's claim to the throne was highly dubious, to say the least.

To an England weary of the ugliness of Richard III's reign, though, any claimant with a drop of royal blood in his veins was welcome. Henry Tudor had the special advantage of being unknown in England. He had not had an opportunity to make enemies. As a boy during the most bitter days of the Wars of the Roses, Henry had remained far from the center of action, spending much of his youth with his uncle, Jasper Tudor, in Wales and all of his adult life across the Channel in Brittany. He had never fought

The Tudor Claim

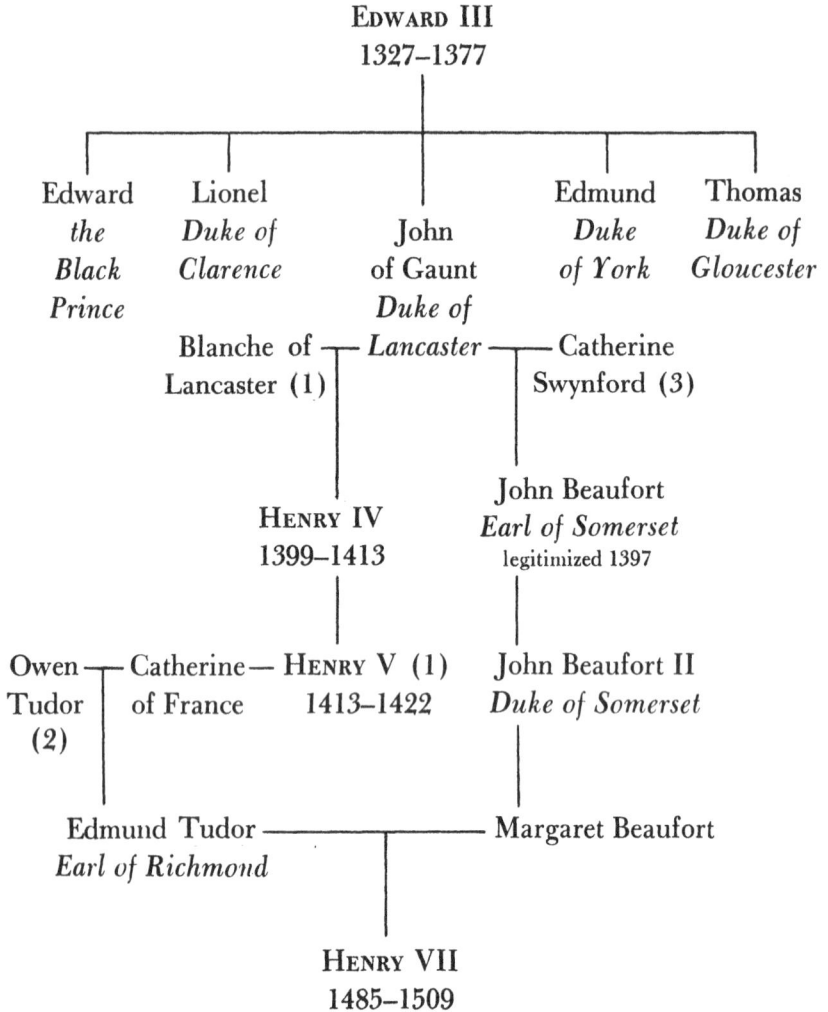

Edward III
1327–1377

Edward *the Black Prince*	Lionel *Duke of Clarence*	John of Gaunt *Duke of Lancaster*	Edmund *Duke of York*	Thomas *Duke of Gloucester*

Blanche of Lancaster (1) —— *Lancaster* —— Catherine Swynford (3)

Henry IV
1399–1413

John Beaufort
Earl of Somerset
legitimized 1397

Owen Tudor (2) —— Catherine of France —— **Henry V** (1)
1413–1422

John Beaufort II
Duke of Somerset

Edmund Tudor —————————— Margaret Beaufort
Earl of Richmond

Henry VII
1485–1509

in any battle. In 1485, at the age of twenty-seven, Henry probably spoke French better than he did English.

Henry had the benefit of two veteran Lancastrian generals in planning his campaign against Richard. One was Jasper Tudor, who had been fighting Yorkists since the first battle of St. Albans in 1455. The other was John de Vere, the thirteenth Earl of Oxford. Oxford had helped to restore Henry VI, and had escaped safely from the field at Barnet the day in 1471 when Warwick was killed. But then, captured by Edward IV in 1473, he had spent ten years as a prisoner near Calais. He bribed his jailer to let him free, at last, and immediately pledged his support to Henry Tudor. This pair of crafty warriors made ready for the invasion.

All during the summer of 1485 Richard III waited, tortured by tales of Henry's immediate arrival. At the head of his troops he patrolled the country, hoping to win public backing if the threatened invasion came. On August 1 Henry set sail for England from the port of Harfleur. He brought with him a small but experienced army made up of French as well as English soldiers. Among his English troops were not only Lancastrians but also many Yorkists who despised Richard III.

A fair wind carried the fleet easily across the Channel. On August 7 the invaders landed at Milford Haven, a harbor in Wales. Richard III's chief captain in Wales was one Rhys ap Thomas, who had taken a vow to keep all rebels from entering Wales, "except they should pass over his belly." But now Rhys found himself torn by conflict, for here was a man of Welsh blood coming to claim the English throne. Rhys did not want to oppose Henry Tudor, but he had no wish to be disloyal to his oath. At length someone

suggested a way for Rhys to admit Henry without breaking his vow. The Welsh captain stood beneath a bridge while Henry walked over the top. Thus the invader passed over Rhys ap Thomas' belly and was greeted joyfully by Wales as a deliverer.

Unmolested, Henry moved eastward through Wales. So poor were communications that Richard III did not learn of the landing until five days had passed. A royal army was dispatched to meet the rebels and check their advance. In command of these troops was Sir William Stanley, an important member of Richard's court.

But Stanley was a man of divided loyalty and a poor choice for such important responsibilities. His older brother, Thomas Lord Stanley, had become the third husband of the widowed Margaret Beaufort, Henry Tudor's mother. Though they had never met, Lord Stanley thus was the stepfather of the invading earl. To Richard that did not seem very important. Sir William, though, hesitated to attack Tudor. Seeing him make no move against the rebels, Richard ordered Sir William's brother, Lord Stanley, to come to court. Lord Stanley replied that he was "ill of the sweating sickness" and could not come, whereupon the king arrested Lord Stanley's son George and held him as a hostage for the loyalty of his father and his uncle. Richard was counting on Lord Stanley and Sir William Stanley both to fight on his side in the coming battle with the Tudor forces.

By August 15 Henry Tudor had come as far east as the town of Shrewsbury. Richard gathered his own army and moved out to meet the invader in person. With him he brought the armies of two of the principal lords of the realm: the Duke of Norfolk and the Earl of Northumberland. Norfolk had received his dukedom from Richard in 1483; as John Howard he had taken part in the plot that made Richard king. Northumberland's earl was the always unpredictable Henry Percy, who often behaved as a law unto himself. The troops of the Stanley brothers accompanied these forces. At the head of this large combined army rode King Richard, mounted on a giant white charger. On Sunday, August 21, the royal army was at Leicester, and that evening it camped near the town of Market Bosworth, virtually in the center of England.

The battle fought at Bosworth Field the next day should have been an easy victory for Richard III. He had some ten thousand men at his command; Henry Tudor's rebels numbered half as many. Richard's soldiers were combat-trained veterans; most of Henry's were Welshmen hastily enrolled in the ranks. Richard was a skilled general who had learned the arts of war at first hand, in the fiercest battles of the reign of Edward IV; Henry had never been in battle at all. Furthermore, the royal army occupied the high ground at Bosworth Field, and the invaders would have to fight uphill to reach Richard, always a difficult matter. "Dismiss all fear," Richard told his men before the battle. "Everyone give but one sure stroke and the day is ours. What prevaileth a handful of men to a whole realm? As for me, I assure you this day I will triumph by glorious victory or suffer death for immortal fame."

He sounded the signal for hostilities to begin.

The great uncertainty on Richard's side was the part Sir William Stanley and his brother, Lord Stanley, would play. The Stanleys stood to one side, holding back from an attack. Richard sent word to Lord Stanley that if he did not charge at once, his son would immediately be beheaded. Lord Stanley proudly retorted that he had other sons. Richard commanded that the execution take place, but the officer charged with the task was bold enough to reply, "My Lord, the enemy is past the marsh. After the battle let young Stanley die." And so the young man's life was spared, for after the battle Richard III's commands no longer mattered.

The armies came together. The Earl of Oxford, commanding Henry Tudor's right wing, did not succeed in getting Richard's left wing, commanded by the Duke of Norfolk, to come downhill to meet the attack. But Norfolk himself was slain. In the early moments of the battle the assault was savage on both sides; the historian Polydore Vergil, working from eyewitness accounts, tells how the royal army "making suddenly great shouts assaulted the enemy first with arrows," and Tudor's men, "nothing faint unto the fight, began also to shoot fiercely; but when they came to hand strokes the matter then was dealt with blades."

Soon, though, a strange pattern was developing. The Earl of Northumberland's army, instead of entering the conflict, stood idle to one side. At the last moment Henry Percy had chosen to remain neutral. As for the Stanleys, they finally made their loyalties clear by dashing across the field and offering their troops to Henry Tudor. They had secretly planned this betrayal with Henry some days earlier.

Seeing the Stanleys desert his cause, Richard knew that all was lost. He had come to his throne through treachery, and he was now undone by treachery. Berserk with rage, he spurred his horse forward, staking his life on one mad hope: to reach Henry Tudor and kill him on the battle-field. "Treason!" Richard roared. "Treason!" With insane fury the king hacked his way through the enemy ranks. His horse was killed, and he jumped free, fighting on foot, mustering a strength that did not seem to be present in his frail body. Shakespeare shows us a bloodied, desperate Richard fighting on against all odds, crying, "A horse! A horse! my kingdom for a horse!"

Sir William Catesby rushes up to say, "Withdraw, my lord; I'll help you to a horse." But the Richard of the play replies:

> *Slave! I have set my life upon a cast,*
> *And I will stand the hazard of the die.*
> *I think there be six Richmonds in the field;*
> *Five have I slain today, instead of him.—*
> *A horse! A horse! my kingdom for a horse!*

At the far side of the field was Henry Tudor, the Earl of Richmond, astonished to see this madman of a Richard

coming toward him. Richard cut down Sir William Bran-
don, Henry's standard-bearer, and killed a strong warrior
named Sir John Cheney. Just as he reached Henry himself,
though, Sir William Stanley's men swept across the field,
separating king from claimant. Richard refused to flee. His
kingdom was lost; he hoped only now for a hero's death
on the field of battle.

That death was granted him. He fought until he could
fight no more, and when the battle ceased, Richard's gashed
and lifeless form lay sprawled on Bosworth Field. He had
worn his crown to the moment of his death. Now that crown
was discovered in the grass, and Lord Stanley lifted it and
placed it upon the head of Henry Tudor, the new King
Henry VII. Richard's naked corpse, stretched across a
horse's back, was carried into Leicester so that all might see
that York's last son was dead.

The wars were over at last. Henry VII would marry
Edward IV's daughter, joining the House of Lancaster to
the House of York in marriage, and from that union would
come a new dynasty that would lead England to greatness.
Henry VII's son, Henry VIII of the many wives, and that
eighth Henry's daughter Elizabeth I, would make the name
of Tudor a glittering one throughout the world; and though
the Tudors died out with childless Queen Elizabeth I, the
blood of Henry Tudor still flows in the English royal family
today.

Henry VII would be a strong, shrewd king. At his request such historians as Sir Thomas More produced books
portraying Richard III as a black villain and defending
Henry's seizure of the throne. He would meet and deal with
rebellions; two impostors would arise, one claiming to be
the Duke of Clarence's son, the other insisting he was Ed-

ward IV's murdered son Richard, and each would lead an uprising. But Henry VII would triumph. A few more heads would fall, and sixty years after Bosworth Field there still would be death sentences for unlucky descendants of Edward III through the wrong lines. But the conflicts of Tudor England are beyond our present concern.

What had the terrible Wars of the Roses accomplished, then?

They had set to rights the tensions produced when Richard II was deposed in 1399. A cycle of usurpation that began with the overthrow of one Richard and ended with the overthrow of another had given England a ruling dynasty, had settled great issues of government, had brought order from chaos.

Oddly, the long years of war produced little hardship for the ordinary Englishman. The battles had been few and far between, concentrated mainly in 1460–61, 1470–71, and 1485. Probably no more than thirty thousand men died in all the warfare, far fewer than those who had died in the war with France. The real carnage had been among the nobility. Between 1455 and 1485—from St. Albans to Bosworth Field—the victims had included three kings (Henry VI, Edward V, Richard III), a Prince of Wales (Queen Margaret's son), nine dukes, a marquis, thirteen earls, twenty-four barons. Whole families, such as the Nevilles and the Beauforts, were extinguished. The Woodvilles rose to power and were largely destroyed. An aristocracy that went back to the eleventh century was cut apart. Most of the ancient noble families of today's England can trace their titles back only to the Tudor dynasty; few indeed are those peers whose noble ancestors survived the Wars of the Roses.

The war was a time of purging for England, a series of

violent revolutions that swept away incompetent kings and
grasping lords, and brought forth the brisk, efficient Tudor
regime. Henry VII was a good king in the sense that he
knew how to govern; Henry VIII also ruled strongly, for
all his bloodthirsty habits; and Elizabeth I was a shrewd
and splendid monarch. Yet the Tudor policies of government did not originate with them. They based their ideas
on the methods of King Edward IV, the unexpected hero
of the Wars of the Roses. Edward, coming to the throne
with so little preparation, proved to be the first modern
king, businesslike and farsighted, with little interest in romantic deeds of chivalry and a keen sense of how a great
kingdom should be ruled. Of all the personalities of that
troubled era—fiery Margaret, dim King Henry, ambitious
York, proud Warwick, faithless Richard—it is Edward IV
who stands out as the most significant figure.

And so the story's pattern was fulfilled. At the beginning a Richard was deposed by a Henry; at the end a
Richard was deposed by a Henry. Between, in a century of
anguish, a new England was created on the splintered ruins
of the old. And when the time was ready, Henry VII
emerged to snatch power from the hands of York. Shakespeare gives noble words to Henry Tudor as he stands
crowned and triumphant on the field at Bosworth:

> *We will unite the white rose and the red:*
> *Smile, heaven, upon this fair conjunction,*
> *That long hath frown'd upon their enmity!*
> *What traitor hears me, and says not amen?*
> *England hath long been mad, and scarr'd herself;*
> *The brother blindly shed the brother's blood,*
> *The father rashly slaughter'd his own son,*
> *The son, compell'd, been butcher to the sire:*
> *All this divided York and Lancaster,*

Divided in their dire division.
O! Now, let Richmond and Elizabeth
The true successors of each royal house,
By God's fair ordinance conjoin together;
And let their heirs—God, if thy will be so,—
Enrich the time to come with smooth-fac'd peace,
With smiling plenty, and fair prosperous days! . . .
Now civil wounds are stopp'd, peace lives again:
That she may long live here, God say amen!

BIBLIOGRAPhy

Chrimes, S. B., *Lancastrians, Yorkists, and Henry VII*. New York: St. Martin's Press, 1964.

Churchill, Winston S., *A History of the English Speaking Peoples, Vol. I, The Birth of Britain*. New York: Dodd, Mead, 1962.

Hamilton, Franklin, *1066*. New York: The Dial Press, 1964.

Hassall, W. O., *They Saw It Happen, Vol. I, 55 B.C.–1485*. Oxford, England: Basil Blackwell, Ltd., 1957.

Jacob, E. F., *The Oxford History of England, Vol. VI, The Fifteenth Century, 1399–1485*. Oxford, England: Oxford University Press, 1961.

Kendall, Paul Murray, *Richard the Third*. New York: W. W. Norton, 1956.

——— *Warwick the Kingmaker*. New York: W. W. Norton, 1957.

——— *The Yorkist Age*. New York: W. W. Norton, 1962.

Lander, J. R., *The Wars of the Roses*. New York: G. P. Putnam's Sons, 1966.

McKisack, May, *The Oxford History of England, Vol. V, The Fourteenth Century, 1307–1399*. Oxford, England: Oxford University Press, 1959.

Myers, A. R., *England in the Late Middle Ages*. London: Penguin Books, 1952.

Previté-Orton, C. W., and Brooke, Z. N., editors, *The Cambridge Medieval History, Vol. VIII, The Close of the Middle Ages*. Cambridge, England: Cambridge University Press, 1959.

Russell, Josiah Cox, *British Medieval Population*. Albuquerque, New Mexico: University of New Mexico Press, 1948.

Shakespeare, William, *The Tragedy of King Richard II*.
——— *The First Part of King Henry IV*.
——— *The Second Part of King Henry IV*.
——— *The Life of King Henry V*.
——— *The First Part of King Henry VI*.
——— *The Second Part of King Henry VI*.
——— *The Third Part of King Henry VI*.
——— *The Tragedy of King Richard III*.

Trevelyan, G. M., *History of England, Vol I, From the Earliest Times to the Reformation*. New York: Doubleday Anchor Books, 1952.

index

About the Author

Franklin Hamilton has been a newspaperman, a radio commentator, and an editor of a national weekly magazine. Currently he spends eight months of the year as a free-lance writer, the rest of the time skin diving in the Caribbean. Mr. Hamilton is married and has two teen-age children. His hobby for many years has been medieval history, and he has accumulated an extensive library of books dealing with the events of the centuries between the fall of Rome and the rise of the modern world. He is the author of *1066* and *The Crusades*.

About the Artist

Judith Ann Lawrence has illustrated several books for children, including *1066* and *The Crusades* by Franklin Hamilton. A graduate of Columbia University, where she received a degree in Fine Arts, she lives with her husband near Washington, D.C. Her illustrations for *Challenge for a Throne* are based on extensive research of the architecture, costumes, weaponry, and heraldry of the period, as well as portraits and descriptions of the people themselves.